Clive Oxenden
Christina Latham-Koenig

ENGLISH FILE

intermediate student's book

OXFORD
UNIVERSITY PRESS

Contents

2

Speaking	Listening	Reading	Writing
Transport: interviewing people Agreeing / disagreeing about driving laws	Travel programme about Lisbon	Newspaper article: *The Rush-hour Grand Prix*	
Cars and car problems	Interview with Sebastian Coe	Two stories: *The Wedding, The Interview*	A nightmare journey
Noise pollution Things that annoy you Defining words	Street interviews	Magazine article: *Invisible pollution*	Adding non-defining relative clauses to a story
Roleplay: asking for and giving directions	Tourists asking for information Following directions	Letter giving directions	A letter to a friend: giving directions
The cinema	Conversation about a film Understanding questions	Film reviews Magazine article: *'I just want to make the film and go home.'* (an interview with Woody Allen)	A film review
Game: 20 questions Sport: interview a partner	Radio programme (strange sport statistics)	Newspaper article: *Who's the fittest?*	
Music: your likes and dislikes 'First times' Retelling extracts from a biography	Understanding an anecdote ♫ *Let it be*	Biography extract: *Many Years from Now* by Paul McCartney	
Roleplay: arranging to go out	Understanding box office information ♫ *Memory*	Signs and notices Reviews of shows	A note to a friend
Describing a tourist town For or against? Family holidays, etc.	Conversation between a tourist and a waiter	Newspaper article: *Where am I?*	Form-filling Describing a place
Your last holiday Roleplay: holiday complaints	Dialogue: complaining about a holiday. ♫ *Daniel*	Travel brochure: New York	
Talking about travel problems	Travel stories	Magazine article: *Welcome to Britain!*	A letter to a friend: giving advice
Roleplay: complaining in a shop	Dialogues: complaining in a shop and in a restaurant.	Signs and notices	A formal letter of complaint
Reading and retelling Talking about the *Titanic*	Radio story: *Titanic*	Magazine article: *The truth about the Titanic*	

4 Practise speaking

Introduction

1 MEETING PEOPLE

a Introduce yourself to as many people as possible.

Hello/Hi, I'm _____.
Nice to meet you.
Where are you from?
What do you do?

b How many names can you remember?

2 NUMBERS

a How do you say these numbers?

13   30   66   102   250   1,000   2,555
7,856   800,000   2,000,000

b **TInt.1** Listen and write the numbers.

1 _____   3 _____   5 _____
2 _____   4 _____

c Ask your partner about numbers.

What's the population of your town/
country? (*About…*)
How much does a flat/good car, etc. cost?
What's the last thing you bought? How
much did it cost?

3 SPELLING

a Complete the chart with the alphabet.

a	*b*	—	—	—	—	—
—	*c*	—	—	—	—	—
—		—	—	—	—	
—		—	—			
—						
—						

b Go to **Vocabulary Builder 14** *English sounds*, *p.142*. Find the seven sounds. What are the other vowel sounds?

c **TInt.2** Listen and write.

1 Surname: _ _ _ _ _ _ _ _ _
2 Flight number: _ _ _ _ _ _ _ _
3 Post code: _ _ _ _ _ _ _
4 Address: _ _ , _ _ _ _ _ _ _ _ _ _ _ _ _ _ _ _
5 Restaurant: _ _ _ _ _ _ _ _ _ _ _ _ _ _ _

d Ask your partner.

How do you spell … your first name?
your surname?
the name of your street?

4 DATES

a How do you say these dates?

1st January 1999   3rd Feb 2001   25.6.76
20th Aug 1905   31/7/88   the 1970s   the 21st century

b Ask your partner about dates.

What's the date today/tomorrow?
When's your birthday?
What days are public holidays in your country?

5 MAKING CONVERSATION

Go to **Communication** *All about you*, **A** *p.121*, **B** *p.125*. Complete the chart.
Ask about your partner's answers.

1 _____
2 _____

5 _____
6 _____

3 _____
4 _____

6 WRITE BETTER

a Read about Antonio. Complete the gaps.

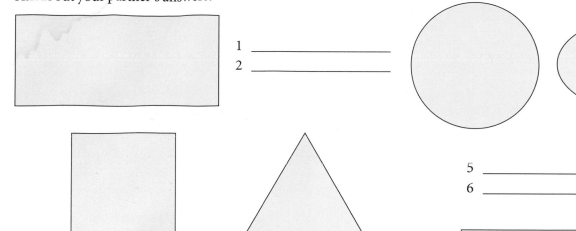

My name's Antonio Pereda and I'm from Mexico. I was 1 born in Mexico City and I've lived there all my life. I'm 2 married, but we haven't got any children.

We 3 live with my parents. Luckily their flat is very big, so there's room for all of us. They are both retired, and they 4 do all the housework, which is great because Ana, my wife, and I both work.

I'm 5 an accountant. I studied Economics 6 at university and then I got a 7 job with a petrol company. Ana is a secretary for the same company — in fact that's how we 8 met.

I'm learning English because we do a lot of 9 work with the USA. I need English 10 to write, to speak on the phone, and sometimes to go out 11 have a meal with American people. Next summer I'm going to do a computer course in the States, so I hope my English will be 12 better enough!

b Write questions.

1 *What's his surname* ? Pereda.
2 Where does he live ? In Mexico City.
3 How lg, has he lived there ? All his life.
4 Is he married ? Yes, but he hasn't who lives with him? got any children.
5 Who does he live with ? His wife and his parents.
6 What does he do ? He's an accountant.
7 What did he study ? Economics.
8 How did he meet his wife ? They work for the same company.
9 Why is he learning English ? Because it's studying important for his job.
10 What is he going to do doing next summer ? A course in the States.

c In **five minutes** write a similar paragraph about yourself. Write about where you live, your family, what you do, and why you're studying English.

1 READ BETTER

a Explain the difference.

1 to know someone/to meet someone
2 a friend/a colleague
3 a friend/a girlfriend
4 a partner/a couple
5 a close friend/a best friend
6 a friendship/a relationship

b Look at the photos. What's their relationship?

c Read the text. Don't worry about new words. Number the questions in the right order.

- [2] How long have they known each other?
- [5] How often do they see each other?
- [4] Why is she his best friend?
- [1] How did they meet?
- [3] Why do they get on well?

d Look at the questions only. Tell your partner what you remember about Dominic and Paulina.

2 BUILD YOUR VOCABULARY

Relationships

a In pairs, underline new words in the text. Guess the meaning.

b Look at the highlighted words in the text. Match them with the meanings below.

1 We began to speak angrily to each other.
   We started to argue.
2 A lot of things about us are the same.
   We've got a lot in common
3 When you know her better.
   When you get to know her
4 We like the same kind of things.
   We've got the same tastes
5 We laugh at the same things.
   We've got the same sense of humour
6 We have a good relationship.
   We've get on very well
7 I can depend on her.
   I can trust her
8 We contact each other regularly.
   We keep in touch.
9 We stopped going out together.
   We broke up.

c Order the verbs below to describe a typical relationship. Compare with a partner. *First you meet, then you...*

- [ ] argue
- [ ] break up
- [ ] fall in love
- [ ] get on well
- [ ] get to know each other
- [ ] keep in touch
- [1] meet
- [ ] go out together
- [ ] stay friends

Just good friends?

I'll never forget our first meeting because it was quite romantic. I had two tickets for a concert in London, but at the last moment the girl who was going to go
5 with me couldn't come. So I went to the concert hall early to get my money back for one of the tickets. Paulina was standing in the queue. We started talking, and I found out that she was
10 there for the same reason. My tickets were better than hers so I suggested that we sat in my seats and we gave her tickets back. After the concert we went for a drink and we've been friends ever
15 since then.

We've known each other for two years. After that first meeting we started going out together and we fell in love. Everything went really well at first but after six months we started to argue
20 a lot and finally we broke up, but we stayed close friends, which isn't always easy.

I think we get on very well mainly because we've got the same sense of humour. We've got a lot in
25 common – we like and dislike the same people and things, and we've got the same tastes in music. Our personalities are quite similar too. Paulina seems quite shy when
30 you first meet her but when you get to know her she's really extrovert and funny.

Café Dôn'chan
3.95

3 MAKING CONVERSATION

Your best friend

a Think about a close friend. Make quick notes in the chart.

	Notes
Who's your best friend? How long have you known each other? How did you meet?	
Why is he/she your best friend? Why do you get on well? Do you ever argue? What about?	
How often do you see each other? How do you keep in touch?	

b In pairs, **A** ask **B** the questions. Get as much information as possible. Swap roles.

4 GRAMMAR ANALYSIS

Present perfect or past simple?

a Correct the sentences which are wrong.

1 Tom has broken his leg yesterday. *broke*
2 They arrived about twenty minutes ago.
3 She's my best friend and I know her for ten years. *I've known.*
4 I've never written a love poem.
5 We've lived here since ten years and we like it.
6 What time has my brother phoned? *did my b. phone*
7 Have you ever worked in a restaurant?
8 I haven't played football since I was 11.

b Explain the difference.

1 I've seen *The Godfather.* → *maybe a long time ago.*
  I saw *The Godfather* last night. → *he remembers very well.*
2 We've been married for five years. → *still*
  We were married for five years. → *finish.*
3 She's been to Britain. → *she is living in B.*
  She's gone to Britain. → *she is leaving (the) B.*

Use the present perfect for:

- **unfinished actions/situations**
  which started in the past and continue now.
  I've lost my car keys.
  How long have you lived here?
  I've lived here for two years.

- **past experiences**
  when you **don't** say, ask, or know when.
  I've travelled a lot.
  Have you ever been to England?
  We've never had a serious argument.

for and *since*
Use *for* + a period of time (long or short).
I've known her for ten years/a long time/ages.
NOT ~~I know her during ten years/since ten years.~~
I've (only) known her for a few weeks.

Use *since* + a point in time (a day, date, year).
We've been married since October/Tuesday/1983.

Use the past simple for:

- **finished actions in the past**
  when you say, ask, or know
  when they happened.
  I lost my car keys
  (yesterday/two days ago).
  How long did you live in Paris?
  I lived in Paris for two years.
  (= I don't live there now.)

I think I call her my 'best friend' because she's a person I can talk to about anything and I know I can trust her. Our friendship is very important to me.

Nowadays, we only see each other about once a month because she's studying at university and I'm working in London, but we keep in touch by e-mail all the time. Some people are surprised when I say that my best friend is a woman, especially an ex-girlfriend. But I think it's perfectly possible for us to be 'just good friends', although maybe when one of us finds a new partner it'll be more difficult. I hope not.

BETTER PRONUNCIATION

Past participles, forms of *have*

a **T1.1** Circle the different sound. Listen and check.

1 gone/won/done
2 paid/said/read
3 spoken/broken/forgotten
4 cut/put/drunk
5 taken/made/fallen
6 bought/caught/hurt
7 looked/watched/invited
8 phoned/needed/arrived

b **T1.2** Listen and write six sentences.

c Go to **Vocabulary Builder 13** *Irregular verbs*, *p.141*. Which ones are new to you? Test each other.

PRACTICE

a Make questions in the past simple or present perfect.

1 When/Pavarotti/born?
2 How long/married/Adua?
3 How long/be/an opera singer?
4 When/start eating too much?
5 When/meet/José Carreras?
6 How long/know/José Carreras?
7 How long/work as one of The Three Tenors?
8 How long/be separated/first wife?

b Ask a partner the questions. Answer from memory.

c Go to **Communication** *Truth or lie?* **A** *p.121*, **B** *p.125*. Practise asking *Have you ever…?* questions.

Luciano Pavarotti

1935	born in Modena, Italy
1961	married first wife, Adua
1961	made opera debut in Italy
1969	started eating too much
1975	met José Carreras in San Francisco
1990	first concert as one of The Three Tenors
1996	separated from first wife
2003	had a daughter with Nicoletta Mantovani

5 LISTEN BETTER

a **T1.3** Listen to Craig talking about an argument he had with his friend, Andy. What was the argument about? Are they still best friends?

b Listen for more detail. Answer with your partner.

1 Where did they meet Tessa?
2 Who spoke to her first?
3 What happened at the end of the party?
4 Who phoned first? What happened?
5 Who phoned second? What happened?
6 How did Andy feel?
7 What was the 'funny thing'?
8 How long did Craig go out with Tessa for?

c Have you ever had a serious argument with a friend? What about?

6 GRAMMAR ANALYSIS
Reflexive pronouns / *each other*

a Look at the pictures. What's the difference between *each other* and *themselves*?

They're hugging *each other*.

They're looking at *themselves* in the mirror.

b Complete the chart.

| **Singular** | myself | _____ | himself /_____ / _____ |
| **Plural** | _____ | yourselves | _____ |

Use *each other*:
- when **A** does an action to **B** and **B** does the same action to **A**.
  They phone each other. We love each other.

Use a reflexive pronoun (*myself, yourself*, etc.):
- when the object of a verb is the same as the subject.
  I cut myself when I was making the dinner.

- for emphasis.
  He built the house himself. = He built it, with no help.

- *by + himself*, etc. = alone
  I live by myself.

! *Enjoy* always needs a reflexive pronoun or another object.
  We enjoyed ourselves. / We enjoyed the film. NOT ~~We enjoyed.~~

PRACTICE

Complete with *myself, himself*, etc. or *each other*.

1 She's selfish. She only thinks of _herself_.
2 My brother and his ex-wife don't speak to _each other_.
3 Have a good holiday, Tom. Enjoy _yourself_.
4 I love travelling by _myself_.
5 He looked at _himself_ in the mirror.
6 We write to ~~herself~~ _each other_ about once a month.
7 This light is automatic. It turns _itself_ on and off.
8 We painted the house _ourselves_.
9 They really enjoyed _themselves_ at the party.
10 They don't understand _each other_.

7 MAKING CONVERSATION
Friends

a Do you agree? Write 1 (strongly agree) to 5 (strongly disagree) in the boxes.

Your best friend can't be a member of your family. [2]

It's difficult to have a best friend of the opposite sex. [5]

It's impossible to stay 'good friends' with an ex-partner. [3]

Men have more close friends than women. [5]

Men keep their friends longer than women. [5]

Women have more serious conversations with their friends than men. [1]

b Compare in groups.

What do you think?
I think (that)…
I agree (with you).
Yes, I think so (too) because…
So do I.
I don't agree / I disagree (with you).
I don't think so because…
Neither do I.

8 WRITE BETTER

Write three paragraphs about your best friend. Use the chart in **3** on *p.9* to help you.

9 SONG ♫

T1.4 *With a little help from my friends*

Caring and sharing?

1 PRESENTATION

a Describe the pictures. Guess what the people are saying.

Picture 1

Picture 2

b **T1.5** Listen and complete.

Conversation 1

A How _____ have you _____ sharing a _____?
B _____ October.
A How do you _____ on with your flatmate?
B Great. We get on really _____.

Conversation 2

A You _____ exhausted. What have you been _____?
B I've been _____ the flat.
A Oh no! I forgot all about it. I'll help you.
B Too late. I've _____ it. Where have you _____?
A I've _____ shopping. I'm really sorry.

2 GRAMMAR ANALYSIS

Present perfect continuous

a Look at Conversations 1 and 2 in **1b**.

  1 How long has she been sharing a flat? Is she *still* sharing a flat?
  2 Why is her flatmate tired? Is she *still* cleaning the flat?
  3 Underline four examples of the present perfect continuous.

b Complete the rule.

> **To form the present perfect continuous, use**
> *have/has* + _____ + (verb + -_____).
>
> **Use the present perfect continuous for:**
> ● **unfinished actions which started in the past and are continuing now, and with**
> ***How long…?* + *for/since*.**
>   **A** *How long have you been studying English?*
>   **B** *I've been studying English for two years.* (= I'm still studying) NOT ~~I am studying …~~
> ● **a continuous action in the past which has recently finished.**
>   **A** *You're very dirty! What have you been doing?*
>   **B** *I've been playing football.*
> **!** We don't use the present perfect continuous with *be*, *have* (possession), and *know*.
>   *I've known her for ten years.* NOT ~~I've been knowing her for ten years.~~

BETTER PRONUNCIATION

Weak forms

a **T1.6** Listen and underline the stressed words.

  1 <u>What</u> have you been <u>doing</u>?
  2 I've been shopping all afternoon.
  3 How long has she been living there?
  4 She's been living there for three years.
  5 How long have you been waiting?
  6 I've been waiting for half an hour.

b What kind of words are not stressed? What happens to the pronunciation of *have/has* and *been*?

c Say the sentences quickly. Emphasize the stressed words.

d **T1.7** Listen and write five sentences.

PRACTICE

a Write *How long…?* questions. Ask a partner.

| two years | 11 o'clock | half an hour | two months | 1980 |

1 _____ ?
2 _____ ?
3 _____ ?
4 _____ ?
5 _____ ?

b What have they been doing? In groups, think of as many answers as you can for each picture below.

Maybe she's been cutting onions or maybe she's been…

1 _____ .
2 _____ .
3 _____ .
4 _____ .

3 BUILD YOUR VOCABULARY

Common verb phrases

a ✐ Complete **Vocabulary Builder 1** *Common verb phrases*, *p.129*.

b Test your memory.

> 1 **Think of three things you can…**
>   do   make   play   have
> 2 **Think of two things you can…**
>   spend   take   catch   miss   lose   keep
> 3 **What does *get* mean in…?**
>   get angry   get to work   get a letter   get a new car   get a taxi
> 4 **What's the difference between…?**
>   go home/get home   be divorced/get divorced
> 5 **What vehicles can you…?**
>   get in(to)   get on

4 READ BETTER

a Imagine you're going to share a flat or a house with two other people you don't know. Which of the following do you think could cause most problems? Why? Can you think of any other possible causes for argument?

watching TV   doing the housework   using the phone   friends   money   food

b Read an article about flat-sharing quickly. Answer the questions without looking back at the text.

1 How many different places has she lived in?
2 Who has she shared with?
3 What were the disadvantages in each place?

Flat-sharing
– the inside story

You've got a problem. You're going to go to university in a different town and you need somewhere to live. Or perhaps you just don't get on with your parents. What can you do? Have you ever thought of sharing a flat?

5 I know all about it because I've been sharing flats for the past four years, since I moved to Edinburgh to study. I must admit my first experience was a bit of a disaster. I saw an advert in the newspaper from a girl who had a flat and was looking for a flatmate. When I met her, she seemed really nice, and I
10 noticed that she had lots of great CDs I wanted to hear and a big TV. However, I changed my mind about her a few days after I moved in. I came home from college one day and threw my books and jacket onto the living room sofa. My flatmate looked at them, looked at me and shouted: 'I hope you're not
15 going to leave those there!' It was then I found out that she was absolutely obsessive about being tidy. It was obvious that we were incompatible, as I'm definitely not the world's tidiest person. I moved out after the first month.

I then decided to try sharing a house with several people. I
20 rented a room in a big old house which I shared with four other girls (two Brazilians, a Russian, and an Italian). It was great because the house was always full of young people from all over the world and we had lots of parties. However, there were three problems. Firstly, it was almost impossible to do any work because the house was so noisy. Secondly, there 25 was only one bathroom, and there was always someone in it, especially first thing in the morning when I was already late for class. But the biggest arguments we had were always the day the phone bill arrived!

After a year the foreign girls went home, and I decided to look 30 for a new, preferably quieter flat! This time I decided to share with a friend, somebody I already knew well. We've been living here now for nearly a year and we get on really well – except for her irritating habits of eating my yoghurts and finishing the coffee! But it's great having someone else to help 35 pay the rent, to share their dinner with you when you're too exhausted to cook, and who, unlike your parents or your partner, doesn't mind what time you get up or if you've left your bedroom in a mess. And best of all, when you've had a bad day or you've broken up with your boyfriend you know 40 there's always someone to talk to.

c In pairs, underline all the new words or expressions in the text, and try to guess their meaning from the context. Now find a word or expression which means:

Paragraph 1
1 having or using something with another person (*v.*) _____

Paragraph 2
2 person you share a flat with (*n.*) _____
3 began living in a flat or house (*v.*) _____
4 discovered (*v.*) _____
5 always worried about (*adj.*) _____
6 having everything in the right place (*adj.*) _____

Paragraph 3
7 some, but not many (*adj.*) _____

Paragraph 4
8 annoying (*adj.*) _____
9 very tired (*adj.*) _____
10 different from (*prep.*) _____
11 untidy, with everything in the wrong place _____

d Now read the text again. Do you think, in general, the writer is for or against flat-sharing? Do you think the problems are the same if you live with your family or a partner?

5 MAKING CONVERSATION

Life at home

In pairs, talk about Circle 1. Ask at least one more question. Get as much information as you can. Then talk about Circle 2, etc.

A *Where do you live?*
B *I live in a flat quite near the centre, near the main square.*
A *How many bedrooms are there?…*

1

WHERE DO YOU LIVE?
House or flat? Where?
What's it like?
How long have you been
living there?
Who do you live with?
Do you get on well?

2

**WHAT HOUSEWORK
DO YOU HAVE TO DO?**
The cooking?
The cleaning?
Tidying your room?
The ironing?
The washing-up?
The shopping?

Anything else?

3

**WHAT CAUSES
PROBLEMS AT HOME?**
Watching TV?
Housework?
Studying?
Going out?
Playing music?
Money?

Anything else?

Who do you argue with most?
What about?

6 GRAMMAR ANALYSIS

Present perfect simple or continuous?

Present perfect simple	Present perfect continuous
Have you ever shared a flat?	How long have you been waiting?
I've had my car for three years.	I've been sharing a flat for a year.
Vicky's lost her job.	What has she been doing?
We haven't finished yet.	She's been crying.

Look at the example sentences above. How do you say them in your language? Read the rules carefully.

Use the present perfect simple (NOT continuous) for:

● **past experiences.**
I've seen that film twice. NOT ~~I've been seeing that film twice.~~

● **unfinished situations with *have* (= possess), *be*, and *know*.**
I've had my car for six months. NOT ~~I've been having …~~

! With some verbs, e.g. *work* and *live*, you can use both tenses.

● **an action in the past which has a result in the present.**
I've broken my leg. NOT ~~I've been breaking my leg.~~

● ***yet, just,* and *already*.**
Have you finished yet? I've already done it. I've just arrived. NOT ~~I've just been arriving~~, etc.

PRACTICE

a Put the verbs in the present perfect simple or continuous.

1 **A** How long _have they had_ their car? (they/have)
  B It's new. _They've just bought_ it. (they/just/buy)
2 **A** _Has she found_ a job yet? (she/find)
  B No, _she has been looking for_ one for ages. (she/look for)
3 **A** How long _has it been raining_? (it/rain)
  B _It has just started_ (it/just/start)
4 **A** You look tired. What _have you been doing_? (you/do)
  B _I've been studying_ all night. (I/study)
5 **A** _Have you seen_ the new Spielberg film yet? (you/see)
  B Yes, _I have already seen_ it. (I/already/see) It's quite good.
6 **A** _Have you finished_ that book I lent you yet? (you/finish)
  B _You have been reading_ it for ages. (you/read).

b Make questions with *How long…?* Use the correct tense.

1 Kevin's got a new car.   _How long has he had it?_
2 They're living in Paris.   _How long they've been living there?_
3 I know Anne very well.   _How long have you been knowing?_
4 Mark's studying English.   _How long has he been studying the English?_
5 David and Vanessa are married. _continuous_
6 I'm waiting for the bus.   _continuous._

c In pairs, ask and answer the questions.

How long/study English?
Where/live? How long/live there?
Drive? How long/drive?
Have/car? How long/have it?
Married? How long/be married?
Where/buy your shirt (shoes, etc.)? How long/have it (them)?
What/favourite possession? How long/have it?

Good relations

1 BUILD YOUR VOCABULARY
Families and describing people

a Do the 'Family' quiz.

> **Who is, in relation to you …?**
> 1 your mother's brother — *my uncle*
> 2 your father's sister — *my aunt*
> 3 your husband's mother — *mother-in-law*
> 4 your husband's sister — *my sister-in-law*
> 5 your brother's daughter — *my niece*
> 6 your sister's son — *my nephew*
> 7 your father's brother's children — *my cousin(s)*
> 8 your mother's father — *my grand-father*
> 9 your daughter's son — *my grandson*
> 10 your father's second wife — *my stepmother (mother-in-law)*

→ husband's mother.

b 📖 Complete **Vocabulary Builder 2A** *Appearance*, p.130.

c Write sentences with *look(s)* or *look(s) like*.

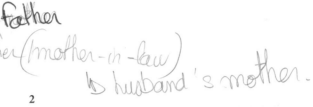

1 Sara _____looks_____ friendly.
2 John _____looks like_____ his father.
3 She _____looks like_____ about thirty.
4 Peter _____looks like_____ a bank manager.
5 You _____looks_____ tired.
6 They _____look_____ French.

1

2

d Say as much as you can about the people.

The adults	The children
What do they look like?	What do they look like?
How old do you think they look?	How old do you think they look?
What nationality do you think they look?	Do the children look like their parents?

2 GRAMMAR ANALYSIS
both, neither, either

a Look at the photos in **1d** again. Which people do the sentences describe?

They *both* have red hair.
Both the mother *and* the son have red hair.
Both of them have red hair.

Neither the father *nor* the son wears glasses.
Neither of them wears glasses.

They look *either* Spanish *or* Mexican.
She doesn't really look like *either* her mother *or* her father.

b Complete the rules.

Use *both*, *neither*, and *either* to talk about two people or things.

- _Neither_ = not **A** and not **B**
  both = **A** and **B**
  Either = **A** or **B**

- After *both* and *neither* the verb must be (+).
  Neither of us is/are tall.
  We both like football.

! *neither* = one or two people, so the verb can be singular or plural.
both = two people, so the verb must be plural.

PRACTICE

a Complete with *both*, *neither*, or *either*.

The person I'm most like in my family is probably my sister Cécile. We look like each other because [1] *both* of us have very dark hair and dark eyes, and we're [2] ~~either~~ *both* more or less the same size, [3] *neither* fat nor slim. We've got similar personalities too. We're [4] *both* extrovert and talkative. When the family gets together, [5] *either* Cécile or I always dominate the conversation. We've also got similar tastes. We [6] *both* love reading, [7] *either* novels or biographies, and [8] *both* of us can play any sport. At *neither*. school we were [9] *both* probably the worst in the class at sport!

b Complete the second sentence so that it means the same as the first. Use *both*, *neither*, or *either*.

1 John lives in the USA and James lives in the USA too.
Both of them live _They both live_ in the USA.

2 Andrea didn't come yesterday, and Gina didn't.
Neither Andrea nor Gina came yesterday.

3 I'd like to go to Rome or Venice this summer.
~~I~~ _We 'd like to go either R or V_ this summer.

4 My sister and I don't smoke.
Neither my sister nor ~~me~~ I smoke.

5 He and his brother live in rented flats.
They both live in rented flats.

6 I don't like this one or that one. _either_
I don't like ~~both~~ of them.
I like neither

3 MAKING CONVERSATION
Your family

In pairs, **A** look at the questions. Tell **B** about your family. **B** listen and ask more questions. Swap roles.

How many people are there in your immediate family?
How old are they? What do they do?
Have you got a lot of other relatives?
Who do you look like in your family?
In what way are you physically similar?

4 READ BETTER

a What's your position in the family? Are you the oldest, the youngest, in the middle, or an only child? Do you like your position? Why (not)?

b Read the introduction to a magazine article about how your position in the family affects your personality. Then read the paragraphs in the order that you find most interesting.

Family
fortunes

Scientists and psychologists agree that although many factors contribute to forming your personality, for example, your sex, class, culture, or lifestyle, one of the most important is your position in the family. So how have *you* been affected?

Are you a first child, a middle child,
5 **the youngest, or an only child?**

First-born children. If you are a first-born child, you are probably self-confident and a good leader – you came first, after all. You may also be bossy and even
10 aggressive if you don't get what you want. You are ambitious, and good at communicating, because you learned to speak from your parents, not from brothers and sisters. On the other hand,
15 you are the oldest and so you have to be the most responsible, and this can make you the kind of person who worries a lot.

Middle children are usually independent and competitive. You had to
20 fight with your brothers and sisters to get what you wanted. You are also co-operative as you always had to negotiate with either your older or your younger brothers and sisters. You are
25 sociable, as you always had someone to play with. On the other hand, you may be jealous and insecure or moody if you felt that your parents preferred your older brother or sister.

30 **Youngest children** are often very charming. You learned very quickly that you could get exactly what you want by being charming – and this can make you manipulative. You are usually affectionate
35 and relaxed because when you arrived your parents were more relaxed themselves. But you are often not very independent, as you always had so many people to help you. This makes it hard for
40 you to take decisions. And you may be lazy, because your parents probably pushed you less and were less strict with you than with your older brothers and sisters.

45 **Only children** are often quite selfish. You had the wonderful luxury of not having to share your parents' attention with anybody else. In fact, you received so much attention as a child that you find it
50 difficult to be interested in other people. On the other hand, you are usually organized and responsible, and often imaginative. But you may find it difficult to communicate with others, and are very
55 sensitive to criticism.

c Underline the adjectives of personality. Write them in the chart.

	First-born children	Middle children	Youngest children	Only children
Positive adjectives	*self-confident* responsible ambitious communicating	independent co-operative sociable	charming affectionate relaxed	organized responsible imaginative
Negative adjectives	bossy aggressive	jealous moody insecure	lazy	selfish sensitive
Positive or negative adjectives	ambitious	competitive	manipulative	sensi

d 📖 Complete **Vocabulary Builder 2B Personality**, *p.130*.

e In pairs, compare opinions on the article. What are you like? What are your brothers/sisters/friends like?

I'm a middle child. I'm competitive, but I'm not really moody. But my younger brother is definitely…

BETTER PRONUNCIATION
Word stress

a Underline the stress.

1 jealous	5 co-operative	9 insecure
2 ambitious	6 affectionate	10 aggressive
3 imaginative	7 independent	11 responsible
4 competitive	8 sociable	12 organized

b **T1.8** Listen and check. Practise saying the adjectives.

Remember: adjectives ending *-ive* = /ɪv/.
adjectives ending *-ous* = /əs/.
adjectives ending *-able* = /əbl/.

c Test a partner on the adjectives of personality in **a** above. Try to pronounce them correctly.

> **A** *This kind of person likes being with other people.*
> **B** *'Sociable'.*

5 LISTEN BETTER

a **T1.9** Listen to a psychologist speaking about other things which affect your personality. What are the main things?

b Listen for more detail. Complete the sentences.

1 If you're a first child and you're a girl, you will be _____ _____ if the second child is a boy.
2 If you're a girl in the middle of three girls, you will probably rebel against _____ _____ and want to wear _____ and play _____.
3 If you're a girl in the middle of boys, you will probably do exactly the opposite and like _____ and pretty _____.
4 Girls who have a lot of attention from their fathers in the early years are usually more _____ and _____.
5 Boys who spend most of their time with their mothers are better at _____ and _____ _____.

c Do you agree with what the psychologist said?

6 MAKING CONVERSATION
Good relations?

a In pairs, look at the topics in the box. **A** write three advantages for each topic, **B** write three disadvantages.

> **ADVANTAGE OR DISADVANTAGE?**
> Having a lot of brothers and sisters
> Being an only child
> Having an older relative living with you (e.g. grandmother)
> Both of your parents working

b Together discuss each point. Do you agree?

> *One advantage/disadvantage is that…*
> *On the other hand…*
> *That's true, but…*
> *I agree/disagree because…*

7 WRITE BETTER

Either:
Write three short paragraphs describing a relative.

Paragraph 1 What does he/she look like?
Paragraph 2 What's he/she like?
Paragraph 3 What does he/she like doing?

Or:
Write three short paragraphs about *one* of the topics in **6**.

Paragraph 1 Advantages
Paragraph 2 Disadvantages
Paragraph 3 Your conclusions/own opinion

Use the **Writing Bank** on *p.145* to help you.

▶ Go to **Check your progress 1**, *p.114*.

Hello and goodbye

1 UNDERSTANDING INFORMATION

a Read this information from a language school brochure. Write **T** (true) or **F** (false).

1 You will receive more information before you leave your country.
2 The best way to get from London to Cambridge is by train.
3 The school will pay for a taxi from the bus station to the family.
4 There are special arrangements for people doing summer courses.
5 On the summer course you will be taken back to the airport on the Saturday after the course ends.
6 Your family will take you to the school on the first day.
7 The Director of Studies will meet you at the school.

b Guess the meaning of the highlighted words in the text. Match them to the definitions.

1 exists for you to use if you want _____
2 a person who receives someone as a guest _____
3 included inside something _____
4 given to you and you don't have to pay _____
5 go with you _____
6 show you all the different parts of _____
7 pay to use for a short time _____
8 a kind of bus which takes you from an airport to another place _____
9 people who work for an organization _____
10 an exam to decide your level _____

WHAT HAPPENS WHEN I ARRIVE?

- Clear instructions sent to you before departure
- Airport pick-up service available
- Guided tour of school
- Level placement test

FROM THE AIRPORT TO YOUR HOST FAMILY

There is an excellent coach transfer to Cambridge city centre from each of the three London airports. You will then find taxis waiting at Cambridge bus station which you can hire to reach your host family. However if you prefer, we can order a taxi straight from the airport to your host family. Prices for this are listed on the enclosed sheet.

Summer Courses – If you are coming on any summer courses and you arrive at Heathrow or Gatwick airports between 09:00 and 18:00 on the Sunday before the beginning of your course, staff from the school will be waiting for you at the airport and will escort you on the transfer coach to Cambridge where a school minibus will take you on to the host family. Transport is provided free of charge to the airport on the Saturday after the end of your course.

YOUR FIRST DAY AT THE SCHOOL

You will need to arrive at the school by 09:15 on your first day (your host family will tell you how to get to us from their house). Here you will be met by our Director of Studies, who will give you all the information you need and show you round the school.

2 MEETING PEOPLE

a T1.10 Listen to Claudia, a foreign student, meeting her host family. Who are the people in the family?

b Listen again. Complete the chart.

Meeting people for the first time	
Usual	**More formal**
Hi!/_____ _____ to meet you. _____ is (my husband). Did you have a _____ _____? Yes, _____ thanks.	Good morning/afternoon. Pleased to meet you./How do you _____?

c Go to **Communication** *Introductions*, **A** *p.121*, **B** *p.125*. Roleplay arriving at the host family's house.

3 LISTEN BETTER

a **T1.11** Listen to a Director of Studies welcoming new language students on their first day. Explain why the following are important:

1 David Hudson
2 Sharon Black
3 from 1.00 till 5.00 p.m.
4 9.30 a.m.
5 10.30 a.m.
6 11.00 a.m.
7 1.30 p.m.
8 2.45 p.m.
9 3.00 p.m.
10 the first floor

b Listen again. Then tell a partner as much as you can about the school. Use the names and times in **a**.

4 UNDERSTANDING SIGNS

Read the signs. Explain where you could see them and what they mean.

1 **OUT OF ORDER**

2 **BEWARE OF THE DOG**

3 **KEEP OFF THE GRASS**

4 **PLEASE QUEUE THIS SIDE**

5 SAYING GOODBYE

T1.12 Listen to Claudia leaving for the Cambridge Language School. Tick (✔)the expressions you hear.

I have to go. ☐
See you (this evening). ☐
Have a nice day. ☐
Bye. ☐
Goodbye. ☐

6 BUILD YOUR VOCABULARY
Common expressions

a Match the responses with the expressions.

Bless you!   Congratulations!   Cheers!   Good luck!
Happy Birthday!   Help yourself.   Yes please./No thanks, I'm full.
The same to you.   See you (tomorrow/later).
Never mind./It doesn't matter.

1 Have a good weekend. _____
2 I've got an exam tomorrow. _____
3 I've left my book at home. _____
4 Atchoo! _____
5 I've got a new job! _____
6 It's my birthday today. _____
7 Would you like some more cake? _____
8 Cheers! _____
9 Could I have another biscuit? _____
10 I must go now. _____

b **T1.13** Listen and check. Repeat and copy the intonation.

c **T1.14** Cover the expressions. Listen and respond with the correct expression.

1 BUILD YOUR VOCABULARY

Daily routine

Write the correct verbs in the chart. Add more words to each column.

Have	take	go	do	get
breakfast a bath/shower a siesta/nap	medicine the children to school the dog for a walk	to the doctor's/ gym to work home	homework sport/exercise housework	dressed to work ready for bed

2 READ BETTER

a Before you read the article, complete the column for your opinion. Complete with **M, A, E,** or **N.** Compare with a partner.

> **M** = 8 a.m. – 2 p.m. (in the morning)
> **A** = 2–6 p.m. (in the afternoon)
> **E** = 6–11 p.m. (in the evening)
> **N** = after 11 p.m. (at night)
>
> | What's the best time of day to …? | Your opinion | Experts' opinion |
> |---|---|---|
> | 1 take vitamins | A | M |
> | 2 have an injection | A | M |
> | 3 write a poem | E | M |
> | 4 have a big meal | M | M |
> | 5 have a siesta | A | A |
> | 6 study | E | M/A |
> | 7 do sport | M | M/A |
> | 8 phone friends | | E |
> | 9 have a bath | E | E |

b Read the article about chronobiology. Do the experts agree with you? Complete the Experts' opinion column with the exact time, e.g. 2–3 p.m.

c Read the text again. Write **T** (true) or **F** (false).
1 The food you eat for breakfast doesn't make you fat. *T*
2 Injections hurt more in the morning. *F*
3 It's best to carry heavy shopping in the morning. *T*
4 You can run fastest in the morning. *F*
5 It's better to eat a large lunch than a large dinner. *T*
6 You have your best ideas in the evening. *F*
7 You concentrate best after midnight. *F*
8 You should be especially careful driving after lunch or late at night. *T*

d In the text, underline words you don't understand. Guess the meaning from the context. Check in the Glossary or a dictionary.

e In pairs, compare your daily routines to the recommendations in the article. What are the main differences?

I never have a good breakfast. At 8 a.m. I only drink a cup of coffee. What about you?

A time

For everything there is a season. The new science of chronobiology tells us the best time of day to do everything,
5 *from writing a poem to taking pills. By following your body's natural daily rhythms, you can get more out of every day.*

MORNING
10 **7 a.m.–9.00** Have a good breakfast. The metabolism is most active in the morning, and everything that you eat at this time gives you energy but doesn't make
15 you put on weight. For the same reason, it's also the best time of day to take vitamins. If you take them before bedtime, some vitamins can keep you awake and others can
20 cause indigestion.
   9–10.00 Go to the doctor's or dentist's. Injections are least painful at this time of day. It is also the best time of day to do weight-training,
25 or heavy physical activity. The back and neck muscles are strongest now and less susceptible to injury.
   10–12.00 Work, study, paint a picture, or write a poem. The brain
30 is at its most creative at this time of day.
   12–2.00 p.m. Eat. This is the best time to have lunch, as the digestive system works very efficiently at this
35 time. You should have your big meal now and not in the evening.

AFTERNOON
2–3.00 Have a siesta. After lunch, the body temperature goes down
40 and the brain works more slowly. Research also shows that there is an increase in road accidents at this time of day because drivers fall asleep at the wheel. Research in
45 Greece shows that men who have a siesta are the least likely to suffer heart attacks.

for everything

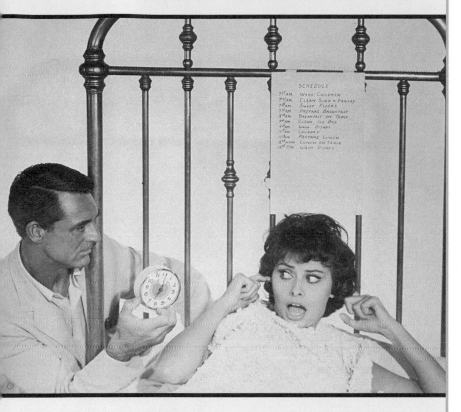

3–5.00 Go to the gym. Physically our bodies are at their daily peak. Body temperature, strength, and flexibility are at their highest, and most Olympic records are broken at this time of day.
4–6.00 Do homework. Research shows that children are faster at doing arithmetic at this time of day.

EVENING
6–8.00 Eat, drink, and enjoy yourself. Although our digestive system works more slowly in the evening, the senses of smell, taste, and hearing are at their best from about 6 p.m to 7 p.m., so now is the time for a light but delicious dinner in good company. The liver is also at its most efficient in dealing with alcohol, so open a bottle of wine! If you're not going out, spend the evening looking after yourself. Put

70 on face and body creams, as the skin absorbs them best at this time of day.
8–10.00 Phone friends. This is the time when people most often feel lonely (and it's also cheaper to 75 phone in most parts of the world!).
10–11.00 Get ready for bed. One of the best ways to make sure you get a good night's sleep is to have a warm bath. This relaxes both your 80 mind and your body.

NIGHT
11 p.m.–7 a.m. Sleep. After 11 o'clock, the metabolism slows down, and body temperature and 85 adrenaline levels drop, preparing us for sleep. If we stay awake after midnight, our attention drops dramatically and even the most careful people often make 90 mistakes. Accidents increase by six times between 3 a.m. and 4 a.m.

BETTER PRONUNCIATION
The letter *i*

a **T2.1** How is the letter *i* pronounced in these words? Put them in the correct column. Underline the stress. Listen and check.

describe   science   dinner   drivers
efficient   highest   injury   vitamins
light   pill   skin   wine

b Look at the spellings. Complete the rules with /ɪ/ or /aɪ/.

i between consonants is usually pronounced _____.
i + **one** consonant + *e* is usually pronounced _____.
igh between consonants is always pronounced _____.

c How do you pronounce these words? Which one is 'irregular'?

twice   likely   written   midnight   routine   since

Glossary
painful (*adj.*) /ˈpeɪnfl/ — something that hurts
research (*n.*) /rɪˈsɜːtʃ/ — work done by e.g. scientists to find out new things
increase (*n.*) /ˈɪŋkriːs/ — a bigger number of
increase (*v.*) /ɪnˈkriːs/ — go up, get bigger
likely (*adj.*) — probable
peak (*n.*) — the highest point of something
drop (*n.*) — a smaller amount
drop (*v.*) — fall, go down
dramatically (*adv.*) — a lot

3 BUILD YOUR VOCABULARY

Body and health

a In pairs, discuss what these words from the text on *pp.22–23* mean.

1 injections   4 painful
2 heart attack   5 skin
3 liver → *Foie*

b 📖 Complete **Vocabulary Builder 3** *Body and health*, *p.131*.

c Do the 'Body and health' quiz.

> - **What organ…?**
>   1 do you use to breathe *lungs*
>   2 sends your blood round your body *heart*
>   3 controls all the other parts *brain*
>   4 is most affected if you drink too much alcohol ~~*heart*~~ *liver*
> - **What part/parts of the body…?**
>   5 goes brown in the sun *skin*
>   6 come in pairs *hands, legs, ears, eyes …*
>   7 do you have 200 of *bones*
> - **What are the symptoms of…?**
>   8 flu → *cough/temperature*
>   9 appendicitis → *stomaches*
>   10 stress → *tired, headache, nervous.*

4 GRAMMAR ANALYSIS

Present simple or continuous?

a **T2.2** Listen. Complete the two questions in each dialogue. What's the difference?

1

What _are_ you _doing here_?
What _do_ you _do_?

2

Where _are_ you _going_?
Where _do_ you _go_?

b Correct the mistakes.

1 **A** Where's Ann? *is watching.*
   B She's in the living room. She watches TV.
2 What time are you usually getting up? *do*
3 What languages do you study at the moment? *are studying*
4 I'm really thirsty. I'm needing a drink.
5 Where lives your brother? *Where does your b. live?*
6 I go to the cinema tonight. *I'm going to*
7 She goes to Italian classes ~~two times~~ a week. *twice*
8 They go hardly ever to the cinema. *hardly ever go.*
9 I play once a week tennis. *I play tennis once a week.*
10 My family has lunch together every Sundays.

c Check with the grammar rules.

> **Use the present simple for:**
> - **permanent situations.**
>   *I live in a flat.*
> - **habitual actions.**
>   *She always has toast for breakfast.*
>   *They go out twice a week.*
> + **time expressions**
>   Adverbs of frequency:
>   *sometimes, never,* etc.
>   Expressions of frequency:
>   *every day, once a year,* etc.
>
> **Use the present continuous for:**
> - **actions happening now.**
>   *It's raining. Prices are going up.*
> + **time expressions**
>   *now, at the moment, this week*
> - **future arrangements.**
>   *What are you doing on Friday night?*
>   *I'm having dinner with friends.*
> + **future time expressions**
>   *this evening, tomorrow night*
>
> 🚫 Some verbs (*be, like, want, know, need, have* (possession)) are not normally used in the present continuous.
> *I need it now.* NOT ~~I'm needing it now.~~
>
> ❗ Adverbs of frequency go before the main verb but after *be*. Frequency expressions (*once a week*, etc.) usually go at the end of the sentence.

PRACTICE

a Write questions in the present simple or continuous.

_ε ē ḗ ī_   Horror. action

Questions		Answers
How often do you go to the c.?	1 How often/go/cinema?	once a month
What are U reading at this m.?	2 What/read/the moment?	a chinese book
W. do u like doing during your	3 What/like/do/free time?	chatting with friends.
W do U usually go on S. night?	4 Where/usually/go/on Saturday night?	sleeping at home
W. time do U usually go to bed?	5 What time/usually/go/bed?	12 o'clock.
Are U studying any other l. this year?	6 Study/other languages/this year?	English
How do u get to work?	7 How/get/work (or school)?	on foot.
W. kind of f. do U like?	8 What kind/films/like?	Funny & horror film
W. are U doing tonight?	9 What/do/tonight?	studying.
When do U watch TV.?	10 When/watch TV?	the evening.

b Cover the **Questions** column. Ask a partner. Note the answers.

c Change partners. Ask and answer questions about your previous partners.

How often **does** Carlos go to the cinema?
He **goes** about once a month.

d Go to **Communication** _Usually or now?_ **A** _p.121_, **B** _p.125_. Ask questions
about life and lifestyles.

5 LISTEN BETTER

a   T2.3   Listen to Esther, a nurse, talking about working
nights. What's the worst thing for her?

b Listen again and complete the notes.

Hours
Has to work nights [1] _____
weeks out of every [2] _____ .
Starts [3] _____ .
Finishes [4] _____ .
Goes to bed at [5] _____ .
Sleeps between [6] _____ and
[7] _____ hours.

Food
Has [8] _____ between
1 and 2 a.m.
Never has [9] _____ .

Problems
Difficult to stay awake, especially between [10] _____
and [11] _____ .
People who work at night [12] _____ _____
more quickly.
When you're on night duty you still have to
[13] _____ _____ _____ _____ _____ .
Another big problem is [14] _____ _____ _____ .

6 MAKING CONVERSATION
How you spend your day

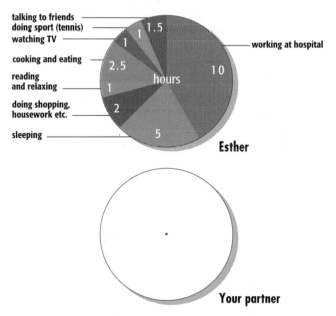

talking to friends
doing sport (tennis)
watching TV
cooking and eating
reading and relaxing
doing shopping, housework etc.
sleeping

1.5   1   1   working at hospital
2.5   10   hours
1   2   5

Esther

Your partner

a Look at Esther's chart showing a typical day. Interview
a partner and fill in the other chart. Ask for more
information.

   A _How long do you spend working?_
   B _Let's see. From 8 to 3, so about seven hours._
   A _What exactly do you do?_

b Compare your charts. Would you like to change
anything about the way you spend your day?

1 LISTEN BETTER

a In pairs, read the newspaper extract.

1 Why are shops going to sell these vegetables?
2 What do the vegetables taste like?
3 Do you think children will like them?
4 Would you like to try them?

Chocolate carrots – tomorrow's vegetables?

HOW many children do you know who really like vegetables? Probably not many. But it has been proved that eating vegetables in childhood helps to protect you against serious illness in later life. So yesterday chocolate-flavoured carrots went on sale in Britain as part of a campaign to encourage children to eat vegetables. The range of products also includes cheese-and-onion flavoured cauliflower, pizza-flavoured sweetcorn, and peas that taste like chewing-gum.

b Underline five vegetables in the text. How many more vegetables can you name? Which do/don't you like?

c T2.4 Listen to a radio programme about the new vegetables. Write **T** (true) or **F** (false).

1 The first chef is against the new vegetables.
2 He thinks the best way to make children eat vegetables is to give them a small portion every day.
3 The second chef thinks that children will like the colour of the new vegetables.
4 James likes the carrots and the peas.
5 He would like to have the vegetables again.

d T2.5 Listen to some extracts from the programme. What do these words mean?

bribe   mixture   disgusting   spoonful

2 BUILD YOUR VOCABULARY
Diet

a 🔥 Complete **Vocabulary Builder 4** *Food and Diet*, *p.132*.

b Do the '5–4–3–2–1 Food' quiz.

- Think of **FIVE** kinds of…
  1 fattening food
  2 vegetables which are often tinned
- Think of **FOUR** kinds of…
  3 food that you usually buy frozen
  4 food that you usually buy fresh
- Think of **THREE** kinds of…
  5 take-away food
  6 spicy dishes
  7 junk food
- Think of **TWO** kinds of…
  8 proteins
  9 carbohydrates
- Think of **ONE** food which can be…
  10 boiled
  11 baked
  12 grilled
  13 fried

3 GRAMMAR ANALYSIS
Quantifiers

a Explain the difference.

Grammatically
1 a few/a little
2 much/many
3 How much?/How many?
4 a lot of/a lot
5 too/too much
6 enough (coffee)/(hot) enough

In meaning
7 I drink a lot of coffee./
  I drink too much coffee.
8 We've got a few eggs./
  We haven't got enough eggs.
9 How much money have you got?
  A little./None.

b Check with the grammar rules.

	Big quantities	**Small quantities**	**Zero quantities**	**More than you need**	**Less then you need**
Countable lots of (−) not many (?) How many	(+) a lot of	a few very few	not…any none (in short answers)	too many	not enough
Uncountable lots of (−) not much (?) How much	(+) a lot of	a little very little	not…any none (in short answers)	too much	not enough

⟶ Ø pluriel

> **!** Use *a lot of* or *lots of* before nouns (*a lot of money*). After a verb use *a lot* (*I eat a lot*).
> *a lot* can also be used in (−) and (?) especially in conversation.
>
> Use *too* + adjective.
> *My coffee's too hot.* NOT ~~My coffee's too much hot.~~
>
> Use (*not*) *enough* before nouns but after adjectives.
> *I haven't got enough time. This soup isn't hot enough.*

PRACTICE

a Correct the sentences which are wrong.
1 Do you eat much fish? Yes, I eat a lot of. ✗ *many*
2 I eat too much sweet things. *many*
3 She doesn't eat vegetables enough.
4 How many milk do you drink a day? *much*
5 I've eaten too many pasta this week. *much*
6 Do you drink much alcohol? No, none. ✓
7 This coffee isn't strong enough. ✓
8 I only eat very few chocolate. It's too ~~much~~ fattening.

b Complete with *much*, *many*, *a lot of*, or *a lot*.
1 **A** Do you eat _a lot of_ fruit?
  B Yes, I eat _many_ apples. I love them. /a lot of
2 **A** How _many_ cups of tea do you have a day?
  B _A lot_. I have at least five, sometimes more.
3 **A** How _much_ mineral water do you drink?
  B Not _a lot_. I usually drink tap water. /much
4 **A** Do you think your diet is healthy?
  B No, I eat too _many_ sweets. I also drink too _much_ coffee.

c Tell a partner how much you eat/drink of these things and why.

> **A** *I eat a lot of green vegetables, especially salad. I love it. I don't eat much red meat.*
> **B** *Why not?*

SUGAR, SWEETS green vegetables
Red Meat e.g. beef   White Meat e.g. Chicken
fish Fruit ALCOHOL
Wholemeal Bread FRIED FOOD
Mineral Water
TAKE-AWAY FOOD Spicy
rice Pasta COKE FOOD

4 READ BETTER

a Read about Michel Montignac's theory about modern eating habits. Answer the questions.

1 Who is Michel Montignac? What's unusual about his method?

2 What makes adults tired and children behave badly?

3 What are most young Americans and a lot of Western Europeans addicted to?

Eat as much as you like – and stay healthy!

My only ambition is 'to teach you how to eat' says Michel Montignac, a French business executive. He has invented a
5 method of healthy eating, which is based on the idea that we should not eat less, we should simply eat the right things – the right carbohy-
10 drates and the right fats – which are traditionally part of a Mediterranean way of eating. The Montignac method is not a diet, it is a
15 philosophy of life, which allows people to be 'fit, healthy, energetic and slim *without* counting calories'.

According to Michel
20 Montignac, traditional methods of cooking and eating are disappearing, and are being replaced by junk food and ready-prepared meals. As
25 a result, he says 'people today (especially children) have a diet which is too high in bad carbohydrates – they have too much sugar, too many sweet
30 drinks, too much white bread, too many potatoes, too much pasta and white rice and too many biscuits'. This makes people's level of blood glucose
35 first go up, but then go down even more. It is this, he says, more than stress and overwork, which causes tiredness, (especially late
40 morning and after lunch) and also irritability, impatience, nervousness and headaches. Among schoolchildren it can also cause low concentration
45 and bad behaviour.

Montignac highlights the fact that:

● most young Americans and a lot of Western Europeans are addicted to sugar.

50 ● the average European consumes 40 kilos of sugar a year compared with the average American who consumes 63 kilos and the average Japanese
55 person who consumes less than 20 kilos.

● the average weight of people in the Western world has increased constantly over the last 50 years.

60 ● one in every five Americans is seriously overweight.

If you follow Montignac's way of eating, he says it will be 'a passport to a new feeling of vitality which
65 will allow you to be more effective in both your personal and professional life'.

b Read the text again. Complete the gaps.

1 In Montignac's method you don't have to worry about how many _____ you're eating.

2 People today are eating _____ fast food than they did in the past.

3 If you eat too many bad carbohydrates, your level of blood glucose goes _____ and then goes _____.

4 Montignac thinks that _____ and _____ are not the main causes of tiredness.

5 The Japanese eat approximately half as much _____ as the Europeans.

c In pairs, read more about Montignac's method. Then cover the text. Say what you remember.

A talk about:
Breakfast and dinner
Fruit
Rice, pasta, and bread

B talk about:
Drinks
Vegetables
Sugar

Sugar – public enemy number one
70 Do not eat sugar, or foods containing sugar, like sweets, biscuits and cakes.

Brown is better than white
Don't eat white bread, pasta or rice. Eat wholemeal bread and pasta and brown rice. Cereals should be wholemeal and 75 without added sugar.

Vegetables, any day, any time
Eat as many vegetables as you like, but don't eat potatoes, carrots, sweetcorn or peas.

80 **Fruit – but always first**
Always eat fruit *before* a meal, if possible 15 minutes before eating anything else. The only kinds of fruit you should eat *after* a meal are strawberries and 85 raspberries. Drink fresh fruit juice, but not commercially-prepared juice, which often contains a lot of sugar.

Goodbye to bread and butter
Never mix 'bad' carbohydrates (white 90 bread, pasta, flour, etc.) with fats or oils during a meal.

Water or wine
Drink as much water as possible, and if you want to drink alcohol, drink a little 95 wine or even champagne, but not beer. And never drink alcohol without eating something at the same time.

Breakfast is king
Have a big breakfast, with fruit juice, 100 muesli or cereal, and wholemeal bread. You can eat as much bread as you like, but only at breakfast, never at lunch or dinner. You can drink coffee, but it's better if it's decaffeinated, and don't drink too much.

105 **Goodbye to big dinners**
Dinner should be the lightest of the three daily meals. And try to have it as early as possible, not at nine o'clock at night.

---

d Tell a partner what you think.

1 Is your diet similar or different to what Montignac recommends?
2 Do you think it's a good method?
3 If you decided to follow it, what would you find most difficult?

BETTER PRONUNCIATION
/uː/ or /ʊ/

a T2.6 Put the words into the correct column. Listen and check.

cook few food fruit good juice put should
soup sugar too would

     _____ _____
     _____ _____
     _____ _____
     _____ _____

b T2.7 Listen and repeat.
1 You shouldn't eat too much sugar.
2 Would you like soup or fruit juice?
3 Very few cooks make good food.

5 MAKING CONVERSATION
Food and diet

a In groups, each person choose one topic. Think of at least five things to say to your group about it.

Men always think that their mothers are the best cooks.

Most young people are addicted to junk food.

People's eating habits are changing a lot.

Women worry more about their diet than men.

Vegetarians are healthier than people who eat a lot of meat.

If you do a lot of exercise, it doesn't matter what you eat.

b Talk to your group for one minute about your topic. The rest of the group listen and then agree or disagree.

6 WRITE BETTER

Write two paragraphs about diet.

Paragraph 1 Your country
What do people usually eat and drink in your country for breakfast/lunch/dinner?
Do they eat at any other times?

Paragraph 2 Your own diet
Is your diet similar to or different from the typical diet in your country?
Do you think it's healthy? Why (not)?

Do we really need to sleep?

1 BUILD YOUR VOCABULARY
Words related to sleep

a Explain the difference.

1 get up / wake up
2 go to bed / go to sleep
3 a dream / a nightmare
4 a clock / an alarm clock
5 a pillow / a blanket
6 awake / asleep

b What do the highlighted words mean? Check in a dictionary or ask your teacher.

1 I fell **asleep** on the sofa last night watching TV.
2 He **yawned** and said, 'I'm tired. I'm going to bed.'
3 My husband **snores** and keeps me **awake** at night.
4 I **overslept** yesterday and was late for work.
5 People with **insomnia** often take **sleeping pills**.

c Look at pictures 1–4. What's happening?

2 MAKING CONVERSATION
Sleeping habits

Interview a partner using the questionnaire. Ask for more information. Swap roles.

The Sleep questionnaire

1 **How many hours do you normally sleep a day?**
2 **How many hours do you need to sleep?**
3 **Can you sleep a) in a bus or plane?**
                          b) with the TV on?
4 **Do you like sleeping in complete darkness?**
5 **How many pillows do you use?**
6 **Do you snore?**
7 **Are you a 'heavy' or a 'light' sleeper?**
8 **What sort of things stop you from sleeping?**
9 **If you find it difficult to go to sleep, what do you do?**
10 **Do you often feel sleepy after lunch?**
11 **Do you often have nightmares?**
12 **Do you remember your dreams?**
13 **Do you always use an alarm clock to wake up?**
14 **When you wake up, do you get up straight away?**
15 **Have you ever a) taken sleeping pills?**
                          b) overslept and missed something really important?
                          c) spent the night in the open air?
                          d) walked in your sleep?
                          e) fallen asleep at work/school/university?
16 **Is sleeping a pleasure for you or a waste of time?**

3 GRAMMAR ANALYSIS

Gerund or *to* + infinitive?

a Complete these questions from the questionnaire.

1 How many hours do you need _____?
2 Do you like _____ in complete darkness?
3 What sort of things stop you from _____?
4 If you find it difficult _____ to sleep, what do you do?
5 Do you always use an alarm clock _____?
6 Is _____ a pleasure for you or a waste of time?

b Read the grammar rules. Match with questions 1–6 in **a**.

Use the gerund (verb + *ing*):		**Use *to* + infinitive:**	
after prepositions	☐	after adjectives	☐
after certain verbs, e.g. *like*	☐	after certain verbs, e.g. *need*	☐
as the subject of a sentence.	☐	to express purpose/reason.	☐

- Some common verbs followed by the gerund are: *like, love, hate, enjoy, mind, finish, stop.*
- Some common verbs followed by *to* + the infinitive are: *would like, want, need, decide, hope, expect, plan, forget, seem, try, promise, offer, refuse, learn, manage.*
- *begin* and *start* can be followed by either the gerund or *to* + the infinitive. *It began raining* or *It began to rain.*
- ! After auxiliary verbs (e.g. *do, will*) and modal verbs (e.g. *can, should*), we use the infinitive without *to*.
  Can you play tennis? NOT ~~Can you to play tennis?~~

PRACTICE

a Complete with *to do* or *doing*. Ask a partner. Answer with a gerund or an infinitive.

1 What do you hate _doing_ in the house?
2 What are you thinking of _doing_ next summer?
3 What do you want _to do_ tonight?
4 What do you like _doing_ in your free time?
5 Are you planning _to do_ anything next weekend?
6 What do you find it difficult _to do_ when you're tired?

b Complete with a verb in the gerund or infinitive.

1 **A** Could you help me make the dinner?
  B Sorry, I'm not very good at _cooking_.
2 **A** Would you like _to go_ to the cinema tonight?
  B I can't. I need _to study_. I've got an exam tomorrow.
3 **A** Why are you going to the supermarket now?
  B _To buy_ some milk. We haven't got any.
4 **A** Why don't we take your car?
  B Because _driving_ in the city centre is a nightmare, and it's impossible _to park_. There aren't enough car parks.
5 I don't really enjoy _doing_ sport, but I don't mind tennis. In fact, my girlfriend's trying _to teach_ me how to play.
6 _Watching_ TV is a waste of time. It's much better _to read_ a book or _to listen_ to some music.
7 Has it stopped _raining_ yet? I forgot _to bring_ my umbrella this morning and I don't want _to get_ wet.
8 He went to the travel agent's _to book_ a holiday in Bermuda. He's hoping _to do_ windsurfing while he's there.

c Go to **Communication** *Gerunds and infinitives*, **A** *p.121*, **B** *p.125*. Practise using gerunds and infinitives.

BETTER PRONUNCIATION

Sentence stress, weak forms

When people speak, they usually pronounce the important words strongly and clearly.

a **T2.8** Listen to six sentences. Just write the important words.

b What do you think the other words are? Listen and check. Write the complete sentences.

c Practise saying the sentences as quickly as possible.

4 READ BETTER

a You're going to read an article about sleep. Before you read, in pairs, predict the answers to these questions.

1 How much of our lives do we spend sleeping?
2 What happens if people don't sleep?
3 Why do you think primitive man slept at night?
4 Why do some animals sleep much less than others?
5 Could we live without sleeping?

b Compare your answers with the information in the text.

Glossary

1 _____	say that something isn't true
2 _____	for example
3 _____	as something/someone says
4 _____	horrible
5 _____	not do what you are told
6 _____	put (documents etc.) in the right place
7 _____	in the end, finally
8 _____	postpone, delay
9 _____	free time
10 _____	strong

DO WE really need to sleep?

Tonight between eleven o'clock and one o'clock millions of people will start yawning. Very soon, they will get undressed, lie down, and close their eyes. A few minutes later, they will be asleep.

5 Sleep is a powerful <u>influence</u> on all our lives, and a 60-year-old person has spent almost twenty years asleep. The traditional theory about sleep
10 is that our brain needs to rest for several hours to refresh itself and to 'file' in our memory everything that has happened to us during the day.
15 We can put off sleeping for a limited period, for instance if we go to an all-night party, but sooner or later we have to sleep. If we are not allowed to
20 sleep, we suffer <u>hallucinations</u>, and eventually die.

However Ray Meddis, a scientist at the Sleep Research Unit at Loughborough
25 University, has a fascinating new theory. He suggests that we don't really *need* to sleep at all. We sleep only because our brain is 'programmed' to make
30 us do so.

He believes that the sleep instinct originates from prehistoric times; primitive man was 'programmed' to
35 sleep to protect himself from the darkness with its many dangers. Animals appear to have been similarly

programmed. The number of
40 hours that they sleep does not depend on physical activity but on how much time they need to eat. Horses, cows, sheep and elephants for example, which
45 spend many hours eating, sleep only 2–3 hours. Cats, on the other hand, who have a lot of spare time, sleep for 14 hours a day, more than half of
50 their lives.

According to Dr Meddis, the 'tiredness' we feel at the end of the day is produced by a chemical mechanism in the
55 brain which makes us sleep. We are 'programmed' to feel 'tired' or 'sleepy' at midnight, even if we have spent the day relaxing on the beach or doing
60 nothing. Dr Meddis believes

that the unpleasant symptoms we suffer when we don't sleep enough are not because we have not rested but because
65 we have disobeyed our brain's programming. The longer we don't sleep, the worse we feel. But Dr Meddis believes that if scientists could locate and
70 'turn off' the sleep mechanism in our brain that produces tiredness, we could live completely normal and healthy lives without sleeping.
75 So is sleeping a waste of time? Well, even Dr Meddis does not deny the great *psychological* value of sleep, and he asks us, 'if scientists
80 invented a pill which, if you took it, would keep you awake for ever, would you take it?'

c Choose from the correct endings a–c to summarize what the text is about.

1 The traditional view is that we sleep because …

_____.

2 Dr Meddis thinks that we sleep only because …

_____.

   a we are programmed to do it.
   b the brain needs to rest.
   c the body needs to rest.

d Look at the highlighted words in the text and match them with their meanings in the Glossary.

e Do you believe Dr Meddis' theory? Would you take a pill to keep you awake for ever? Why (not)?

5 LISTEN BETTER

a T2.9 Listen to the story of Mr Gordon Pringle.
Choose a, b, or c.

1 He hasn't slept since
   a 13.12.87.
   b 30.9.87.
   c 13.9.87.
2 He had an accident
   a at work.
   b going to work.
   c going home from work.
3 He had _____ injuries.
   a neck b leg c head
4 After the operation he
   a had a lot of pain. b couldn't sleep.
   c felt fine.
5 At night he
   a lies in bed and thinks. b does the housework.
   c reads.
6 a He doesn't want to sleep.
   b He desperately wants to sleep.
   c He doesn't mind not sleeping.

b Listen again for more detail. Write the missing words.

GORDON Well, I had an 1_____, and when I 2_____ up after the operation I found I was suffering from 3_____ insomnia. I couldn't sleep. The doctors gave me all 4_____ of drugs, but I'm afraid 5_____ of them worked. And since then I haven't been 6_____ to sleep at all. I often feel 7_____, but I just can't sleep.
KEITH Is this 8_____ Angela?
ANGELA Yes, I can 9_____ say I haven't seen my husband 10_____ since 1987.

6 SONG

T2.10 *Moon over Bourbon Street*

This song, originally written and recorded by Sting, was inspired by the novel *Interview with a Vampire*. The novel was later made into a film. Sting said that he wrote the song in the voice of Louis, the vampire.

a Look at the words above each verse and put them into rhyming pairs.

b Read the song and complete the gaps with words from the box.

call   lamplight   all   strong   tonight   wrong

There's a moon over Bourbon Street _____
2 I see faces as they pass beneath the pale _____.
I've no choice but to follow that _____
4 The bright lights, the people and the moon and _____.
I pray every day to be _____,
6 For I know what I do must be _____.
Oh, you'll never see my shade or hear the sound of my feet
8 While there's a moon over Bourbon Street.

moon   beast   lamb   am   noon   priest

It was many years ago I became what I _____.
10 I was trapped in this life like an innocent _____.
Now I can never show my face at _____,
12 And you'll only see me walking by the light of the _____.
The brim of my hat hides the eye of a _____.
14 I've the face of a sinner but the hands of a _____.
Oh, you'll never see my shade or hear the sound of my feet
16 While there's a moon over Bourbon Street.

above   love   means   moonlight   New Orleans   night

She walks every day through the streets of _____.
18 She's innocent and young from a family of _____.
I have stood many times outside her window at _____
20 To struggle with my instinct in the pale _____.
How could I be this way when I pray to God _____?
22 I must love what I destroy, and destroy the thing I _____.
Oh, you'll never see my shade or hear the sound of my feet
24 While there's a moon over Bourbon Street.

c Listen to the song and check.

▶ Go to **Check your progress 2**, *p.115.*

Checking and apologizing

1 CHECKING INFORMATION

a **T2.11** Listen to Meltem, a Turkish student staying with a British family.

1 Where's she from in Turkey?
2 Has she been to Oxford before?
3 Does she like Oxford?
4 Does she smoke? Does she mind if other people smoke?

b Listen again. Complete the gaps.

Question tags	Short answers
You're from Ankara, _aren't_ you?	Yes, _I am_.
That's the capital, _isn't_ it?	Yes, it is.
You haven't been to Oxford before, _have_ you?	No, _I haven't_.
You don't smoke, _do_ you?	No, I _don't_.

Checking if information is correct
When we want to check if information is correct, we often use a question tag at the end of a sentence (*do you? isn't it? have you?* etc.).

● The auxiliary you use depends on the tense of the verb in the sentence, e.g. *do you? doesn't he?* for the present simple, *did she?* for the past simple.

● If the sentence is (+), the question tag is (−).
You're from Ankara, aren't you?
If the sentence is (−), the question tag is (+).
You don't smoke, do you?

Short answers
We often use short answers (*Yes/No* + an auxiliary verb) when we answer yes/no questions or tag questions.
Have you been here before?　　　*Yes, I have/No, I haven't.*
You don't smoke, do you?　　　*Yes, I do/No, I don't.*

! You can answer only *Yes/No*, but this often sounds abrupt or unfriendly.

c **T2.12** Listen to ten questions. Answer with a short answer.

BETTER PRONUNCIATION

Intonation

When you check information that you're certain about, the intonation in the question tag **doesn't** go up.

a **T2.13** Complete the sentence with a question tag. Listen and check.

1 He's French, _isn't he_?
2 This is the train to London, _isn't it_?
3 Banks don't open on Saturdays, _do they_?
4 You've been to London before, _haven't U_?
5 You're in my class, _aren't U_?
6 She doesn't eat meat, _does she_?
7 You went on the excursion, _didn't U_?
8 He's got a car, _hasn't he_?
9 You aren't coming tonight, _are U_?
10 You didn't come to class yesterday, _did U_?

b Listen again and repeat. Copy the intonation.

c Go to **Communication** *I know you, don't I?* **A** *p.122,* **B** *p.126.*
Roleplay two students in the coffee bar.

2 APOLOGIZING

a What do you say in these situations? Write *Excuse me*, *Sorry*, or *Sorry?*

1 You want to ask somebody you don't know for some information.

_____

2 You step on somebody's foot.

_____

3 You want to pass and somebody is standing in your way.

_____

4 You don't hear or understand what somebody says to you.

_____

5 You're late for class.

_____

> ● **Use:**
> *Excuse me* **before** you ask / do something.
> *Sorry* **after** you've done something wrong.
> *Sorry?* when you don't hear or understand something.

b **T2.14** Listen. Match the dialogues 1–4 with pictures A–D.

c Listen again. Complete the gaps.

Apologizing		
Usual	**Stronger**	**Responses**
Sorry.	I'm very sorry.	_____ OK / all right.
I'm sorry.	I'm _____ sorry.	_____ mind.
I'm _____ (*I've broken a glass*).	I'm _____ sorry.	It doesn't _____.
		Don't _____.

d In pairs, practise the dialogues.

3 UNDERSTANDING INFORMATION

a Read the signs. In pairs, explain where you could see them and what they mean.

1 LONDON TRANSPORT APOLOGISES FOR DELAYS ON THE NORTHERN LINE. THIS IS DUE TO URGENT REPAIRS. WE REGRET THE INCONVENIENCE CAUSED.

2 We regret that we only repair computers which were bought here.

3 WE REGRET TO ANNOUNCE THAT TONIGHT'S PERFORMANCE HAS BEEN CANCELLED.

b Which two verbs are formal ways of saying *sorry*?

4 WRITE BETTER
A letter to a friend

Write a letter to a friend.

You have arranged to stay with an English friend at their home for a week in June. Because of a last-minute problem, you can't go.

● Use the **Writing Bank**, *p.143* to help you start and finish a letter to a friend.

● Explain why you can't come (invent a reason).
I'm afraid I've got some bad news…

● Apologize.

The day that changed my life

1 PRESENTATION

a Describe the woman in the photos. What do you think her job was? Why do you think her life changed on 31 August 1997?

b **T3.1** Listen to a radio interview with her. Were you right?

c Listen again. Complete the sentences with one word.

	In the past	Now
Job	She used to impersonate _lady_ _Diana_. She used to _open_ new shops. She used to give _interview_ on TV.	She's doing a _computer_ course.
Appearance	She used to _be_ like her. She used to have _short_ hair.	Her hair is _shorter_ and it's a different _colour_.
Lifestyle/ personality	She didn't use to spend enough time with her _children_. She used to _worry_ too much about the future.	She _takes_ them to school every day. She lives for _today_.

2 GRAMMAR ANALYSIS

used to / didn't use to

> (+) I used to work in a restaurant.
> (−) I didn't use to drive to work.
> (?) Did you use to play with dolls when you were a child?

Look at the sentences in the box above.

1 Does *used to* refer to the **present** or the **past**?
2 Does it refer to actions that happened **once** or **many times**?
3 Does it refer to actions that we **still** do or that are **finished**?

Use *used to* for:

● **past habits** that have changed.
I used to drive to work. (but I don't now)

● **past situations or states** that have changed.
She used to be a Diana lookalike. (but now she isn't)
She used to have short hair. (but now it's a different style)
The form of *used to* is the same for all persons.

! *Used to* does not exist in the present tense. To talk about a present habit, use *usually* + present simple.
I used to eat a lot of meat but now I usually eat fish.
NOT ~~I use to eat fish.~~

! Don't confuse *I used to* + infinitive with *I'm used to* + gerund.
I used to work hard. = I worked hard in the past but now I don't.
I'm used to working hard. = I'm accustomed now to working hard.

BETTER PRONUNCIATION
used to, /j/ and /dʒ/

a **T3.2** Listen and repeat seven sentences about Nicky. Remember, *used to* = /juːstə/.

b **T3.3** Listen and write the words in the correct column.

yesterday	January
music	village
————	————
————	————
————	————
————	————

c Look at the spelling. Can you see any rules?

PRACTICE

a Make sentences with *used to*.

1 _I used to have long hair_ when I was younger. (I/have long hair)
2 _Did U use to smoke_ when you were a teenager? (you/smoke)
3 _he used to ski a lot_ until he broke his leg last year. (he/ski a lot)
4 _we didn't use to have a car_ but then we bought one last year. (we/not have a car)
5 _Did she use to be good at sport_ when she was a child? (she/be good at sport)
6 _he didn't use to drive_ when he lived in London. (he/not drive)
7 _Did they use to go out more_ before they were married? (they/go out more)
8 _I used to wear glasses_ until I got contact lenses. (I/wear glasses)

b In pairs, **A** ask about changes in **B**'s life. Find out as many details as possible. **B** answer the questions. (Use *used to* to talk about your *past* actions or situations.)

> **A** *Has your appearance changed in any way?*
> **B** *Yes, I used to have really long hair.*
> **A** *How long?*

CHANGES IN YOUR LIFE

Appearance
Has your appearance changed in any way?

Job/studies
Have you always worked/studied in the same place?

Lifestyle
Have you always lived in the same town/street?
Have any of your hobbies/interests changed?
Has your lifestyle changed in any other way?

Personality
Has your personality changed much since you were a child?

3 READ BETTER

a Talk to a partner. Did you use to go on holiday with your family? Did you use to enjoy it? Do you still go?

b Quickly read an extract about family holidays from Bill Bryson's travel book, *The Lost Continent*.

1 Did he use to enjoy family holidays? Why (not)?
2 Where did they go on this trip?
3 What was the only good thing about it?

My father was born in Iowa, and lived there all his life, but every year he used to get a mad uncontrollable desire to go out of the state and go on vacation. Every summer, he used to pack everything into the car,
5 including my mother, my sister and I, and drive for miles and miles through the states of America to some distant point. Every year it was the same. Every year it was awful.

The worst thing for us children was the boredom.
10 Iowa is 1,000 miles from the sea, 400 miles from the nearest mountain, and 300 miles from skyscrapers or anything of interest. We used to drive for miles with nothing to see out of the window except fields. The only exciting thing we ever saw were billboards.
15 American highways used to be full of them, advertising anything from milk to a bowling alley and often some coming attraction, like the magic words VISIT SPOOK CAVERNS! OKLAHOMA'S GREAT FAMILY ATTRACTION! JUST 69 MILES! As soon as we saw
20 one like this, we children would begin suggesting that we stop and have a look, taking it in turns to say, in a sincere and moving way, 'Oh *please* Dad, oh *pleeeease*.'

My father's reaction was always perfectly predictable, and was always the same. First he said, 'No, because
25 it's too expensive, and anyway your behaviour since breakfast has been disgraceful.' A few miles later he changed, and asked my mother in a quiet voice what she thought of the idea (she never gave her opinion). Then he ignored us for a few miles, hoping that we would

30 forget about it. Then he changed again and said that perhaps we could go. Then he changed back to 'Definitely no!' (because we had started fighting), until he finally said, 'All right. We'll go.' It was always the same. He always said 'yes' in the end. I never
35 understood why he didn't just say 'yes' in the first place and save himself thirty minutes of arguing. But he always had the last word. 'We're only going to stay for half an hour. And you're not going to buy anything. Is that clear?' This seemed to make him feel that he was
40 in control.

When we found them at last, Spook Caverns turned out to be an enormous disappointment. The only possible compensation was to buy a plastic knife and a bag of plastic dinosaurs in the gift shop. So, as the sun
45 went down and my father realised that it was now late, and going to be difficult to find a room for the night, we children spent the time in the back of the car having noisy and aggressive fights, only stopping at intervals to cry, accuse each other of injuries, and complain of
50 hunger, boredom and the need for the toilet. It was a kind of living hell. There aren't any billboards along the highways any more. What a sad loss!

c Read again. Number the events in the right order 1–11.

- [4] The children asked their father if they could go.
- [3] The children saw a billboard advertising an attraction.
- [6] Their father asked their mother what she thought.
- [5] Their father said they couldn't go.
- [1] Their father put everything in the car.
- [9] Their father said they could go.
- [11] They bought some things in the gift shop.
- [2] They drove for miles without seeing anything.
- [10] They visited Spook Caverns.
- [7] Their father said that perhaps they could go.
- [8] Their father said they couldn't go for the second time.

d Underline the words you don't know. Guess the meaning from context. Check in the Glossary or with a dictionary. Then find three phrases which show how the author feels about family holidays.

Glossary

vacation (*n.*) /veɪˈkeɪʃn/		holiday (US)
boredom (*n.*) /ˈbɔːdəm/		noun from *boring*
skyscrapers (*n.*) /ˈskaɪskreɪpəz/		tall buildings typical in New York
billboards (*n.*) /ˈbɪlbɔːdz/		advertisements beside the road (US)
highway (*n.*) /ˈhaɪweɪ/		road (US)
spook (*n.*) /spuːk/		ghost (US)

4 BUILD YOUR VOCABULARY
Noun-building

We often make nouns from verbs by adding:

- **-ment**   disappoint – disappointment
- **-ation**   imagine – imagination
- **-ion**   attract – attraction

a Make nouns from these verbs. Underline the stress.

advertise argue combine concentrate connect
excite govern protect react organize

b What other nouns do you know with these endings?

5 GRAMMAR ANALYSIS
any more / any longer

> There aren't any billboards along the highways **any more**.
> My father doesn't take us on holiday **any more**.

Look at the two sentences. What does *not… any more* mean?

Use *any more*:
- at the end of a sentence with a (–) verb to say that a past situation doesn't exist now.
  I don't work there any more. = I used to work there but I don't now.

  any longer/no longer mean the same as *any more. No longer* is more formal.
  This credit card is no longer valid.

PRACTICE

a Rewrite the sentences with *any more*.

1 I used to like coffee but now I don't.
   I _don't like coffee anymore_

2 He used to be a teacher but now he isn't.
   He ~~doesn't~~ _isn't a teacher anymore_

3 Alice used to live here but now she doesn't.
   Alice _doesn't live here anylonger_

4 They used to love each other but now they don't.
   They _don't love each other anymore_

5 She used to smoke but now she's stopped.
   She _don't " anymore._

6 We used to keep in touch but now we don't.
   We _don't keep in touch anylonger._

b Write three similar sentences about yourself.

6 MAKING CONVERSATION
Your childhood

Ask a partner about his/her childhood with *Did you use to…?* + an expression from the box. Ask for more information.

A *When you were a child, did you use to watch a lot of TV?*
B *Yes, I did. But I don't watch much TV any more.*
A *What was your favourite programme?…*

When you were a child, did you use to…?	
share a bedroom	watch a lot of TV
be ill a lot	hate any particular food
do any sport	fight with your brothers/sisters
play in the street	visit your grandparents
like school	be afraid of anything
eat a lot of sweets	have a favourite pop group/singer

Another brick in the wall

1 PRESENTATION

a Describe the photo. Where do you think it was taken?

b Read the text carefully. Then go to **Communication** *Test your memory*, **A** *p.122*, **B** *p.126*. Remember details about the text.

c What do you think are the advantages and disadvantages of this education system?
How different is it from the system in your country?

AT SCHOOL FOR 17 HOURS A DAY

It is 6.30 a.m. and the sun has only just come up when the two alarm clocks next to Jie Sun's bed ring simultaneously. She gets out of bed and goes to the kitchen. Her eyes half 5 closed, she hardly says a word while she eats breakfast. Next to the table is her blue Benetton school bag which she packed the night before. It weighs just over six and a half kilos. At 7 a.m. she says goodbye to her 10 parents and sets off to her school, just outside the capital city, Seoul. She returns home at 6 p.m. for dinner, but half an hour later she sets off again for a private academy where she studies for another four hours. On 15 a typical night she gets home at midnight and falls asleep, completely exhausted.

Studying for up to 17 hours a day is a fact of life for South Korean secondary school pupils. They live in a society where 20 education is very important, and there is great competition for a place at university. Getting a good degree from a top university is the only way to be sure of getting a professional well-paid job. The normal 25 secondary school day, as in most other countries, lasts eight hours. But after that most parents make their children stay at school for extra classes. In theory these classes are optional, but in practice they are 30 compulsory. When the school day ends, the children are not allowed to relax and enjoy themselves. Most of them have to study all evening in libraries, with private tutors or at private academies.

35 Classes of 50 are not uncommon and the teachers are strict. Pupils have to repeat after the teacher and memorise everything. 'Teachers at my school don't give you any individual attention because they haven't 40 got time,' says Jie Sun. 'They don't let us ask questions because they say it wastes time.'

Young people like Jie Sun have almost no social life. They rarely have time to see their friends, and having a boyfriend or girlfriend 45 is unthinkable. 'I've never had a boyfriend and neither have any of my friends,' says Jie Sun. 'Our studies come first.'

This lifestyle may seem very hard to many European schoolchildren, who are 50 accustomed to going out most weekends, and watching TV every evening. But on the other hand, in many British schools, up to 40% of teenagers leave school with no qualifications and the prospect of 55 unemployment. So which system really is better?

2 GRAMMAR ANALYSIS

make / let / be allowed (to)

Most parents **make** _____ at school …
The children are **not allowed** _____
They **don't let** _____ …

a Complete the three example sentences from the text in **1**.

b Match expressions 1–3 with their meaning a–c.

1 I'm allowed to/not allowed to *b*   a I have to
2 They let me *c*   b I can/can't
3 They make me *a*   c They give me permission

c Look at the grammar rules.

make and *let* take an object + infinitive without *to*.
be allowed takes *to* + infinitive.

Past tense

make	*made*
let	*let*
be allowed	*was/were allowed*

PRACTICE

a Rewrite the sentences using the verbs in brackets.

1 She isn't allowed to wear make-up.   Her parents _don't let her wear make up_ (let)
2 We had to memorize everything.   Our teachers _made us memorize everything_ (make)
3 They couldn't have lunch at home.   They _weren't allowed to have lunch at home_ (be allowed to)
4 I have to do my homework before I go out.   My mother _makes me do my homework_ (make)
5 I couldn't watch TV during the week.   I _wasn't allowed to watch TV_ (be allowed to)
6 We can use calculators in class.   The teachers _let us use calculators in class_. (let)

b Ask a partner six questions from the chart. (If your partner has finished school, use the past tense, e.g. *Did your parents let you… / Were you allowed to…?*)

At your school… / When you were at school…?			
Do Did Are Were	your teachers your parents you	let you make you allowed to	smoke? go out during the week? stay in at weekends to study? wear what you like at school? do a lot of homework? ask questions in class? call teachers by their first names? memorize everything? watch TV in the evening? go to extra classes?

3 BUILD YOUR VOCABULARY

Education

a Complete **Vocabulary Builder 5** *Education*, p.133.

b Test your memory.

- **What's the difference between …?**
  1 a primary school / a secondary school
  2 a state school / a private school
  3 your exams / your marks
  4 a pupil / a student
  5 do an exam / pass an exam
- **What do you call …?**
  6 the qualification you get when you finish university
  7 the parts of the school year
  8 a school for children under three
  9 a school where pupils live and sleep
  10 the work scientists often do at universities
- **Name …**
  11 five subjects you can do at school

BETTER PRONUNCIATION

/ʌ/ **or** /juː/

Be careful with the pronunciation of *u*. Between consonants it is usually pronounced /ʌ/ or /juː/.

a **T3.4** Put the words in the correct column. Listen and check.

lunch pupil result student study subject tutor
uniform university nuns

/ʌ/	/juː/

b **T3.5** Listen and repeat.
1 I studied music at university.
2 All the pupils wear uniforms.
3 The students study unusual subjects.

4 MAKING CONVERSATION

Your education

In pairs, talk for at least three minutes about your education. Choose either primary school or secondary school. **A** Say as much as you can about the topics in the box. **B** Listen and ask questions. Swap roles.

A *I went to primary school from when I was 4 until I was 11.*
B *Was it a state school or a private school?*
A *It was a state school, called…*
B *Did you like it?*

> Kind of school…? When…? Good or bad?
> Your uniform
> Your favourite/least favourite teacher/Why?
> Your best/worst subjects/Why?
> Something that you liked a lot at your school
> Something bad that you used to do at school (copying in exams, breaking rules, etc.)
> Discipline/punishment at your school

5 GRAMMAR ANALYSIS

Definite article *the*

a Correct the sentences which are wrong.

1 I started school when I was four.
2 I'm going to university the next year.
3 I hate the exams. I always fail them.
4 The nearest school is only for boys.
5 Teachers earn less than lawyers.
6 When I was at school, I had to play hockey.
7 I was very good at the maths.
8 She learned to play guitar.
9 Do you have the breakfast before you go to work?
10 The government isn't spending enough money on education.

b Check with the grammar rules.

Use *the*:
● to talk about *specific* people, places, or things, e.g. *the books I bought yesterday.*
● when there's only one of something (e.g. *the sun, the post office*) or if it's clear what you're talking about (*She opened the door and went into the flat.*).
● with musical instruments.

Don't use *the*:
● to talk about things or people in general, e.g. *books, politics, life.*
● after the verbs *go to, get to, start, finish, leave, be in/at* with *school, university, work, bed, hospital, church, prison* (the institution NOT the building).
● with *next/last + week/month/year/summer/Monday*, etc.
● with sports, meals, and school subjects.

PRACTICE

Write *the* where necessary.

1 Were you good at _____ geography when you were at _____ school?
2 He always practises _____ piano before he has _____ dinner.
3 I used to go to _____ church every Sunday.
4 I like _____ pop music, _____ Chinese food, and _____ tennis.
5 I think _____ women are better teachers than _____ men.
6 Go straight on until you get to _____ church on _____ corner.
7 I like having _____ lunch at _____ home.
8 _____ next Saturday I'm going to _____ cinema.

6 LISTEN BETTER

a In pairs, write **T** (true), **F** (false), or **?** (I don't know) for **Your country**.

	Your country	England
1 All schools used to be only single sex.	☐	☐
2 Nowadays a lot of schools are mixed.	☐	☐
3 Today many parents prefer mixed schools.	☐	☐
4 Girls do better academically in single-sex schools.	☐	☐
5 Girls worry more about their appearance in mixed schools.	☐	☐
6 Boys do better at single-sex schools.	☐	☐
7 Girls do better academically than boys at both kinds of school.	☐	☐

b **T3.6** Now listen to Susan Powell, the head teacher of a London school. Complete the chart for England.

c Listen again for more detail. Correct the false sentences.

7 SONG 🎵

Another brick in the wall

a **T3.7** Listen to the song. Complete the gaps.

> WE DON'T NEED NO _____.
> WE DON'T NEED NO THOUGHT CONTROL.
> NO DARK SARCASM IN THE _____.
> _____, LEAVE THEM KIDS ALONE.
> HEY _____, LEAVE THEM KIDS
> ALONE.
> ALL IN ALL, IT'S JUST ANOTHER BRICK
> IN THE WALL.
> ALL IN ALL, YOU'RE JUST ANOTHER
> BRICK IN THE WALL.

Glossary	
kids	children
all in all	in conclusion
brick	block you use to build (a house / wall)

b What are the grammar mistakes? Why are they there?

c In pairs, translate the song.

8 WRITE BETTER

Write three paragraphs about either the school you go to now or a school you used to go to.

Paragraph 1
- Kind of school?
- Where?
- How long / there?

Paragraph 2
- Number of pupils in the class
- Teachers (old-fashioned / liberal / strict, etc.)
- School rules / discipline
- Subjects (good / bad at)

Paragraph 3
- Say in general if you enjoy(ed) your school. Why (not)?
- Give examples of things you like(d) / you don't (didn't) like.

Still me

1 MAKING CONVERSATION

a Look at the photos. What are all the different things you can read?

b Interview a partner. Ask for more information.

THE READING QUESTIONNAIRE

IN YOUR LANGUAGE

1 What kind of things do you read?
2 What's your favourite time and place to read?
3 What's the first book you can remember reading?
4 What was the last book you read?
5 What are you reading at the moment?
6 Do you read more or less than you used to?
7 Have you got a favourite book or author?
8 Do you think people will read less in the future?

IN ENGLISH

9 How often do you read in English? What kind of things do you read?
10 Which of these things do you do when you read in English (✓ or ✗)?
I read things I'm interested in. ☐
I read regularly (e.g. 10 minutes a day). ☐
I take an English book with me when I travel. ☐
I always read until the end of a chapter or section. ☐
I try to understand groups of words or sentences, not just individual words. ☐
I try to guess unknown words from the context. ☐
I use a dictionary when I can't guess important words. ☐
I highlight important words and write them down in a notebook. ☐

2 READ BETTER

a Read the book review quickly. Answer each question in one sentence.
1 What kind of book is it?
2 What is it about?
3 Why does the reviewer think it's worth reading?

b Number the paragraph topics in the right order.
☐ His family's reaction to the accident
☐ What the reviewer thinks of the book
☐ Who the book's about
☐ His life before the accident
☐ What he has been doing since the accident

c Look at the highlighted words and phrases in the review. In pairs, guess the meaning from the context. Complete the Glossary.

Book of the month

STILL ME
by
Christopher Reeve

Something people always asked Christopher Reeve when he made the first **Superman** film was 'Can you give us your
5 definition of a hero?' He used to answer that it was a person who did something heroic without considering the consequences. Now, he says,
10 his definition is different: a hero is an ordinary person who finds the strength to go on living in spite of enormous obstacles. By that definition,
15 he himself is a hero, perhaps even a superhero, since the day in May 1995 when he fell off a horse, hit his head on the ground, and broke his neck.

20 Before that day, he seemed to be an exceptionally lucky person. He was born into a rich family, went to an expensive private school, and
25 was tall, good-looking, and talented. Apart from his acting ability, he was also very good at sports. He could sail, fly a plane, ski, and even do scuba
30 diving, and had recently become fascinated by horses and horse-riding.

d Many words can have more than one meaning. Look at the definitions. Decide which is correct in the context of the text.

1 lift (*line 35*)
  a (*n.*) a machine which takes you up and down
  b (*v.*) move something up

2 key (*line 42*)
  a (*n.*) a thing you use to open a door
  b (*n.*) the most important thing

3 raise (*line 47*)
  a (*v.*) move up, e.g. your hand
  b (*v.*) collect for a purpose, e.g. money

4 positive (*line 50*)
  a (*adj.*) opposite of *negative*
  b (*adj.*) very sure

5 funny (*line 58*)
  a (*adj.*) making you laugh
  b (*adj.*) strange, unusual

6 moving (*line 59*)
  a (*adj.*) changing position
  b (*adj.*) affecting you emotionally

e Read the review again.

1 How has Christopher Reeve's definition of a hero changed?
2 What was his life like before the accident?
3 How did his family react after the accident?
4 What has he been doing since the accident?
5 What example does he give to explain why he sometimes finds it hard to be positive?

Just after the accident, Reeve's mother thought he should be allowed to die. Her son, who used to be able to do almost any
35 sport, now could not even lift his arms or turn his head. She could not imagine that he would want to live in a wheelchair for the rest of his life, and Reeve himself, just 40 years old, was not sure either. The only person who was able to convince him that life was still worth living was his wife Dana, when she
40 told him, 'It's your life and you have to make the decision. But I want you to know that I'll be with you. You're still you and I love you.' This was the key to his recovery.

Although even today Reeve still cannot breathe without artificial help, he has never given up hope. Just three months
45 after he left hospital he was able to appear at the Oscars ceremony in a wheelchair, and since then he has been working hard both to raise money for research into spinal injuries, and as a film director. He knows he will never be able to ride and ski again, or even walk, but he tries to be optimistic about the
50 future, although it is difficult for him to be positive every day. Many days he looks back at the past with nostalgia. 'When I

see a beautiful view, like the one from my house, I think yes, it's beautiful, but I can only see it as a spectator. I can never be part of it.'

55 When I opened this book I was expecting a sentimental Hollywood story about a famous star and a tragic accident. When I got to the end, I was left with a feeling of profound admiration for a brave, intelligent and funny man. I have rarely read any book as moving as this one.

Glossary

_____ (*adj.*) /ɪˈnɔːməs/	very big
_____ (*n.*) /ˈɒbstəkl/	difficulty
_____ (*n.*) /ˈwɪəltʃeə/	a chair with wheels for people who can't walk
_____	good enough to live for
_____ (*adj.*) /ɑːtɪˈfɪʃl/	not natural
_____	lost hope
_____ (*n.*) /spekˈteɪtə/	a person looking at sthg
_____ (*adj.*) /prəˈfaʊnd/	deep

3 GRAMMAR ANALYSIS

can, could, be able to

> He **cannot** (**can't**) breathe without artificial help.
> She **could not** (**couldn't**) imagine that he would want to live in a wheelchair.
> He **will** (**'ll**) never **be able** to ride and ski again.
> He **used to be able to** do almost any sport.

a Look at the four sentences from the review. Why *don't* we use a form of *can* in the last two?

b Complete the chart with a form of *can* where possible. If it isn't possible, put –.

	can	be able to (+ inf.)
present simple	*can*	am/is/are able to
future (will)	–	will be able to
past simple		was/were able to
present perfect		has/have been able to
infinitive		(to) be able to
gerund		being able to

Use *can/could* + infinitive:
- to say that something is/was possible or that someone has/had the ability to do something.

Use *be able to* + infinitive:
- when there is no form of *can*, e.g. in the present perfect or infinitive.

! Use *could/ was able to* to talk about a general ability. Use *was/were able to* when someone did something in **one particular situation**, although it was difficult.
My grandfather could play the piano and the violin.
Reeve was able to appear at the Oscars ceremony. NOT ~~Reeve could appear…~~

PRACTICE

Complete with *can*, *could*, or *be able to*.

1 If we get up early, we'll _____ catch the first train.
2 Mozart _____ play the piano brilliantly when he was five.
3 She hasn't _____ find a job yet.
4 They _____ buy the flat because it was too expensive.
5 I used to _____ speak Russian well, but now I _____.
6 There was a lot of traffic but we _____ get there on time.
7 I've always wanted _____ dance the tango.
8 I hate travelling abroad without _____ speak the language.
9 Chimpanzees _____ communicate in sign language.
10 _____ you take me to the party? If not, I won't _____ go.

BETTER PRONUNCIATION

Sentence stress, strong and weak forms

a **T3.8** Listen and write six sentences.

b Listen again and repeat. Underline the stress.

c Write true sentences. Read them to a partner.

1 I can _____ very well.
2 I can't _____.
3 I couldn't _____ until I was _____ years old.
4 I used to be able to _____ very well.
5 I've never been able to _____.
6 If I go to Britain, I'll be able to _____.

4 MAKING CONVERSATION
Skills

a Add to the circle two things you can do and two things you'd like to be able to do well.

b Talk to a partner about the skills.

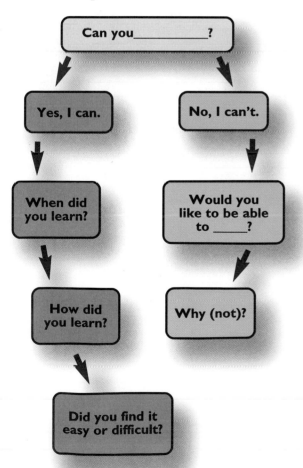

5 BUILD YOUR VOCABULARY
Strong adjectives

Some adjectives have the same meaning as others but are stronger.
awful = very bad, *brilliant* = very good, etc.
*Christopher Reeve was **fascinated** by horses.* = very interested

With strong adjectives we use *absolutely* or *really*, **not** *very*.
The film was absolutely awful. NOT ~~very awful~~.

a Write synonyms for the strong adjectives.

1	He has had **enormous** problems.	= very _____
2	He had a **tragic** accident.	= very _____
3	I'm absolutely **exhausted**. I've been working all day.	= very _____
4	The water's **freezing**. We can't possibly swim.	= very _____
5	It's **boiling** today. At least 40 degrees.	= very _____
6	I'm **starving**. I haven't eaten all day.	= very _____
7	My new baby is really **tiny**.	= very _____
8	He's **furious** because she forgot his birthday.	= very _____
9	I was **amazed** at the news. It was completely unexpected.	= very _____
10	I'm **positive** he's going to win. He's the best.	= very _____

b Cover **5a**. Complete with a strong adjective.

1	Are you hungry?	Yes, I'm _____.
2	Is it cold outside?	Yes, it's absolutely _____.
3	Was your father angry?	Angry? He was _____.
4	Are you sure it starts at six?	Yes, I'm _____.
5	Are you tired?	Tired? I'm _____.
6	Is your coffee hot enough?	Yes, it's _____.
7	Did you think the ending was sad?	Yes, it was _____.
8	Were you surprised?	I was absolutely _____.
9	Your suitcase is very big!	Yes, sorry. It's _____.
10	Is his flat small?	Yes, it's _____.

c In pairs, **A** read the questions. **B** answer from memory. Swap roles.

6 WRITE BETTER

Write a review of a book you've read recently.

Paragraph 1
Start *A book I've read recently is…*
What's it called? Who's it by? What kind of book is it?

Paragraph 2
What's it about?
What's the most exciting/funniest/saddest/most interesting part of the book?

! Use the present tense.
  *It's about a girl who **lives** with her aunt. Her aunt **is** very unkind and…*

Paragraph 3
What did you think of it? Why?

> ▶ Go to **Check your progress 3**, *p.116*.

Could you do me a favour?

1 UNDERSTANDING INFORMATION

In pairs, explain what the hotel signs mean.

1
> *Visitors are requested to vacate their room before 12.00 on the day of their departure*

2
> **NO VACANCIES**

3
> **The Management does not accept responsibility for any valuables left in the room. All valuables should be given to the hotel receptionist to be placed in the safe.**

2 BUILD YOUR VOCABULARY
Common verb phrases

a Complete the sentences with a verb from the list.

book	check into/out of	do	fill in	leave	make
send	sign				

1 _____ me a favour
2 _____ a form
3 _____ a phone call
4 _____ a fax

5 _____ a table in a restaurant
6 _____ your name
7 _____ a message
8 _____ a hotel

b Cover the verbs. Remember the phrases.

3 READ BETTER

Read about four Edinburgh hotels. Then go to **Communication *Choosing a hotel*, p.122.**
Choose the best hotel for the people.

1
★★ ORWELL LODGE
29 Polwarth Terrace, Edinburgh EH11 1NH

This Victorian mansion is situated in a quiet residential area in the south-west of the city, and is convenient for transport to the city centre. Bedrooms offer good facilities for both the business guest and tourists.
10 rooms, all no smoking. CTV in all bedrooms. No dogs (except guide dogs). Weekly live entertainment.
No smoking in restaurants. Last dinner 8.30 p.m.
ROOMS (incl. breakfast) s £45 d £75

2
★★★ CHANNINGS
South Learmonth Gardens, Edinburgh EH4 1EZ

This discreet club-like hotel consists of five beautiful Edwardian houses with a comfortable, elegant atmosphere. The restaurant serves Scottish and French cuisine.
48 rooms. No dogs. No smoking in restaurant.
Last dinner 9.30 p.m.
ROOMS (incl. breakfast) s £105 d £130

3
★★ THRUMS PRIVATE HOTEL
14 Minto Street, Edinburgh EH9 1RQ

Friendly and informal service is provided at this family-run hotel on the south side of the city. Small bar and dining room serving mainly British food for residents and their guests only. There are 6 cheerful modern bedrooms in the hotel itself and 8 magnificent period rooms in the next-door house, 5 of which are family rooms.
14 rooms, last dinner 8.30 p.m.
ROOMS (incl. breakfast) s £40 d £60

4
★★★ MALMAISON
1 Tower Place, Leith EH6 7DB

This stylish hotel offers a French-influenced brasserie where traditional Mediterranean cuisine can be enjoyed until late in the evening. The hotel is medium-sized and very comfortable, well connected by public transport.
60 rooms, (6 family). No coaches. Last dinner 10.30 p.m.
ROOMS s £65 d £85

4 MAKING REQUESTS

a **T3.9** Listen to a guest checking into a hotel. Write his four requests. Which is the most polite?

b Listen again and complete the expressions in the chart. **R** = receptionist **G** = guest

Asking somebody to do something		
Usual	**Very polite**	**Responses**
R Could I have _your passport please._ ?	**R** Would you mind _Filling in this form._	Yes, of course.
R Could you _sign here please_ ?	**G** Do you think you could _send this fax_ ?	Sure./No problem.
G Can you _put in on my_ ?	_for me._	I'm sorry but…
bill		No, of course not.

- When you ask somebody to do something which is not a normal part of their job, or you ask a friend for a special favour, you often use a very polite expression.

c Look at the pairs of gapped requests below. Who would you say them to? For which one (a or b) do you think you should be very polite?

1a _Would U mind asking_ (ask) the chef to cook this a bit more?
b _Could I have_ (have) another bottle of mineral
Can " " water?

2a _Would U mind keep_ (keep) this sweater for me until 4.30?
b _Could U take_ (take) the price off? It's a present.

3a _Could U take_ (take) me to Piccadilly?
b _Do U think U could_ (hurry)? I need to be there in
hurry fifteen minutes.

4a _Do U think U could_ (change) my room for one
change with a balcony?
b _Could U order_ (order) me a taxi for 8.30?

d **T3.10** Listen and complete the gaps.

e Cover the requests. Can you remember them?

5 ASKING PERMISSION

a Complete the chart on the right with:
Could I…? Can I…? May I…?
Do you think I could…?

b Look at the pictures of people asking permission. Imagine what they're saying.

Asking permission		
Normal	**Very polite**	**Responses**
_____	_____	Sure. Go ahead. ✓
_____	_____	Of course. ✓
		I'm sorry but… ✗
	Do you mind if I…?	No, not at all. ✓
		I'd rather you didn't. ✗
		('d = would)

1   2
3   4

6 WRITE BETTER

A fax

Write a fax to the manager of a hotel.

You have just spent two weeks in Channings Hotel in Edinburgh. When you got home, you realized that you didn't have your alarm clock and you think you left it in your hotel room.

- Use the **Writing Bank**, *p.145* to help you write a fax correctly.
- Explain exactly when you stayed at the hotel, and your room number.
- Say where you think you left the alarm clock.
- Ask him/her to send you the alarm clock.
  If you find my clock, I would be very grateful if you could send it to me at the following address:
  (your address)

c **T3.11** Listen and check. Copy the polite intonation.

househusband

1 LISTEN BETTER

air-traffic controller

au pair

travel
courier

a Look at the four photos. What do you think are …?

- the most important personal qualities they need (to be able to get on with people, etc.)
- the special qualifications/abilities they need (a degree, to be able to drive, etc.)
- the good/bad sides of the job

b **T4.1** Listen to two of the people talking. Who are they?

c Listen again. Make notes in the chart.

	1	2
Personal qualities	Patient, good with people	love children, be good at getting on with them
Abilities/qualifications	languages	a bit of english
Good side	travelling, meet nice people	children learn english / free time
Bad side	stressful, not very well paid, low salary	parents of the children argument / housework
Worst experience at work	a customer complaining	woman in love with the husband.

2 BUILD YOUR VOCABULARY
Jobs and work

a Complete **Vocabulary Builder 6** *Work*, p.134.

b Do the 'Jobs' quiz.

> - **What's the difference between …?**
>   1 job/work
>   2 a part-time job/a full-time job
>   3 a temporary job/a permanent job
>   4 an employer/an employee
>   5 a cook/a cooker
>   6 earn money/win money
>   7 resign/retire
>   8 work overtime/go on strike
>   9 be sacked/get promoted
>   10 qualifications/experience
> - **Name three jobs ending in …**
>   -er -or -ist -ian

BETTER PRONUNCIATION
/ɜː/ or /ɔː/?

a **T4.2** Listen and repeat.

first	_____	more	_____
turn	_____	saw	_____
her	_____	daughter	_____
work	_____	floor	_____
learn	_____	talk	_____

b Put these words in the correct column.

worse walk law nurse earn
verb third caught boring door

c **T4.3** Listen and repeat.

1 Her first birthday is on Thursday the third.
2 He works for the worst boss in the world.
3 I saw his daughter at the door talking to the porter.
4 The more he talks, the more bored I get.

3 MAKING CONVERSATION

What do you do?

a Think of someone in your family who works. Complete the circles about him/her.

b Talk to another student about his/her relative's job.

> **A** *I'm going to talk about my uncle.*
> **B** *What does he do?*
> **A** *He's an electrician.*
> **B** *Where does he work?*

c In pairs, talk about what **you** do.

JOB

PLACE OF WORK

ADJECTIVES THAT DESCRIBE THE JOB

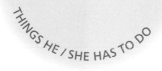
THINGS HE / SHE HAS TO DO

MAIN ADVANTAGE — MAIN DISADVANTAGE

4 GRAMMAR ANALYSIS

Future forms: *will*, *going to*, present continuous

a Look at the pairs of sentences (a/b). In pairs, decide which are possible.

1 What are your plans for the future?
　a I'm going to start my own business.
　b I'll start my own business.
2 The phone's ringing!
　a OK, I'll answer it.
　b OK, I'm going to answer it.

3 Who do you think is going to get the job?
　a I think Martin will get it.
　b I think Martin's going to get it.
4 What are you doing tonight?
　a I'm going to meet some friends after class.
　b I'm meeting some friends after class.

b Check with the grammar rules.

Three different forms are commonly used in English to talk about the future. The one you use depends on the situation.

- **Plans**
  For something you have already decided to do, use *going to*.
  What are you going to do when you finish school? (= What are your plans?)
  I'm going to work for my father. (= I've already decided)

- **Unplanned decisions**
  For a decision at the moment of speaking, or making an offer, use *will/won't* + infinitive.
  A *I've got a problem.* **B** *I'll help you.* NOT ~~I help you.~~

! For questions with *I* and *we*, use *Shall…?*
  Shall I help you?

- **Predictions**
  For predictions, use either *will* or *going to*.
  I think they'll win./they're going to win.

- **Future arrangements**
  For something in the future we have already arranged (e.g. written in our diary), use the **present continuous**, especially with the verbs *go, come, see, meet, leave, have* (*dinner*, etc.).
  I'm having dinner with Ann tomorrow. (= We've already booked the restaurant).

! *I'm going to have dinner with Ann tomorrow* is also possible.

PRACTICE

a Ask a partner about future plans. Choose a box and make a question with *going to*. Ask for more information.

What/do/next summer?	What/the next film/see?	Go away/next weekend?
What/the next CD/buy?	Go out/tonight?	What/do after class?
What time/get up tomorrow?	Do any sport/next week?	Watch TV/tonight?

A *What are you going to do next summer?*
B *I'm going (to go) to Ibiza with some friends.*
A *Where are you going to stay?*

b In pairs, respond to the statements. Use *I'll…*, or *Shall I…?*

1 'It's very hot in this room.'
2 'I'm hungry.'
3 'It's very dark in here.'
4 'This case is too heavy for me.'
5 'We need some milk and potatoes.'
6 'I need to get to the airport urgently.'

c In pairs, ask and answer questions. Say why.

Do you think you'll ever…
  work in another country?
  have your own business?
  marry a foreigner?
  write a novel?
  be in *Hello* magazine?
  adopt a child?
  run a marathon?
  live on your own?
  become a vegetarian?

I'm sure I will.
I think so./I hope so.
I don't think so. I hope not.
Maybe I'll…
I doubt it.

d Cross out the wrong verb.

1 Do you think **you'll finish/you're finishing** work late tonight?
2 **Shall I help you/Am I going to help you** with that letter?
3 I can't help you. **I'll go/I'm going** shopping.
4 Have you heard the news? Jean **is going to/will** be sacked!
5 I think **I'll apply/I'm applying** for the job at Ford.
6 **I'll/I'm going to** buy a new flat soon.
7 Oh no! I forgot to phone him. **I'm doing it/I'll do it** now.
8 **I'm having/I'll have** dinner with Mark tonight.

5 READ BETTER

a Read the dictionary definition. What kind of people do you think go to clairvoyants? Have you ever been to one, or do you know anyone who has?

clair·voyant /kleə'vɔɪənt/ *n* a fortune-teller, someone who predicts the future.

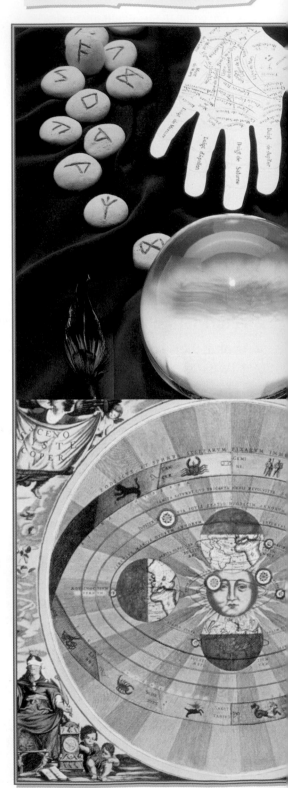

b Quickly read about three people who have been to a clairvoyant. Write **A**, **B**, and **C**.

1 Who is very worried because of a prediction? ____
2 Who uses clairvoyants in their job? ____
3 Who made a last-minute decision which saved their life? ____

c Read again. Write the missing words.

LOOKING
into the future

Ⓐ Tiziano Terzani, journalist

I work ¹_____ the German magazine, *Der Spiegel*, as the foreign correspondent. In 1992 I went to a fortune-teller just as a joke, and he ²_____ me, 'Next year you will be involved in a flying accident.' I didn't ³_____ him but in March 1993 I was supposed to go on an assignment for the United Nations. At the last moment I decided ⁴_____ to go, and another journalist went in my place. The helicopter they were travelling in crashed, and all fifteen journalists on board were killed.

Ⓑ Namita Panjabi, restaurant owner

I regularly go to palmists, astrologers and clairvoyants. I know a ⁵_____ of people may think it's a bit strange, but for me it's a normal part of life. I go ⁶_____ six months, and I'd never start a new business project without consulting one. But I'm not the ⁷_____ person who does this. I know many successful businessmen and women ⁸_____ go to fortune-tellers. But you have to be careful. Most of them are charlatans. The really good ones are very rare.

Ⓒ George Leith, scientist

I'm a very analytical, realistic sort of person. But ten years ago when I was ⁹_____ some research in India I visited a palmist who said to me, 'You're going to die when you are 34.' I didn't believe him, but a year later when I ¹⁰_____ working in Africa a Zimbabwean witch doctor ¹¹_____ exactly the same thing. I haven't been to a clairvoyant since. I try not to think about it, but I have started to worry. I keep thinking that each day might be my ¹²_____. I was 34 last October ...

6 GRAMMAR ANALYSIS
might / may + infinitive

a Look at the cartoon. Explain the difference between *You're going to…*, and *You might…*.

b Check with the grammar rules.

I	might (not) may	go to the party. I'm not sure.

Use *might* (or *may*) + infinitive:

● to say when you ***aren't sure*** about what is going to happen.
It might rain. (= It's a possibility)
might/may is the same form for all persons.

! *might* and *may* are the same, but *might* is more common in spoken English.

PRACTICE

Answer these questions with *might* giving two possibilities.

EXAMPLE
I'm not sure. I might… or I might…

1 What are you going to do tonight?
2 Where are you going to go next summer?
3 What are you going to buy your mother for her birthday?
4 What car are you going to buy?
5 What film are you going to see?
6 What are you going to call your first child if it's a boy?

7 MAKING CONVERSATION
Fortune-telling

Go to **Communication *Clairvoyant*, A** *p.122*, **B** *p.126*. Make predictions about each other's future.

1 READ BETTER

a You're going to read a short story called *The Firing Line*. Before you read, match a word in **A** with a definition in **B**.

	A		B
e	1	company	a a doll you can control
g	2	document	b note
h	3	Personnel	c quickly
	4	fault	d not able to relax
b	5	memo	e business
c	6	promptly	f understand
a	7	puppet	g important file/paper
f	8	realize	h department in charge of employing people
d	9	tense	i I'm sure
i	10	I bet	j mistake

b **T4.4** Read and listen to Part 1 of *The Firing Line*. Cover the text. Answer the questions.

1 Who or what do these names refer to?
Keeler   *employee*
Bowles   *head of Personnel*
Walford *name of company*
Stamford → *will be sacked*

2 What does Keeler have to do on Friday afternoon?

3 Why can't he do it before then?

Part 1

The Firing Line

by Henry Slesar

WEDNESDAY

Bill Keeler, marketing manager of Walford International, knew from experience that company meetings could be called at any time and in any place, even in the lifts. As he was going up to his office
5   on Wednesday morning, Cliff Bowles, the head of Personnel, got into the lift with him. 'We had a meeting last night, Bill,' he said. 'One of your department has to be sacked.'
'Oh?' Keeler said. 'Who?'
'Stamford. He's not the right man for the job. Tell him as soon as
10 you can.'
'Of course,' Keeler said, desperately trying to remember who Stamford was. 'I'll tell him now.'
'Wait a moment, no,' said Bowles. 'I think it'll be better if you wait until Friday. And do it in the afternoon, after most people have gone
15 home. It's not good for the company to have sacked employees complaining to everyone. They might even go on strike.'
Keeler wasn't pleased. It wasn't the first time he'd had to tell someone to go, but he didn't enjoy it. And sometimes there were unpleasant scenes. Even the carefully-written company document
20 (*How to Sack a Walford Employee*) wasn't much help when the victim became emotional. The lift stopped and Keeler got out.
'Right,' he said. 'I'll tell him when I get back from lunch on Friday.'

c **T4.5** Read and listen to Part 2. Cover the text. In pairs, say why the following are important. **A** answer 1–4, **B** 5–8.

1 Friday afternoon	5 a memo
2 'How long have you been working here?'	6 a puppet
	7 "the old man"
3 two years	8 5.10
4 Bob	

Part 2

FRIDAY

25 Thursday was a busy day for Keeler, and he completely forgot that he had to sack one of his men. But on Friday, he returned from lunch feeling tense. He knew the moment had come, and couldn't wait any longer. He called Eve, his secretary, and told her to tell Bob Stanford to come to his office. Stanford arrived promptly, a slim young man with a sensitive face.

30 'Sit down,' Keeler said with a friendly smile. 'How long have you been working here, Stanford?' This was the standard first question, recommended by the company document.
'Almost two years,' the young man said. 'Let's see, it'll be exactly two years this November.'

35 Keeler smiled. 'And how do you feel about these two years?'
'Fine,' the young man said, 'Just fine, Mr Keeler.'
The manager sighed deeply. 'Well, I suppose it must be our fault then,' he said sadly.
'Your fault? What do you mean?'

40 'Look, Bob,' Keeler said confidentially. 'You're a good man and you've got great prospects. When you leave here, your experience with Walford will be a really good recommendation. We'll give you a good reference. You can be sure of that.'
'But I wasn't thinking of leaving, Mr Keeler.'

45 'Bob,' Keeler said sadly, 'sometimes a man has to think about leaving.'
Stanford suddenly realized the truth. 'You mean I'm sacked?' he said incredulously.
'Look Bob…'

50 'Don't call me Bob. You've never called me Bob in your life, Keeler. I bet you never even knew my first name until now.'
'I'm only trying to make this easy for you…'
'I'm the best salesman you've ever had, you told me that yourself.'
'Did I?'

55 'You certainly did. Last year. You sent me a memo, remember? Or didn't you know who you were sending it to? I've got the best record in the department, and now you're sacking me! I don't believe it!'
'There are a few factors,' Keeler said seriously. 'The Personnel

60 department…'
'To hell with them!' the young man said furiously, standing up.
'And to hell with you!' he shouted. 'You're just a puppet!' He turned and walked towards the door. 'I'm going to see the "old man". I'm going to get some answers. I won't accept it unless he

65 gives me a really good reason.'
'Wait a minute!' Keeler shouted. 'You'll only make things worse if you go and see him…'
But he couldn't stop him. Keeler sighed deeply and went back to the letter he was writing. At 5.10 he filled his briefcase with unread

70 documents and went home.

2 LISTEN BETTER

a In pairs, decide what's going to happen to:
1 Stanford.
2 Keeler.

b **T4.6** Listen to Part 3.
1 Where does Keeler go on Monday morning?
2 What happens in the end? Why?
3 Do you think something like this could really happen?

BETTER PRONUNCIATION
Word stress

Always underline the stress on new words you learn, especially when it's different to a similar word in your language.
Remember the way stress is marked in a dictionary, e.g. /ˈlæŋgwɪdʒ/. Stress the syllable *after* the stress mark.

a **T4.7** Underline the stress. Listen and check.

Personnel	carefully	recommend
experience	afternoon	department
unpleasant	completely	document
manager	employer	employee

b Say these sentences.
1 The manager of the Personnel department had an unpleasant experience this afternoon.
2 I recommend that you read this document very carefully.

3 BUILD YOUR VOCABULARY

Human sounds

a Look at the highlighted verbs. Guess from the context what kind of sound they are.

1 'Wait a minute!' Keeler shouted.
2 He sighed deeply, and went back to the letter he was writing.
3 The old man looked up, and coughed before speaking.
4 'Stamford,' he whispered. 'Oh my God!'

b **T4.8** Listen and match each sound 1–8 with a verb.

sigh /saɪ/ ☐
scream ☐
cough /cɒf/ ☐
whistle /'wɪsl/ ☐
snore ☐
shout ☐
yawn /jɔːn/ ☐
whisper ☐

4 GRAMMAR ANALYSIS

when / as soon as, first conditional

> Tell him **as soon as** you can.
> I think it'll be better **if** you wait until Friday.
> I'll tell him **when** I get back from lunch.
> I won't accept it **unless** he gives me a good reason.
> You'll only make things worse **if** you go and see him.

a Look at the five sentences from the story. What tense are the verbs after *as soon as/if/ when/unless*? Do they refer to the present or to the future?

b Which three are first conditionals?

- **Use the present tense after *if*, *when*, *as soon as*, *unless*, and *until* although you are talking about the future.**

  We'll stay here until she comes.
  NOT ~~until she'll come.~~
  Turn off the TV when you go to bed.
  NOT ~~when you'll go to bed.~~
  The other verb in the sentence is usually in the future (*will/won't*) or an imperative.
  I'll come and see you when I have time.
  Come and see us when you have time.

! *unless* + positive verb can be used instead of *if… not*.
You'll be late unless you go now/if you don't go now.

PRACTICE

a Rearrange the words to make sentences.

1 you as 'll soon as know we tell ~~We~~
   We _'ll tell you as soon as we know._
2 he late arrives he again 'll sacked ~~If~~ be
   If _he arrives late again he'll be sacked._
3 go the can home ~~You~~ exercise soon as as finish you
   You _can go home as soon as you finish the exercise._
4 back won't relax able ~~I~~ to until be children the go school to
   I _won't be able to relax until the children go back to school._
5 unless miss 'll we ~~We~~ hurry train the up
   We _'ll miss the train unless we hurry up._
6 town ~~Visit~~ you when 're me in
   Visit _me when you're in town._
7 ~~I~~ be 'll if he the doesn't job surprised get
   I _'ll be surprised if he doesn't get the job._
8 we give won't us the ~~They~~ them tickets pay until for
   They _won't give us tickets until we pay for them._

b Complete with the correct form of the verb.

A Hi, Clare, it's Jane here. Listen, if I [1] _tell_ you a secret [2] _will_ you _promise_ not to tell anyone? (tell, promise)
B Of course. What is it?
A I've applied for a new job but my boss [3] _will be_ furious if he [4] _finds out_. (be, find out)
A But unless you [5] _tell_ him, he [6] _won't give_ you a reference. (tell, not give)
B Well, I [7] _'ll tell_ him when I [8] _am_ sure I've got it. (tell, be). I [9] _'ll know_ next week (know). I [10] _'ll phone_ you as soon as I [11] _hear_ anything. (phone, hear) So don't say anything until I [12] _say_ it's OK. (say)
A OK, I promise.

c Go to **Communication** *As soon as possible*, **A** *p.123*, **B** *p.126*. Ask and answer questions about the future.

d Play 'Three in a row' in small groups.

One team is **X** and one is **O**. Choose a square in turn. Finish the sentence so that it's grammatically correct and makes sense. If you are right, put your **X** or **O** in the square. The first team to get 'three in a row' is the winner.

Unless we hurry, ... *we will miss the train*	I'll leave home when... *I have enough money*	I won't get married until... *you can raise yourself*
I'll give you the money as soon as ... *you come to my house*	If I see him, ... *I will ask for money from him*	When I can speak English fluently, ...
He'll lose his job if ... *he always chat with others*	As soon as he gets here, ... *he will see hopes*	You'll never be rich unless ...

5 WRITE BETTER

WANTED! TOURIST GUIDES

We're looking for part-time tourist guides to show foreign students around the city.

We need people:
◆ who know the city well
◆ with a good level of spoken English
◆ with an open, friendly personality.

Write (enclosing CV and colour photo) to
Mr Tony Grant, P.O. Box 4679

Write a letter of application.

● Use the **Writing Bank**, *p.144* to help you begin and end a formal letter.

Paragraph 1
Say why you are writing.

Paragraph 2
Give personal information (age, job/ studies, level of English, etc.) and details of any relevant experience you've had.

6 SONG 🎵

T4.9 *Stand by me*

Living in the material world

1 BUILD YOUR VOCABULARY

Money

a Match the two halves of the quotations.

1 Time is
2 Money is always there
3 Save a little each month
4 I'd like to live
5 I've been rich, and I've been poor
6 The person who said money can't buy happiness

a but the pockets change.
b like a poor man with lots of money.
c didn't know where to go shopping.
d and I know which one I prefer.
e money.
f and you'll be surprised how little you have at the end of the year.

b Complete **Vocabulary Builder 7** *Money*, *p.135*.

c Test your memory.

- **Can you think of…?**
  1 five things you can do with money
  2 two places where you can keep money
- **What do you call…?**
  3 the money you borrow from the bank *a loan*
  4 the money you get from a job *a salary*
  5 the money you pay the government *tax*
  6 all the money you receive in a year *income*
- **What's the difference between…?**
  7 lend/borrow
  8 win/earn
  9 spend/waste
  10 inherit/invest
  11 wealthy/broke
- **Explain…**
  12 *I can't afford* to buy a new coat.
  13 He's *given* all his money *away*.
  14 I *owe* you $5. I'll *pay* you *back* later.

2 PRESENTATION

a In pairs, imagine yourself in these situations. Explain your answers.

HOW IMPORTANT IS MONEY TO YOU? WHAT WOULD YOU DO…

1 **if a very wealthy person, who you liked but who you didn't find attractive, wanted to marry you?**
   a) I'd marry him/her.
   b) I wouldn't marry him/her.
   c) It depends.

2 **if you were offered a job which was very well paid but incredibly boring?**
   a) I'd accept it.
   b) I wouldn't accept it.
   c) I'd think seriously about it.

3 **if you won 1,000 euros?**
   a) I'd spend most of it on myself.
   b) I'd share most of it with my friends/family.
   c) I'd save most of it.

4 **if an old woman asked you to give her some money for a sandwich?**
   a) I wouldn't give her any money.
   b) I'd give her some money.
   c) I'd buy her a sandwich.

5 **if you lent a friend some money but he/she forgot to pay you back?**
   a) I'd ask him/her for it immediately.
   b) I'd forget about it.
   c) I'd wait a few days and then ask him/her for it.

b Go to **Communication** *Quiz answers*, *p.123*. Work out your score. Do you agree?

3 GRAMMAR ANALYSIS
Second conditional

(+)	If I **won** 1,000 euros,	I'd (**would**) spend it.
(−)	If she **asked** me for money,	I **wouldn't** give her any.
(?)	**Would** you spend it?	Yes, I **would**./No, I **wouldn't**.

1 Look at the sentences and the question in the box.
  Are the situations real or imaginary?
2 Underline the verbs after **if** in the questionnaire. What tense are they?

Compare the first and second conditionals:
1st *If I have time, I'll help you.* (= Maybe I'll have time. Then I'll help you.)
2nd *If I had time, I'd help you.* (= I haven't got time so I can't help you.)

! With the verb *be*, we can say *was* or *were* for *I* and *he/she*.
  *If I/he **was** rich…* or *If I/he **were** rich…*

PRACTICE

a Match 1–8 with a–h.

1 If I had better qualifications,
2 If he wasn't so mean,
3 If she didn't work overtime,
4 If I knew more about money,
5 The boss would sack me
6 I wouldn't lend a friend money
7 He wouldn't work
8 It'd be safer

a if she found out about the document I lost.
b if he didn't have to.
c I'd invest in the stock market.
d if you kept your money in a bank account.
e unless I knew he'd pay me back.
f people would like him more.
g I'd apply for that job.
h her salary wouldn't be enough to live on.

b Cover a–h. Try to remember how the sentences end.

c Make second conditional sentences.

1 I *'d lend* you the money if I *had* it. (lend, have)
2 If she really *loved* him, she *wouldn't waste* all his money. (love, not waste)
3 We *'d buy* a bigger house if we *could* afford it. (buy, can)
4 If he *didn't earn* so much, he *wouldn't pay* so much income tax. (not earn, not pay)
5 You *'d be able to* buy a car next year if you *saved* a bit of money each week.
  (be able to, save)
6 If I *was* my own boss, I *'d have to* work longer hours. (be, have to)

d Choose from the list below. Make true sentences about yourself.
  Begin *If I…*

EXAMPLE
If I were at home now, I'd go to sleep on the sofa.

> be at home now
> can choose a job
> have more free time
> speak English fluently
> can have dinner with a famous person
> inherit a fortune
> fall in love with a foreigner
> need to borrow some money
> can go abroad this summer

BETTER PRONUNCIATION
Contractions in first and second conditionals

a **T4.10** Listen to six conditional sentences. Write *1st* or *2nd*.

1 ☐ 3 ☐ 5 ☐
2 ☐ 4 ☐ 6 ☐

b Listen again. Write the sentences.

c Practise saying the sentences with contractions.

4 MAKING CONVERSATION

If …

Go to **Communication** *What would you do if …?*
A *p.123*, **B** *p.127*. Ask and answer questions about
imaginary situations.

5 READ BETTER

a Read about three very rich people: an aristocrat who
inherited a fortune, a self-made millionaire, and a
lottery winner. Before you read, guess who said …

1 "Money alone will not make you any happier, you will
just find something else to worry about."

2 "If I lost my fortune, the worst thing for me would be
that I wouldn't be able to do exactly what I want, but
would have to start working for a living."

3 "The most important thing that money gives me is
security, but on the other hand I sometimes live in fear
of losing it all."

b In groups of three, **A** read 'The Aristocrat', **B** read
'The Self-Made Millionaire', and **C** read 'The Lottery
Winner'. From memory, tell your partners about
your text. Were you right about the sentences in **a**?

c In your groups, find out who:

1 has bought a lot of luxurious things.   _____
2 hasn't been changed by money.   _____
3 never thinks about money.   _____
4 seems to have the most relaxing life.   _____
5 thinks that money doesn't stop you
   from worrying.   _____
6 used to save money for things when
   he/she was a child.   _____
7 worries about if his/her friends are
   real friends.   _____
8 worries about who to give money to.   _____
9 wouldn't like to work.   _____

d Ask in pairs.

1 Which of the three people do you think is the
   happiest? Why?
2 Do you know anyone who:
      has won a lot of money (e.g. on the lottery)?
      earns a lot of money from their job?
      has inherited a lot of money?
      has made a lot of money from their own
         business?
      has married a wealthy person?
3 Do you think being rich would make you happy?

Rich … and happy?

THE ARISTOCRAT

THE Marquess of Bath was 18 when he inherited £23 million. Now
the 65-year-old aristocrat lives surrounded by young women, and
spends his time painting, writing, and generally enjoying himself.
5 'I have never really thought about having money, because I've
always had it. But I have never been extravagant, in fact I've been
rather mean. For example, I've never bought any Ferraris. I just try
to buy what I need. Am I happy? Well, I'm not unhappy. The most
important thing money gives you is freedom. If I lost my fortune,
10 the worst thing for me would be that I wouldn't be able to do
exactly what I want, but would have to start working for a living. If
there was a revolution and I had to choose a job, I suppose I would
like to be a long-distance lorry driver. First, because I love
travelling, and second because you are your own boss. I suppose I
15 could have a more or less happy existence like that, but the idea of
losing everything is not very pleasant.'

THE SELF-MADE MILLIONAIRE

JOHN MADEJSKI is the director of a car magazine and the owner
of Reading Football Club. He has a fortune of about £250 million.
20 'I remember saving my pocket money for things when I was a boy,
and being really excited when eventually I was able to buy what I
wanted. But the funny thing is that the easier it is to buy things, the
less attractive they become. Although I enjoy some things I've
bought, like my paintings and my collection of exotic cars, I hardly
25 ever use them. The most important thing that money gives me is
security, but on the other hand I sometimes live in fear of losing it
all. Financial security alone does not bring happiness. Most things
that make you happy can't be bought. Also having a lot of money
can mean that you live in a superficial world where you are never
30 sure if the people around you are really telling you the truth or not.
Money will never buy the genuine affection of other people.
However, if I had to choose, I would still prefer to have money than
not, but nobody should ever think that it's the answer to all their
dreams.'

THE LOTTERY WINNER

ELAINE THOMPSON won £2.7 million on the national lottery in
December 1995. That night Elaine had a party with her neighbours,
waiting for her husband to come home from a football match.
When he arrived, the party went on all night. But when she was
40 interviewed three months later she said, 'We've spent all the time
worrying about what to do with the money: how much we should
give away and who to, and how our neighbours and friends would
react to us now. Has it made me happier? To be honest, no. We
were very happy before, and we're very happy now so the money
45 has really made no difference at all. I have been married for nearly
20 years, we have two children and we already had a lovely life. I
think anybody who is unhappy now will still be unhappy after
winning the lottery. Money alone will not make you any happier,
you will just find something else to worry about.'

6 LISTEN BETTER

a Describe the photo. Where do you think it was taken?

b **T4.11** Listen to Caroline de Bendern, the girl holding the flag. Choose a, b, or c.

1 Her grandfather was very rich because
   a he was a brilliant businessman.
   b he had a lot of land in France.
   c he won a fortune in Monaco.
2 He wanted her to
   a be an artist.
   b be a musician.
   c marry a king or prince.
3 In 1968, Caroline was
   a not interested in politics.
   b a communist.
   c an anarchist.

4 She was holding the flag because
   a she was a leader in the demonstration.
   b someone asked her to.
   c it was hers.
5 When her grandfather saw the photo, he was
   a very angry.
   b very surprised.
   c very proud.
6 He decided
   a to leave her less money.
   b to leave her more money.
   c to leave her no money.

c Listen again. Complete with **one** word.

1 He chose her as his heir because she was _pretty_.
2 She was going to inherit _everything_.
3 In New York she worked for a short time as a _model_.
4 In Paris there was a lot of street fighting and _demonstrations_
5 She became intoxicated with the _atmosphere_
6 A friend carried her on his _shoulders_.
7 She didn't _realize_ there were photographers everywhere.
8 The photo was on the _cover_ of magazines all over the world.
9 Her grandfather was _furious_ with her.
10 She didn't inherit _anything_.

▶ Go to **Check your progress 4**, p.117.

Getting what you want

1 BUILD YOUR VOCABULARY

Shops

Match the things with the shops where you can buy them.

baker's   butcher's   chemist's   department store   gift shop   greengrocer's   newsagent's   stationer's

1 apples and potatoes — *green grocer's*
2 bread and cakes — *baker's*
3 chicken and sausages — *butcher's*
4 clothes and furniture — *department store*

5 envelopes and pens — *stationer's*
6 medicine and shampoo — *chemist's*
7 newspapers and cigarettes — *newsagent's*
8 presents and souvenirs — *gift shop*

2 EXPLAINING WHAT YOU WANT

highlighter pen   *shower cap*

a T4.12 Listen to two conversations.

1 What do they buy? Tick the correct pictures above.
2 What shops are they in?

b Listen again. Complete the gaps in the chart.

Explaining what you want		
I don't know what it's called in English but…		
	Conversation 1	**Conversation 2**
What's it like?	It's a kind of (*hat*).	It's a sort of (*pen*).
	It's made of (*plastic*).	It's (*small* and *fat*).
What's it for?	It's a thing you use to (*cover*) your hair when you (*have a shower*).	It's (a thing) for (*marking import words*).

c Write a similar dialogue for one of the other objects.

d Go to **Communication** *Explaining what you want*, **A** *p.123*, **B** *p.127*.
   Roleplay asking for things in a shop.

3 UNDERSTANDING INFORMATION

a Read the signs. In pairs, explain what they mean.

1
   SALE ends 15th

2 **SHOPLIFTERS WILL BE PROSECUTED**

3 **ALL PRICES REDUCED THIS WEEK**

4 **WE REGRET WE CANNOT ACCEPT PAYMENT BY CREDIT CARD FOR SALES UNDER $20**

5 **WE WILL ONLY GIVE A REFUND IF GOODS ARE FAULTY.**

b Quickly read about shopping in London.

1 What time do most shops close on Saturdays? *17.30*

2 What days can you go shopping after seven o'clock? *Wednesday / Thursday*

3 What kind of shops usually open on Sundays? *supermarket / department store (shops)*

4 Where should you go if you want to buy, e.g. an old clock or a painting?

5 Name one place where you can go if you want to buy:

   a camera   a dictionary   a CD
   a scarf

6 If you come from Japan, can you get a refund on VAT? *Yes in some shops.*

c Read the text again. Underline words or expressions you don't know. Guess their meaning from the context. Check with the Glossary or the teacher.

4 SHOPPING

a **T4.13** Listen to someone shopping.

1 What kind of shop is she in?
2 What does she ask for first?
3 Does she buy one?
4 What does she try on?
5 Why doesn't she buy the first one?
6 How does she pay?

b Listen again. Complete the gaps.

1 *Have* *U* *got* any lipsticks?
2 I'm sorry, we've *sold* *out*.
3 I'm *just* looking, thank you.
4 What *size* are you?
5 Can I *try* it on?
6 The *changing* rooms are over there.
7 It doesn't *fit* very well.
8 Have you got it in *other* colour?
9 I'll *have* it.
10 Your *receipt*'s in the bag.

c In pairs, roleplay a conversation buying clothes. **A** is the customer, **B** the shop assistant. **B** begins *Can I help you?*

5 UNDERSTANDING PRICES

a **T4.14** Listen to a man shopping.
Write the prices you hear.

1 *£4.99*
2 *3.50*
3 *4.60*
4 *15.99*
5 *8.30*

b Listen again and check. How much did he spend altogether?

SHOPPING IN LONDON

London's main shopping areas are Oxford Street/Regent Street/Bond Street, Knightsbridge, Kensington High Street, and Covent Garden. Normal Monday to Saturday shopping hours are 09.00 to 17.30, although some shops are now opening and closing a bit later, i.e. 10.00 to 18.00. Many shops have one day a week when there is late-night closing, usually Wednesday or Thursday, when they don't close until 20.00. Shopping hours are extended in the period before Christmas. Many shops in central London now open on Sundays, including most supermarkets and many department stores.

Shopping in London generally gives good value for money, but certain goods are particularly worth buying if you are a visitor to Britain: antiques (Camden Passage, Bond Street, King's Road), sweaters and other clothes especially made of wool (Marks and Spencer, Scotch House), books (Foyles, Waterstones), CDs and tapes (Virgin Records, HMV), hi-fi and photographic equipment (Tottenham Court Road).

Visitors to Britain who are not resident in EU countries receive a refund on VAT paid in this country for certain goods. Information on how this is done is available in the stores which operate the scheme.

Glossary

extend	make longer
goods	things you can buy
receive a refund	get money back
VAT	value added tax

1 BUILD YOUR VOCABULARY

Vehicles and traffic

a Describe the photograph. What forms of transport can you see?

b ✎ Complete **Vocabulary Builder 8A** *Vehicles and traffic*, *p.136*.

c Answer these questions with a partner.

Have you been in a sports car / van / lorry? When?

When's the rush hour in your town / city?

Are there enough car parks / parking spaces?

Are there any cycle lanes? Do people use them?

2 READ BETTER

a Read the introduction below quickly. In pairs, answer the questions from memory.

1 Why did *The Times* organize the race?
2 Who took part in the race? What vehicles were they using?
3 Where did it start? Where did it end?
4 How far was it? When was it?
5 What were the rules?
6 Who do you think won the race? Why?

The Rush-hour Grand Prix

Do you live in a city or a large town? How do you get to work or get to class? Do you drive or go on a motorbike, do you use public
5 transport or a bike, or do you just walk?

Every day more than 500,000 people travel across the city of London to get to work or school.
10 But what's the best way for them to get around the city? To find the answer to this question, *The Times* newspaper decided to organize a race.
15 The four contestants in the race, Linda, Nick, Alan and Dalya, all *Times* journalists, had to choose between a bike, a scooter, a car, and public transport (the London
20 underground or 'tube').

The race started at Belsize Park underground station in north London, about 12 kilometres away from *The Times* offices. The start of
25 the race was 8.36 on a sunny morning in June, right in the middle of the London rush hour. The objective was to see who would arrive first at the office, and in what
30 condition (stressed, exhausted, etc.). There were only two rules: 'you mustn't break the law, and you have to be considerate to other travellers'.

b Read the rest of the article and complete with *car, bike, scooter,* or *underground*. What problems did they each have?

They set off at exactly 8.36 a.m.

35 *Nick* went by ___bike___.
'Although you don't have to wear a helmet in Britain, I always wear one. People who use this form of transport are famous for not
40 obeying traffic signs or traffic lights. But I remembered the rules of the race and I tried to behave impeccably. However, I was stopped by a policeman who said:
45 "Excuse me sir, but you've just turned right where it said no right turn. Next time I'll fine you." I had to listen to a five-minute lecture.'

Alan chose the ___car___.
50 'I had the most comfortable journey, but the race was over for me at the first traffic lights. While I was sitting in traffic jams, I turned

on the air-conditioning and listened
55 to classical music to relax. On the journey I noticed that very few drivers were carrying more than one passenger, which I suppose is the reason why there's so much
60 traffic on the roads during the rush hour.'

Dalya went by ___tube___,
on the Northern line, which London commuters call the Misery line. Her
65 journey was a nightmare (although she said it wasn't the worst she has had.)
  'The one I wanted to catch left just as I arrived, so I had to wait for
70 ten minutes. The next one was too crowded to get on, and when the next one came there were still no

seats so I had to stand. Then we had a delay of a few minutes
75 because of 'problems on the line'. I tried to forget my frustration by studying the face of the woman opposite me who was wearing earrings in all sorts of strange
80 places…'

Linda chose the ___scooter___.
'When you travel like this, it's a good idea to go behind someone on a big motorbike, because they
85 protect you – but you shouldn't stop next to them at traffic lights – they look down at you as if you were inferior! I was wearing a leather jacket, gloves and a helmet
90 so I got a bit hot as it was a sunny day.'

---

c In what order do you think they arrived? Go to *p.127* and find out.

d Read the text again quickly and find words in the text for the following definitions. There are two in each paragraph.

1 a hard hat which protects your head _____
2 perfectly _____
3 was finished _____
4 saw _____

5 people who travel to a city to work ___commuters___
6 irritation when you can't do anything ___frustration___
7 not as good ___inferior___
8 material made from animal skin ___leather___

e If you organized a similar race in your city, which form of transport would win and which would come last? Why?

3 MAKING CONVERSATION

Survey: How do you get around?

Interview three people about how they get around. Write the information in the chart.

Name	Getting to school/work/university			Getting around at night	
	How	Time taken	Problems	How	Problems
1 Maria	bus, underground	3/4	Traffic (bus)	car	
2					
3					

How do you usually get to work/school?
How long does it take you?
What problems do you have?
How do you usually get around when you go out at night?

4 GRAMMAR ANALYSIS

Modals of obligation / recommendation

a Match sentences 1–7 with their meanings a–g.

1 You **mustn't** stop on the motorway.
2 You **have to** wear a seat-belt in a car.
3 You **shouldn't** go by car in the rush hour.
4 I **had to** stand on the bus, because there were no seats.
5 You **should** cycle to work – it's good exercise.
6 You **must** be careful when you cross the road!
7 Cyclists **don't have to** wear helmets, only motorcyclists.

a It's not necessary / obligatory.
b Do this. I think it's very important.
c It's not allowed. Don't do it.
d An obligation or necessity in the past.
e Not a good idea, I don't recommend it.
f It's a good idea. I recommend it.
g It's the law.

b Answer with *must*, *have to*, or *should*.

1 Which verb needs *do/did* to make questions and negatives? _____
2 Which verbs don't need *to*? _____ _____
3 Which verb has present, past, and future forms? _____
4 Write the three forms. _____ _____ _____

c Complete the chart with *must/mustn't*, *have to/don't have to*, *should/shouldn't*.

Obligation/ strong recommendation (+)	Recommendation/ advice (+ and –)	No obligation/ no necessity	Not allowed/ strong recommendation (–)
have to	_____	_____	_____
_____	_____		

! ***mustn't / don't have to***: Remember that *mustn't* and *don't have to* are completely different.
You mustn't use a dictionary. = It's not allowed. Don't do it.
You don't have to use a dictionary. = It's not necessary. The text is very easy.
● When *mustn't* = is not allowed, it is the same as *can't*.
You mustn't park here. = You can't park here.

PRACTICE

a Complete with the correct form of *must*, *have to*, or *should*.

1 You _____ tell anybody. It's a secret.
2 It's Sunday so I _____ go to work.
3 That skirt is perfect for you. I think you _____ buy it.
4 We _____ wear a uniform at our school. I hate it.
5 I _____ remember to give you back the money I borrowed.
6 You _____ eat too much white bread. It's not very good for you.
7 Peter bought the cinema tickets and dinner last night. I _____ pay for anything.
8 Our car broke down on holiday so we _____ rent a car for a week.

b You are going on a long car journey. In pairs, make true sentences for your country with *you have to*, *you should*, *you don't have to*, *you shouldn't*, *you mustn't*.

check your oil and water	clean your car
drive slowly in the fast lane	go over the speed limit
stop at traffic lights	use a mobile phone while you're driving
stop and rest every two hours	let children sit in the front
wear a seat-belt in the front	wear a seat-belt in the back

5 LISTEN BETTER

a **T5.1** Listen to a travel programme about Lisbon. Number the topics in the order you hear them.

☐ **nightlife**
best area? *barrio alto*
dancing? _____

☐ **getting around**
best way to see Lisbon? _____

☐ **accommodation**
easy to find? _____
hostels? _____

☐ **sightseeing**
must see _____
and _____

☐ **shopping**
best area? _____
best souvenir? _____

b Listen again. Complete the notes for each heading.

BETTER PRONUNCIATION

The letters *ea*

a *ea* is usually pronounced /iː/, but there are many exceptions.

Look at these three words from the text on *pp. 64–65*: *break, seats, leather.* What is the sound of the *ea* in each word? Put them under the correct sound picture.

🌳	e	🚂 eɪ

_____ _____ _____
_____ _____ _____
_____ _____
_____ _____
_____ _____
_____

b **T5.2** Now put these words in the correct column. Listen and check.

cheap breakfast please dead head pleasure
season steak sweater great leader each

c **T5.3** Repeat these sentences after the tape. Then practise saying them.

1 This season the sweaters are cheap but great.
2 It's a pleasure to have steak for breakfast.
3 Don't break the leather seats, please.
4 He isn't dead. He's only hurt his head.

6 MAKING CONVERSATION

Driving laws

a Choose the best answer.

1 The minimum age for driving motorbikes or scooters should be _____.
a 14   b 16   c 18

2 The speed limit on a motorway should be _____.
a 100 kph   b 120 kph   c 140 kph

3 People who drink and drive should lose their driving licence for _____.
a 6 months   b a year   c life

4 People should have to stop driving when they reach the age of _____.
a 65   b 75   c 80

5 People should wear seat-belts _____.
a only in cars
b in cars and taxis but not in coaches
c in all vehicles

6 Mobile phones _____.
a should never be used by drivers
b should be used only if they are 'hands free'
c can be used by drivers if they're careful

7 Helmets should be worn by _____.
a people on motorbikes
b people on motorbikes and scooters
c people on motorbikes, scooters, and bicycles

b In groups of three, compare your choices and explain why.

A *I think the speed limit on motorways should be 140 kph.*
B *Why?*
A *Because nobody drives at 120. It's too slow.*
B *I don't agree. I think 140 is dangerous. That's why there are so many accidents.*

Dream cars and nightmare journeys

1 BUILD YOUR VOCABULARY
Cars and driving

a 📝 Complete **Vocabulary Builder 8B** *Cars and driving*, p.136.

b Do the 'Car' quiz.

1 What can you put in the *boot* of a car?
2 How many *gears* do cars usually have?
3 What do you have to do if you get a *puncture*?
4 What two things protect the driver in an accident?
5 How many *wheels* does a car have?
6 What are three problems you can have on a car journey?
7 When do you use the *brakes*?
8 When mustn't you *overtake*?
9 What's the *steering wheel* for?
10 What do you have to turn on before you can drive?

2 PRESENTATION

Sebastian Coe is one of Britain's most famous and most successful athletes. Born in 1956, he won two Olympic gold medals and two silver medals and broke the 800 metres world record in 1981. When he retired from sport he became a Member of Parliament, but then lost his seat when the Labour Party won the general election in 1997.

a **T5.4** Listen to Sebastian Coe's answers to some questions about cars and driving. Number the questions in the correct order.

☐ What's your dream car?
☐ Do you like driving?
☐ 1 When did you first learn to drive?
☐ Do you ever go over the speed limit?
☐ What car have you got now?
☐ What do you hate most about other drivers?
☐ What's your favourite car advertisement?

b **T5.5** Listen and check. Try to remember his answers.

c Ask a partner these questions.
1 What's your 'dream' car? Why do you like it?
2 Can you drive a car or ride a motorbike or scooter? Do you enjoy it?
3 Are there any cars you really ***don't*** like?
4 What's your favourite car advertisement?

3 GRAMMAR ANALYSIS
Past perfect

a Which did Sebastian Coe do first: win an Olympic medal, or get his driving licence?

'When I got my driving licence, I **had** already **won** an Olympic medal.'

b Is the picture below sentence 1 or 2? Check with the grammar rules.

1 When Jane got home, her parents **went** to bed.
2 When Jane got home, her parents **had gone** to bed.

Use the past perfect (*had*/*hadn't* + past participle):
- when you are talking or writing about the past and you want to say that one action happened earlier than another, e.g. *I called you this morning but you had already gone to work.* (= you went to work *before* I called you)

! The contraction of *had* is *'d*. Be careful not to confuse it with *'d = would*.

PRACTICE

a Complete the sentences. Use the past simple or past perfect.

1 I was too late. When I arrived, the meeting _____. (finish)
2 She was so exhausted last night that she _____ this morning. (oversleep)
3 She didn't want to come with us because she _____ the film before. (see)
4 I didn't realize that I _____ through a red traffic light, until a policeman stopped me! (go)
5 He was furious. Someone _____ the car window and _____ radio. (break) (take)
6 He woke up when the alarm clock _____. (ring)

b Complete the sentences. Use the past perfect.

1 When she got to the airport, she realized that
_____.

2 When he turned on the TV, he saw that
_____.

3 When the waitress finally brought the bill, the couple
_____.

BETTER PRONUNCIATION
Contractions and linking

T5.6 Say these sentences. Listen and check.

1 I'd already put on my seat-belt.
2 She realized she'd run out of petrol.
3 They'd always wanted a sports car.
4 He hadn't turned on the engine.
5 I'd never been on a motorbike before.
6 We thought we'd missed it.

4 READ BETTER

a Read two mixed-up stories: *The Wedding* and *The Interview*.
Which four paragraphs belong to each story? Write the correct order 1–4.

The Wedding   1   *E*   2   ~~H~~   3   D   4   ~~B~~

The Interview   1   G   2   ~~F~~   3   C   4   ~~A~~

Nightmare journeys

We asked our readers to send us their 'nightmare' journeys.
Here are this week's two best stories called **The Wedding** *and* **The Interview**.

 A   After a few agonizing minutes of indecision I decided to abandon the car and take a taxi. But even the taxi took ages to get there because there was a terrible traffic jam. I eventually arrived, ten minutes late, hot, sweaty and really stressed. When I walked into the manager's office, the first thing she asked me was, 'Did you have a good journey?' 'Oh, yes,' I said. 'It was fine.' But at least the story has a happy ending, because I got the job!

 B   Finally, with my car repaired, I reached the village at two o'clock in the afternoon, but the wedding had already finished. My friend was furious because I'd missed one of the most important moments in his life. 'Why don't you buy a *normal* car,' he said, 'which doesn't *always* break down when you really need it?'

 C   I started to change the wheel myself, but I was wearing a very tight white skirt and jacket and was afraid of getting dirty. Time was running out, and I knew that being late for the interview would be disastrous. They might not even believe what had really happened.

 D   But when I arrived at the first crossroads, I took the wrong turning and I soon found myself completely lost. The engine was beginning to get very hot and suddenly black smoke began coming out. Five minutes later the car broke down. In my elegant suit I began walking towards the nearest village to find a mechanic. Luckily, a passing car stopped and gave me a lift to the garage.

 E   The worst journey I've ever had was three years ago when I was going to my friend's wedding at a small village in Scotland. I was the best man so it was very important for me to arrive early.

 F   First of all, I saw that I'd almost run out of petrol, and had to stop at a garage. Then, as I was driving towards the centre, another car hooted at me and I realized that I had a puncture. I couldn't believe it!

 G   My nightmare journey happened last year. I'd been unemployed for about six months but I had just been called for an interview for a job. The interview was at 4.15 in the centre of town. But as soon as I got into the car, everything started to go wrong.

 H   The ceremony was at 1 p.m., but my car, an old sports car which I loved, was eighteen years old and sometimes used to break down. Although it was only an hour's journey from my home in Aberdeen, I'd decided to set off at 11.00 in the morning.

b Look at the highlighted words and expressions in the text. Guess the meaning from the context. Check with your dictionary or the teacher.

c Underline any more words or expressions you don't know. Check the meaning.

5 MAKING CONVERSATION

Car problems

In groups of three or four, talk about your experiences of car journeys.

Have you ever…

got really lost in a car?
run out of petrol?
had a puncture?
broken down?
missed something important because of traffic problems?
been stopped in a car by the police?
stopped to pick up a hitch-hiker?

If someone has had one of the experiences, ask him/her more questions.
When? Where were you going? What did you do? What happened in the end?

6 WRITE BETTER

a Write a composition called *A nightmare journey.*
If you can't think of a bad journey, invent one. First make notes using these headings.

Paragraph 1
1 When was the journey?
2 Where were you going? Who with? Why?

Paragraph 2
3 What went wrong? What happened?

Paragraph 3
4 What happened in the end?

b Write the composition using your notes. Use the **Writing Bank** *Telling a story*, *p.145* to help you. Start like this…

My nightmare journey was (two years ago). I was going to…

What drives you mad?

1 PRESENTATION

a What do you think of when you hear the word *pollution*?

b Read the article. What kind of pollution is it about?
Is this a problem where you live?

Invisible pollution

What do you think of when you hear the word *pollution*? Factories with black smoke coming out of the chimneys, dirty rivers and beaches, piles of rubbish? But what many people don't realize is that there is another kind of pollution you can't see but which affects us all wherever we live, at any time of day or night, and which can make our lives a misery – noise. According to the Environmental Health Department, noise pollution is now one of the worst problems in cities and towns.

The 10 noises which most annoy people in Britain are, in order:

1 *Neighbours who make a lot of noise.*
2 *Building sites.*
3 *Shops or pubs where they play loud disco music.*
4 *Burglar or car alarms whose owners don't switch them off.*
5 *Noisy parties which go on until very late.*
6 *Roadworks.*
7 *Dogs which bark when people walk past the house or during the night.*
8 *Heavy traffic and drivers hooting.*
9 *People who play their car radios at full volume with the windows open.*
10 *Planes which fly low over towns and cities.*

c **T5.7** Listen. What noises can you hear?

d Choose the three which most annoy you. Compare with a partner and explain why. Are there any other noises which annoy you a lot?

2 GRAMMAR ANALYSIS

Defining relative clauses

a Cover the text in **1**. Complete phrases 1–5 with *which, whose, where, who*.
Then check with the text.

1 Neighbours __who__ make a lot of noise.
2 Noisy parties __which__ go on until very late.
3 Shops or pubs __where__ they play loud disco music.
4 Car alarms __whose__ owners don't switch them off.
5 A kind of pollution __which__ you can't see but which affects us all …

b In which phrase in **a** is the relative pronoun possible, but not necessary?

c Check with the grammar rules. Then cover the rules. Can you remember them?

Use defining relative clauses to give essential information about a person, place, or thing.

1 Use *who* for people, *which* for things or animals, and *where* for places.
2 *whose* = *of who* or *of which*. It can't be omitted.
3 In conversation you can use *that* instead of *who/which*.
4 *who, which,* and *that* are often omitted when the verb after the relative pronoun has a **different** subject, especially in conversation.
The woman (who) I met last week has six children.
(The subject of *met* is *I*, NOT *the woman*.)

PRACTICE

a Complete with *who* or *which* if necessary.

1 Is that the film ___ø___ you saw last week?
2 Is that the film __which__ won seven Oscars? ✓
3 The man ___ø___ you met is our neighbour. ✓
4 The man __who__ lives next door makes a lot of noise. ✓

5 A close friend is someone ___ø___ you can trust. ✓
6 A close friend is someone __who__ will help you in a crisis. ✓
7 I work for a company __which__ makes furniture. ✓
8 That's the company ~~which~~ ø I work for. ✗

b Make sentences with *which, who, whose,* or *where*.

EXAMPLE
That's the shop. They sell Italian food there.
That's the shop where *they sell Italian food.*

1 We stopped to help a man. His car had broken down.   *whose car had broken down.*
2 It's a new kind of car. It doesn't use petrol.   *of car which doesn't use petrol. /that*
3 I like restaurants. They don't play music there.   *restaurants where they don't ...*
4 At the party I met a girl. Her father's a millionaire.   *I met a girl whose~~her~~ father's a millionaire.*
5 She's the person. She won the competition.   *the person who won the competition.*
6 I complained to the man. His dog was always barking.   *the man whose dog was always barking.*

c Go to **Communication** *The defining game*, **A** *p.124,* **B** *p.127.*
A defines a word to **B** who writes the word. Swap roles.

3 LISTEN BETTER

a You are going to listen to people in the street being asked about things which really annoy them. In pairs, guess what they might say in 1–6.

1 Drivers who _drives slowly_.
2 People on trains who _talks on mobile phone_.
3 Computer or video manuals which _you can't understand_.
4 Shops where _the shop assistant follows you everywhere_.
5 Advertising leaflets which _coming inside magazine or newspaper_.
6 Plastic shopping bags which _break (on the pavement)_.

b **T5.8** Listen and complete the sentences. Which of these things also annoy you?

4 MAKING CONVERSATION

Things that annoy you

a In groups of three or four, talk about people, places, and things which really annoy you. Make a list of the things your group found most annoying.

What really annoys me is/are…	*who…*
What drives me mad is/are…	*which…*
What I hate is/are…	*where…*
	whose…

b Read out your list to other groups. Are any of the things the same?

5 BUILD YOUR VOCABULARY

Compound nouns

In English we often use two nouns where the first noun describes the second, e.g. *bus stop, traffic lights, front door, noise pollution.*

a Can you remember these compound nouns?

1 A place where builders are working
   Building site

2 An alarm which protects your house
   _____

3 Something you use to carry shopping
   _____

4 A book which teaches you to use a computer
   _____

b Match words in **A** with words in **B** to make compound nouns.

A		B	
traffic	soap	agent's	attack
heart	alarm	car	hour
sleeping	junk	limit	clock
state	sports	food	jam
speed	science	fiction	school
travel	rush	pill	opera

BETTER PRONUNCIATION

Compound nouns; /ʃ/ and /tʃ/

a **T5.9** In compound nouns, the first noun is usually stressed, e.g. *junk food.*

Listen and repeat the compound nouns in **5b**.

b Cover box **B** in **5b**. Say the nouns from memory.

c **T5.10** Listen and repeat the words in the columns below. Then put the words from the list in the correct column.

 crash
station
sociable
expression

 coach
puncture
match
future

_____   _____
_____   _____
_____   _____
_____   _____
_____   _____

pollution   chimney   beaches   shops   furniture   church
competition   depression   especially   which

d Look at the spelling of the /ʃ/ and /tʃ/ sounds. Add some more words to each column.

6 PRESENTATION

a What kind of noise pollution is there in the country?

b Read this true story about Mr and Mrs Fussey and answer the questions.

1 Why did they buy their house?
2 Why did they complain to the local environmental health department?
3 What do they want to do now?

Margaret Fussey and her husband Christopher bought their house in the country 12 years ago because it was so peaceful. The house,
¹_____, was just what they had always wanted. However, last spring Fred Kennedy,
²_____, built two aviaries in his garden. In the aviaries, ³_____, he put 45 budgies. 'We had expected a certain amount of noise from neighbours, but not this. The birds started singing at eight in the morning and didn't stop until the evening. We were getting no peace and felt permanently stressed,' says Mrs Fussey. The couple complained to the local environmental health department, ⁴_____. They took Mr Kennedy to court – but lost. 'We'd like to sell the house now,' says Mrs Fussey, ⁵_____
_____, 'but nobody wants to buy it with all these birds next door.'

c Put these pieces of extra information into the text above. Write a–e in spaces 1–5.

a who lives next door
b who is now suffering from depression
c who agreed that the noise was unacceptable
d which has a large garden
e which were two metres high

7 GRAMMAR ANALYSIS
Non-defining relative clauses

> 1 The house, which has a large garden, was just what they had always wanted.
> 2 The house which I like best is the small one.

Which sentence has some extra information which could be omitted, and the sentence would still make sense? Check with the grammar rules.

Use non-defining relative clauses to give some *extra* information about a person or thing. This information is not essential.

1 Non-defining relative clauses always have a comma before ***who/which/where/whose*** and a comma (or full stop) at the end of the clause to separate this extra information from the main information.
My mother, who is 65, has just retired.
Finally I arrived home, where my mother was waiting for me.
2 In non-defining relative clauses, you ***can't*** use *that*.

PRACTICE

a Read the sentences. Put commas where necessary.

1 The hotel where we stayed was very noisy.
2 Mrs Black whose daughter goes to my school has just won the lottery.
3 People who earn a lot of money should pay higher taxes.
4 The giant panda which lives mainly in China is in danger of extinction.
5 The author whose book you're reading has just won a prize.
6 My sister who's a doctor is arriving tonight.
7 Buckingham Palace where the Queen lives is now open to the public.
8 Windscreen wipers are things which you switch on when you're driving in the rain.

b In pairs, put in as many non-defining relative clauses as possible to make the story longer and more interesting.

> *A man called James went to London to see a friend. When he got to his house, a strange woman opened the door. She invited him into the living room and gave him a drink. After a short time he fell asleep in an armchair. When he woke up he was on a boat.*

A man called James, who was a farmer, went to London, where he used to live, …

c Read out your stories. Whose story is the best?

> Go to **Check your progress 5**, *p.118*.

Finding your way

1 ASKING POLITELY FOR INFORMATION

a **T5.11** Listen to some tourists asking for information. Complete the questions.

> **Asking politely for information (indirect questions)**
> 1a   Where's the bus station?
> b   Could you tell me _____ _____ _____ _____ _____?
> 2a   What time does the bank open?
> b   Do you know _____ _____ _____ _____ _____?
> 3a   Does this bus go to Piccadilly?
> b   Could you tell me _____ _____ _____ _____ to Piccadilly?

b Look at questions 1–3 in **a** and answer the questions below.

1 Which questions are more polite, a or b?
2 What happens to the verb *be* in sentence 1b?
3 What happens to the auxiliary *does* in 2b and 3b?
4 Which word do you have to add to the yes/no question in 3b?

Use indirect questions when you want to ask a question very politely.

! In an indirect question the second verb is not in question form,
  NOT ~~Could you tell me what time does the last bus leave?~~

c Rewrite the questions in the correct order.

1 could is me next tell the time train what you ?
   _____

2 to bus do if know centre goes the this you ?
   _____

3 bank do is know nearest the where you ?
   _____

4 train you to tell could me if this Bristol goes ?
   _____

d Look at the picture. Ask questions 1–8 politely.

1 Could you tell me *if there's a post office near here* ?
2 Do you know _____?
3 Could you tell me _____?
4 Do you know _____?
5 Do you know _____?
6 Do you know _____?
7 Could you tell me _____?
8 Could you tell me _____?

e **T5.12** Listen and repeat. Copy the polite intonation.

1 Is there a post office near here?
2 Where's the British museum?
3 Which floor is the café on?
4 Do the shops open on Sunday?
5 What time do the shops close?
6 How long does the journey take?
7 Where do I have to get off?
8 Does this train stop at London Bridge?

2 BUILD YOUR VOCABULARY
Prepositions of movement

across   along   down   over   past   round   through   under   up

Look at the pictures. Give directions using prepositions from the list.

a   **b**   **c**

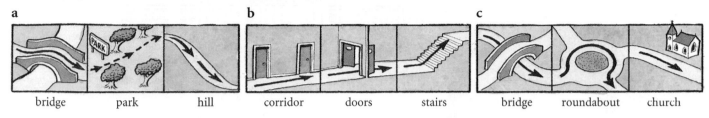

bridge   park   hill   corridor   doors   stairs   bridge   roundabout   church

3 ASKING FOR AND GIVING DIRECTIONS

a **T5.13** Listen to the conversation. Tick (✓) Caroline's house on the map.

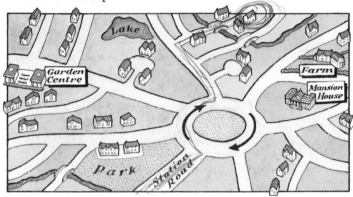

b Listen again. Write the missing words.

> **Giving directions**
> How do I ___get___ to your house?
> Go ___along___ Station Road, ___past___ the park
> until you ___get to/until___ the big roundabout.
> Go ___round___ the roundabout and take the first,
> second, third ___exit___.
> ___keep___ going along that road.
> Take the third ___turning___ on the ___right___.
> Go ___straight___ on down that road.
> You can't ___miss___ it.

c In pairs, **A** choose a house. **B** ask **A** for directions to his/her house and tick (✓) it on the map. Swap roles.

4 WRITE BETTER
Giving directions

a Read Nick's letter and label as much as you can on the map, including a cross where his house is.

> The easiest way to get here is to take the number 24 bus, which you can get at either Victoria or Trafalgar Square, but make sure it's going north, towards Hampstead, and not south! Get off at Hampstead Heath (ask the driver to tell you when you get there). The bus stop is next to the tube station, and there's a newsagent's on the corner. Go down that road (where the newsagent's is) — I can't remember what it's called — for about 100 metres, and then turn left, and you're in Constantine Road. Number 107 is about halfway down the street on the left.

b Go to the **Writing Bank**, *p.143*. Check how to write a letter to a friend.

c Write a letter to a friend explaining how to get to your house. Include a map. Start like this:

> *Dear...,*
>   *I'm so glad you're coming next Saturday. I'm really looking forward to seeing you. The easiest way to get here is...*

Set in the Wild West, shot in Spain

1 PRESENTATION

a Look at the film titles. What kind of films are they (cartoons, love stories, etc.)?

b In pairs, ask these questions.

How often do you go to the cinema?
What kind of films do you like? Are there any that you hate?
What's the best film you've seen this year? Why did you like it?
What's the next film you'd like to see?

c Read about a critic's five favourite classic films. Do you know which films they are?

1

This enchanting story has been filmed twice, the first time as a cartoon, and the screenplay is based on a novel which was written by an English writer, Dodie Smith. The second version, which was made in 1996, was for me a bit disappointing. It starred Glenn Close as the evil woman whose hair is half black and half white – but the real stars of the film, of course, are not people…

2

This film is set 'a long time ago in a galaxy far, far away' and it was originally intended to be the fourth in a series of nine films. It was rejected by two studios before 20th Century Fox decided to take a risk with it, and it became the first in a series of three. The film is about a young farmer who rescues a princess who is being kept prisoner, with the help of various people – well, perhaps 'people' is not the right word. The cast includes famous actors such as Alec Guinness, and the whole series was re-released in 1997 with improved sound and colour.

3

This film, a drama, was set in Britain and Paris in the 1920s. It starred two unknown actors, Ben Cross and Ian Charleson, and co-starred Ian Holm who played the part of a coach. The film won several Oscars in 1981, including best film. The scene which will always be remembered is that of the young athletes running along the sea shore to the accompaniment of the unforgettable soundtrack.

4

Although it is based on a real event, this dramatic film is really a mixture of a Hollywood love story and a disaster movie. At the time of its production it was the most expensive film ever made, in spite of not having well-known stars. This was partly because of the amazing special effects, but also because of numerous problems while it was being filmed, which resulted in several months delay. Although the end of this film is no surprise, it is still incredibly moving. It was nominated for 14 Oscars, including best film, best director and best actress.

5

The most famous scene in this classic thriller takes place in the shower of a cheap motel on an American highway. This film was directed by one of the best-known British film directors, who always appeared for a few seconds in his own films. A sequel, which came out 30 years after the first version had been released, was made with the same main actor but a different director. It was not nearly as thrilling or as successful as the original film.

d Do you agree with the choice?
Which would be your five favourite films?

2 BUILD YOUR VOCABULARY
The cinema

a Guess the meaning of the highlighted words in the texts.

b Complete **Vocabulary Builder 9** *The cinema*, *p.137*.

c Test your partner's memory.

A (Book open) Describe a word or phrase.   B (Book closed) Say the word or phrase.

3 GRAMMAR ANALYSIS
The passive

ACTIVE		PASSIVE
1a Spielberg directed *ET*.	→	**1b** *ET* was directed by Spielberg.
2a They nominated the film for 14 Oscars.	→	**2b** The film was nominated for 14 Oscars.

a Look at the sentences in the box above.

In **1**, in which sentence (**a** or **b**) are we more interested in the film than in the director?
In **2**, in which sentence (**a** or **b**) is the film more important than the people? Do we know who *they* are?

Use the passive:
- when we are not especially interested in the person or people who did an action, e.g. *The film was made in 1990* (we are not interested in the people who made it).

If the person who did the action is also important use *by*.
The film was made in 1997 **by** *James Cameron*.

b Look at the texts on *p. 78* and underline all the verbs in the passive. What tenses are they?

c Complete the table with passive forms of the verb *make*.

	Active	Passive
Present simple	*make*	*is made* ~~being~~
Present continuous	*is making*	was made
Future (*will*)	*will make*	will be "
Future (*going to*)	*is going to make*	is going to be made
Past simple	*made*	was made
Past continuous	*was making*	was being made
Present perfect	*has made*	has been made
Past perfect	*had made*	had been made
infinitive (with *to*)	*to make*	*to be made*

PRACTICE

a Put the verbs in brackets into the passive.

1 In 1963, 26,000 costumes _were used_ in the film *Cleopatra*. (use)
2 Before 1927, films used to _be made_ without sound. (make)
3 Classic films, like Hitchcock's *Rear Window*, _have been seen_ by millions of people since they first came out. (see)
4 Marilyn Monroe died while her last film, *The Misfits*, _was being shot_. (shoot).
5 After her death, some people thought that she _had been murdered_ by the CIA. (murder)
6 Nowadays many special effects _____ by computer. (create)
7 At this moment, all over the world hundreds of films _are being made_. (make)
8 In the mid-21st century many more films _will be seen_ on home videos and computers than in the cinema. (see)

b Choose the correct form.

The Piano [1](won/ ~~was won~~) the Palme d'Or at the Cannes film festival in 1993. It [2](~~directed~~/ was directed) by Jane Campion, and it [3](stars/ ~~is starred~~) Holly Hunter and Harvey Keitel. It [4](~~set~~/ is set) in New Zealand in the 19th century, and is about a Scottish woman, Ada, who [5](~~sends~~/ is sent) there by her parents to marry a local man. She only [6](brings/ ~~is brought~~) two things with her: her daughter, and her piano. Ada never [7](speaks/ ~~is spoken~~) and [8](has/ ~~is had~~) a very unhappy time until she [9](falls/ ~~is fallen~~) in love with a neighbour. Finally, she [10](~~rescues~~/ is rescued) by him from her violent husband and, in her new life, she [11](learns/ ~~is learned~~) to speak again. The soundtrack [12](~~wrote~~/ was written) by Michael Nyman, and millions of copies of the CD [13](~~have sold~~/have been sold) all over the world.

c In pairs, write a text like 1–5 in **1c** for the rest of the class to identify.

4 LISTEN BETTER

a **T6.1** Listen to a man asking a woman about a film she's just seen. Who's it directed by? What does the man think of the director?

b Listen again. What five questions does he ask about the film?

1 _____?
2 _____?
3 _____?
4 _____?
5 _____?

c What are her answers?

5 MAKING CONVERSATION

Talking about films

In pairs, ask each other about films you've seen recently.

A *I saw* (name of film) *at the cinema/on TV* (when?).
B *What's it like? Who's in it?*

6 READ BETTER

a Have you seen any Woody Allen films? Did you like them?

b Read the interview with Woody Allen quickly. Answer questions 1–3.

1 Why doesn't he go to the opening nights of his films?
2 Why did he try to stop one of his films from being seen?
3 Does he enjoy the Hollywood lifestyle?

c Look at the highlighted words and expressions in the text. In pairs, guess their meaning. Check with a dictionary or the teacher.

d Read the text again. Which of these words would you use to describe him? Why?

a perfectionist   cheerful   extrovert   hard-working
insecure   neurotic   optimistic   sociable

'I just want to make the film and go home'

an interview with Woody Allen

Woody Allen, whose real name is Allen Konigsberg, was born in 1935. He is an actor and director, and specializes in adult comedies set in New York. Among his best known films are *Annie Hall* (1977), *The Purple Rose of Cairo* (1985) and *Mighty Aphrodite* (1995). Apart from his films and his sense of humour, he's famous for his glasses and his marriage in 1997 to Soon Yi, the adopted daughter of Mia Farrow, his ex-partner. When he isn't making films, he plays the clarinet in a New York jazz club.

5

M ost people are convinced that the characters that Woody Allen plays, which tend to be very similar, are based on his own personality. He has always denied this, but there is some evidence to the contrary.
Like many of the characters he plays, he is genuinely shy. 'For me the real pleasure is writing. Making the movie is this: you're out there in the cold and rain, you're freezing, the clock is ticking, you're spending thousands of dollars, and people keep saying, "Hurry up". The nicest feeling I know is that the film is opening in Chicago and I'm not there – I'm in bed, relaxing, reading, playing my clarinet. All my life I've enjoyed <u>not</u> being at the opening night. I used to have a joke: "I don't mind dying, but I don't want to be there when it happens." That really is about me. When I'm invited to parties, I almost never go. Sometimes I get to the door and I just can't go in. It's nothing to do with being famous, I was like that before. Not being there, but

10

15

20

25

BETTER PRONUNCIATION
/d/, /ð/, and /θ/

director

clothes

think

_____   _____   _____

_____   _____   _____

_____   _____   _____

a Look at the three columns. How do you pronounce the words? What are the three sounds?

b **T6.2** You're going to hear nine words, three for each sound. Listen and write the words in the correct column.

c **T6.3** Repeat the sentences after the tape. Practise saying them.

1 The director made this film in three months.
2 I think the end of the thriller was disappointing.
3 The third film in the series was dubbed.

7 WRITE BETTER

Write a review of a film you've seen recently.

● Write three paragraphs, answering the following questions. Include other information if you want.

Paragraph 1
What's it called? Who does it star? Who's it directed by? Where is it set?

Paragraph 2
What's it about? Use the present tense, e.g. _It's about some men who_ **are** _unemployed and_ **want** _to earn some money so they_ **decide** _to …_
What's the funniest/saddest/most exciting scene? What's the soundtrack like?

Paragraph 3
What did you think of it? Why?

● Start _A film I really enjoyed was …_
● Use **Vocabulary Builder 9** _The cinema_, _p.137_ to help with vocabulary.

knowing people like the film – that's perfect for me.' He stays away from Hollywood, its romances and its glamorous lifestyle. 'I hate all that. I just want to make
50 the film and go home.'
    Woody Allen is also very insecure about his films. 'The idea in my mind is always superb, but by the time the film's made, it's never exactly as I wanted it. I always want to say to people, "You don't realize what a great
55 film I nearly made here." ' In fact, he was so disappointed with _Manhattan_ that he tried to buy the movie back from United Artists, and promised that he would make another film for free if they destroyed it for him or threw it away. They refused, and the film was nominated for an
60 Oscar.
    The big question is, is he happy? 'What does that mean? My basic position is pessimism. Some people are naturally cheerful, some aren't. I naturally expect the worst. It's just the way I am.' ■

Survival of the fittest

1 BUILD YOUR VOCABULARY

Sport

a How many Olympic sports can you name? Which sports are **not** Olympic sports?

b 📖 Complete **Vocabulary Builder 10** *Sport*, p.138.

c In pairs, explain the difference between:

1 a court and a pitch   3 win and beat
2 a coach and a referee   4 nil and love

d Play '20 questions'. In groups of three or four, **A** thinks of a sport. The others can ask up to twenty *yes/no* questions to identify the sport.

   A *OK, I've thought of one.*
   B *Is it an indoor sport?*
   A *No, it isn't.*
   C *Do you play with a ball?*
   A *Yes, you do,* etc.

2 LISTEN BETTER

a How do you say these numbers and scores?

200 m   150 kg   175 kph   1.65 m   4.6 km   64.5 kg
4–1, 2–0, 3–3 (football, basketball, etc.)

b **T6.4** You're going to listen to a radio programme about strange sporting statistics. The first time you listen, cover the texts. What were the world records for?

c Listen again and complete the missing information.

STRANGE SPORTING STATISTICS

Athletics

The ¹ _____ marathon runner in the world was Dimitrion Yordanidis from Greece who completed the Athens marathon in 1976 in 7 hours ² 31 minutes aged ³ 98 .

The world's ⁴ hardest sport is probably the triathlon, where competitors have to swim ⁵ 3.8 km, cycle ⁶ 180 km, and run a marathon (42.195 km).

Basketball

The ⁷ tallest basketball player was Suleiman Ali Nashnush who played for the Libyan national team in 1962. He was ⁸ 2 m tall.

The ⁹ highest number of points scored by one player in a basketball match was achieved by a Swedish player, Mats Wermelin, who scored all the points in his team's victory in a tournament in Stockholm in 1974. The final score was ¹⁰ 272 – 0.

Football

The ¹¹ largest crowd at a football match was in the Maracanã municipal stadium in Rio de Janeiro, Brazil on 16th July, ¹² 1950 for the match between Brazil and Uruguay. There were almost ¹³ 200 000 spectators.

The ¹⁴ heaviest international goalkeeper on record was Willie 'Fatty' Foulke who played for England. He was ¹⁵ 1.90 tall and weighed ¹⁶ 165 kg. He once stopped a game when he broke the bar of the goal.

3 GRAMMAR ANALYSIS

Comparatives, superlatives, *as ... as*

a In pairs, do the comparatives and superlatives quiz.

Part 1 What's the opposite of...?

Comparative adjectives		Superlative adjectives	
1 longer	*shorter*	8 the slowest	*fastest*
2 smaller	*bigger*	9 the coldest	*hottest*
3 cheaper	*more expensive*	10 the safest	*most dangerous*
4 more difficult	*less* ✗	11 the saddest	*happiest*
5 more interesting	*less* ✗	12 the rudest	*more polite*
6 better	*worst*	13 the best	*worst*
7 more	*less*	14 the most	*the least*

Part 2 Correct the mistakes

1 She can't swim as fast ~~than~~ *as* her sister. ✓
2 I think skiing is the ~~more~~ *most* enjoyable winter sport.
3 He plays squash much better ~~that~~ *than* me.
4 That was the ~~better~~ *best* match I've ever seen.
5 Their team's shirt is the same colour ~~than~~ *as* ours.
6 He's the most exciting footballer ~~of~~ *in* the world.

SCORE: /20

b Check your answers with the grammar rules.

ADJECTIVES	COMPARATIVES	SUPERLATIVES
1-syllable	+ er	+ est
2-syllable	*more* + adj.	*the most* + adj.
ending in *y*	+ ier	+ iest
3-syllable	*more* + adj.	*the most* + adj.

ADVERBS	COMPARATIVES	SUPERLATIVES
regular	*more* + adverb	*the most* + adverb

IRREGULAR ADJECTIVES AND ADVERBS

good/well	better	the best
bad/badly	worse	the worst
far	further	the furthest

! 1-syllable adjectives which end in 1 consonant + 1 vowel + 1 consonant = double the final consonant.
slim – slimmer – the slimmest

To compare two things, use:
- a comparative adjective/adverb + *than*.
  Boxing is **more** dangerous **than** rugby. I can run **faster than** you.
- *not* + *as* + adjective + *as*.
  Rugby **isn't as** dangerous **as** boxing. I can't run **as fast as** you.

To express maximums or minimums, use:
- *the* + a superlative adjective/adverb.
  She's the **tallest/most** exciting player **in** the team.
  She plays **the best**.

To say that two things are the same, use:
- *as* + adjective/adverb + *as*.
  Our team is **as** good **as** yours. He can play **as well as** me.
- *the same as*.
  My racket is **the same as** yours.

c Now check with the teacher. What was your score?

PRACTICE

a Complete with the comparative or superlative.

1 He was the *worst* referee we've ever had. (bad)
2 I think swimming is *more relaxing* than jogging. (relaxing)
3 The new sports centre is much *better* than the old one. (good)
4 It was the *biggest* crowd of the season. (big)
5 I'm much *fitter* than I used to be. (fit)
6 One of the *easiest* sports to do is cycling. (easy)
7 Cross-country skiing is *more tiring* than normal skiing. (tiring)
8 It was the *most exciting* match I've ever seen. (exciting)

b Compare the following using *not as ... as* + the adjective.

1 motor racing/motorcycling   (dangerous)
2 live sport/sport on TV   (exciting)
3 golf/cycling   (boring to watch)
4 swimming/aerobics   (good for you)
5 watching sport/doing sport   (enjoyable)
6 squash/tennis   (tiring)
7 being a player/being a coach   (difficult)
8 winning/taking part   (important)

Compare your sentences with a partner.
Do you agree?

taking part isn't as important as ...

motor racing isn't as dangerous as
live sport isn't as exciting as
golf isn't as boring to watch as
swimming isn't as good for you as
watching sport isn't as enjoyable as
tennis isn't as tiring as squash
being a player isn't as difficult as

BETTER PRONUNCIATION
The /ə/ sound in words and sentences

a Remember that unstressed words and syllables are often pronounced /ə/. Underline the stressed syllable in the following words. (Circle) the /ə/ sound.

1 footballer 2 medal 3 exercise 4 centre
5 referee 6 motor racing 7 spectator 8 corner

b **T6.5** Listen and check. Say the words. Focus on getting the stress and the pronunciation of the /ə/ sound right.

c **T6.6** Listen to these sentences and underline the stressed words. Listen again and (circle) the /ə/ sound.

1 A <u>tennis</u> <u>player</u> isn't as <u>strong</u> as a <u>footballer</u>.
2 <u>Players</u> earn more than <u>referees</u>.
3 <u>The</u> last time I beat him was two weeks ago.
4 <u>The</u> swimming pool's about a mile away.
5 There's a sports <u>centre</u> on the corner.

d Now say the sentences. Focus on getting the stress and the pronunciation of the /ə/ sound right.

4 READ BETTER

a Look at the photos. Have you ever done any of these sports?

b Read **Part 1** of an article about five students who do the sports in **a**. Answer the questions.

1 What do the boys study?
2 What's their house like?
3 How do they earn extra money?
4 How often do they do sport a day?
5 Who do you think is the fittest?

Part 1

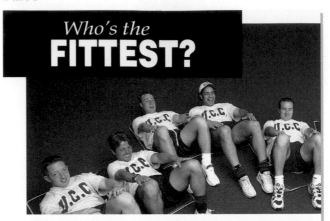

Who's the **FITTEST?**

When you walk into number 4 Walpole Street, Chester, in the north of England, you have to be careful you don't fall over the mountain bikes, sports bags and various pieces of sports
5   equipment all over the hall. The house is occupied by five sports science students from University College, Chester, who eat, live and breathe sport. They work hard to keep fit. Karl, the canoeist, describes a typical day: 'In the
10 morning, we go for a run before breakfast, and then we have lectures at college. Then we go running again or swimming, and then a quick lunch. In the afternoons we do coaching to earn some extra money, and evenings are spent in
15 the gym or playing football.'

All five boys are obviously fit. But who is the fittest? We asked them to do a series of tests to find out the answer.

c Look at the questions and in pairs, guess the answers before you read **Part 2**. Choose from:

the footballer   the tennis player   the canoeist
the runner   the shot putter

1 Who had the least body fat? _____
2 Who could keep running the longest time? _____
3 Who was the most flexible? _____
4 Who jumped the highest? _____
5 Who was the fastest sprinter? _____
6 Who was the slowest? _____
7 Who could do the most sit-ups? _____
8 Who did the fewest? _____

d Read **Part 2** of the text. Check your answers.

Part 2

Body fat

20 The testing started by measuring body fat. Not surprisingly, the one with the most was the shot putter, and the one with the least was the tennis player.

Endurance

25 The athletes had to run at a speed which was controlled by an audio signal from a cassette. After each minute, the signal got faster, and they had to try to keep going for as long as possible. The first to get tired was the shot putter who
30 lasted 10 minutes followed by the canoeist ('you don't have to run in a canoe!'), and the runner, not surprisingly, lasted the longest.

Flexibility

When they had recovered, they had to do some
35 stretching. This gave the shot putter the chance to win some points, and he was the most flexible, followed by the runner.

Strength

The next test involved lifting weights to test the
40 strength of their arms. Logically, the shot putter was the strongest. Then leg strength was measured using a jump test, and the runner jumped the highest, 1cm more than the canoeist.

Speed

45 An electronic timing system was used to measure sprinting speed and the result, a surprise, was that the tennis player was the fastest, just ahead of the footballer, and the shot putter was last.

Abdominal muscles

50 To complete the fitness test, their abdominal muscles were tested by doing continuous sit-ups. The footballer only managed two minutes, and after five minutes the only one left was the tennis player who lasted the full eight minutes.

e Read **Part 3** of the text. Who was the fittest? Who was the least fit? Are you surprised?

Part 3

So, at the end of the day, who was the fittest? Using a points system for each of the tests, the result was as follows:
    In last place, the shot putter, then the canoeist, then the footballer. In second place was the tennis player, and the winner was Robert, the runner.

f Read the text again. Underline any words you don't know. Guess the meaning or find them in the Glossary.

5 BUILD YOUR VOCABULARY

Noun-building

Write the nouns for these verbs and adjectives.

1 strong   s_____ /streŋθ/
2 high   h_____ /haɪt/
3 fit   f_____ /'fɪtnəs/
4 weigh   w_____ /weɪt/
5 fast   s_____ /spiːd/
6 long   l_____ /leŋθ/
7 wide   w_____ /wɪdθ/
8 deep   d_____ /depθ/

6 MAKING CONVERSATION

Sport

Choose a topic from the box below and interview a partner. Swap roles.

> **AT SCHOOL**
> 1 What sports do/did you have to do at school? Do/did you enjoy it? Why (not)?
> 2 Do you think sport is as important as maths or languages?
> 3 Do you think everybody should play a team sport at school?
>
> **AS A HOBBY**
> 1 Do you do any sports? Which?
> 2 How often do you do them? Where?
> 3 Do you think there are enough sports centres in your town?
> 4 Do you think you're fit? Would you like to be fitter?
> 5 Is there any sport you'd like to be able to do? Which?
>
> **PROFESSIONAL SPORT**
> 1 Do you watch sport on TV? Which?
> 2 What's the most exciting live sports event you've been to?
> 3 Do you think referees in your country are usually fair?
> 4 What do you think are the advantages/disadvantages of being a professional athlete?

Glossary

measure (v.)/'meʒə/	find the height, length, width, etc. of something
endurance (n.) /ɪn'dʒurəns/	the ability to keep doing something difficult
last (v.)	to continue for a certain amount of time, e.g. *the film lasts 2 hours.*
stretch (v.)	to push out your arms, legs, etc. as far as possible
ahead (adj.) /ə'hed/	in front
manage (v.) /'mænɪdʒ/	to be able to do something with difficulty
be left (v.)	be still existing, e.g. *there's only one egg left.*

Let it be

1 BUILD YOUR VOCABULARY

a Do the '20th century pop' quiz in pairs.

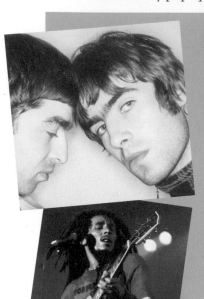

1 Where did the pop group Abba come from?

2 What kind of music did Bob Marley and the Wailers make famous?

3 Which Michael Jackson album sold 38 million copies in 1982?

4 Which Irish group couldn't find what they were looking for in the 1980s?

5 Which British group do the Gallagher brothers belong to?

6 Which British group couldn't 'get no satisfaction' in the 1960s?

7 Which hit single made the Spice Girls famous in 1997?

8 Which Californian group made surfing famous in the 1960s and 1970s (although only one of them could surf)?

9 Which song by Los del Rio did President Clinton dance to in 1995?

10 Who wrote the lyrics for the Beatles' songs?

b Match the words with their definitions. Look at the phonetics. How do you pronounce the words? What's the difference between *record* as a verb and as a noun?

1 record /rɪˈkɔːd/ (*v.*) a a person who likes a group or singer
2 tune /tjuːn/ (*n.*) b a collection of songs on CD or tape
3 lyrics /ˈlɪrɪks/ (*n.*) c the best-selling singles at the moment
4 hit /hɪt/ (*n.*) d the music of a song
5 album /ˈælbəm/ (*n.*) e a CD with only one song
6 record /ˈrekɔːd/ (*n.*) f the words of a song
7 single /ˈsɪŋɡl/ (*n.*) g not recorded
8 the top 20 h a plastic disc with recorded music on it
9 fan /fæn/ (*n.*) i put music onto a tape or CD
10 live /laɪv/ (*adj.*) j a success

c Talk to a partner.

What kinds of music do you like?

What kinds of music do you hate?

Who is your favourite group or singer?

When and where do you listen to music?

Do you listen to music when you study? What kind?

How often do you buy CDs or cassettes?

What CD or cassette would you take with you to a desert island?

Sir Paul McCartney is probably the most famous pop musician of the 20th century. Together with John Lennon he formed the Beatles, and since their break-up has had a
5 long solo career. Altogether he has written over 500 songs including *Yesterday*, the most played pop song of all time. He has recently also written a classical piece called *Standing Stone* which was premièred in
10 1997. His wife Linda died of cancer in 1998. He has four children.

1 _____?

'In 1957 when I was 15 and he was 16 and we were both still at school. We had a lot in
15 common, we were both mad about music and we both lost our mothers when we were teenagers. My mother had died of cancer the year before and John's mum was run over by a car a year after we'd met. So there was always
20 that special bond between us.'

2 READ BETTER

a Read the introduction to the text and look at the photos showing moments in Paul McCartney's life. Who are the other people?

b Read some extracts from Paul McCartney's recent biography, *Many Years from Now*. Match the questions to the extracts.

Are any of your lyrics about real people and events?

Are you disappointed that none of your children are musicians?

When did you and John begin to write songs together?

How did you feel about becoming Sir Paul McCartney in 1997?

When did you and John Lennon meet?

Why did you decide to make your wife a member of your group Wings?

c Now read the paragraphs again and number the events in chronological order.

John Lennon's mother died.	☐
Paul and John formed the Beatles.	☐
Paul formed the group Wings.	☐
Paul McCartney's mother died.	☐
Paul met John Lennon.	☐
Paul became Sir Paul McCartney.	☐
Paul wrote *Let it be*.	☐
The Beatles broke up.	☐

d Cover the text. In pairs, look at the questions in **b**. Remember his answers.

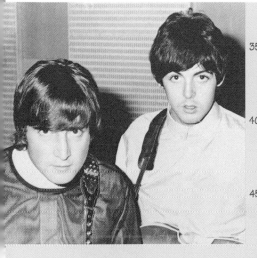

3 _____?

35 'Usually the Beatles' songs which were my idea weren't personal, but there were some exceptions, for instance I wrote *Let it be* about my mother, whose name was Mary. One night, when the Beatles were breaking up and I was
40 feeling very depressed, I had a dream where I saw my mum, who had died when I was fourteen. It was great to see her again and in the dream she said, 'Don't worry. Everything'll be all right.' It was such a nice dream I woke up
45 and I felt much better and I started to write *Let it be*. Afterwards, thousands of people wrote to me saying that the song had helped them in difficult times. Later, after the Beatles had broken up, I formed Wings and I wrote a lot of
50 songs to my wife Linda, like *Silly Love songs* and *The Lovely Linda*.'

2 _____?

'It was when I was still at school and John was at art college. We used to write at my house in the afternoon when my dad was working. We
25 had about three hours before my dad got home. John had a second-hand guitar and I played a bit on the piano. We had an old school notebook and I used to write at the top of the page *A Lennon and McCartney original*.
30 We always said to each other that we'd be the greatest songwriting team in the world, which is funny because that's exactly what we became. We formed the Beatles in 1960.'

5 _____?

'It was one of the best days of my life. When I arrived at Buckingham Palace I realized that I'd forgotten my invitation, but luckily it didn't
65 matter. They recognized me. When the Queen touched me on the shoulder with the sword, my daughter Stella who was in the audience started crying. I felt incredibly proud that someone who started life in a poor street in
70 Liverpool had come so far.'

6 _____?

'Not at all. On the contrary, I'm incredibly proud of them all, because they're all really creative. Stella, who's now a fashion designer,
75 will probably end up being more famous than me.'

4 _____?

'I persuaded her to do it. I needed her there, we were a partnership and I wanted her with
55 me on the stage. She wasn't very happy about being in the group at all in the beginning, I suppose because she felt she wasn't a musician. But for me, it was really important to have her there. I know a lot of people didn't
60 like it but that's their problem.'

3 GRAMMAR ANALYSIS
Narrative tenses

> One night, when the Beatles were breaking up and I was feeling very depressed, I had a dream where I saw my mum, who had died when I was fourteen.

a Read the sentence in the box and look at how the narrative tenses are used. Which tense is each of the highlighted verbs?

b Complete the rules with the **past simple**, **past continuous**, or **past perfect**.

1 **Use the** _____ to talk about consecutive actions in the past.

2 **Use the** _____ to talk about something which happened *before* the past time we are talking about.

3 **Use the** _____ to describe a longer past action.

BETTER PRONUNCIATION
was/were weak and strong forms

a **T6.7** Listen and repeat. Notice how the pronunciation of *was* and *were* changes when they aren't stressed.

I was <u>still</u> at <u>school</u>. My <u>dad</u> was <u>working</u>. We were <u>both</u> <u>mad</u> about <u>music</u>.

She <u>wasn't</u> very <u>happy</u>.

<u>Most</u> of the <u>songs</u> <u>weren't</u> <u>personal</u>.

b **T6.8** Listen and write five sentences.

PRACTICE

a Read another extract from Paul McCartney's biography. Put the verbs on the right in the past simple, past continuous, or past perfect.

How did you hear of John Lennon's death?	
It ¹_____ early in the morning and it ²_____.	be, rain
I ³_____ at my office when I ⁴_____ a phone call.	work, get
It ⁵_____ an American journalist who ⁶_____ me that	be, tell
John ⁷_____. A fan ⁸_____ him when he	be killed, shoot
⁹_____ into a hotel in New York. I ¹⁰_____ horrified.	go, be
First I ¹¹_____ thinking, 'Will I be next?' But then	start
I ¹²_____ that it was the end of everything. When I ¹³_____	realize, get
home that night I ¹⁴_____.	cry

b Go to **Communication** *How the Beatles broke up*, **A** *p.124*, *How Paul McCartney wrote 'Yesterday'*, **B** *p.128*. Read two more extracts from his biography.

4 MAKING CONVERSATION
The first time

In pairs, **A** choose two 'first times'. Tell **B** about what happened. **B** listen and ask for more information. Swap roles.

A *I'm going to tell you about the first time I drove a car. I was staying in the country with my uncle and he had an old Renault 4…*
B *How old were you?*

The first time I…
bought a record or CD
went to a live concert
smoked a cigarette
fell in love
travelled by plane
went abroad
drove a car
saw a lot of snow
earned some money
had to go to hospital

5 LISTEN BETTER 🎵

a **T6.9** Listen to a woman called Jennifer telling an anecdote about the time she met a famous singer. Listen twice and make notes. Tell your partner everything you remember. Together try to retell the whole story.

b Pop songs often contain 'ungrammatical' or very colloquial language. What do the highlighted words mean in these song lyrics?

1 Yeah, I love you babe.
2 I'm gonna make you mine.
3 Do you wanna be my girl?
4 I gotta see you again.
5 He ain't coming back to me.
6 I'm sad 'cos it's over.

c **T6.10** Read the lyrics of *Let it be* with the Glossary, and then listen to the song. Is it positive or negative? Can you remember what made Paul McCartney write it?

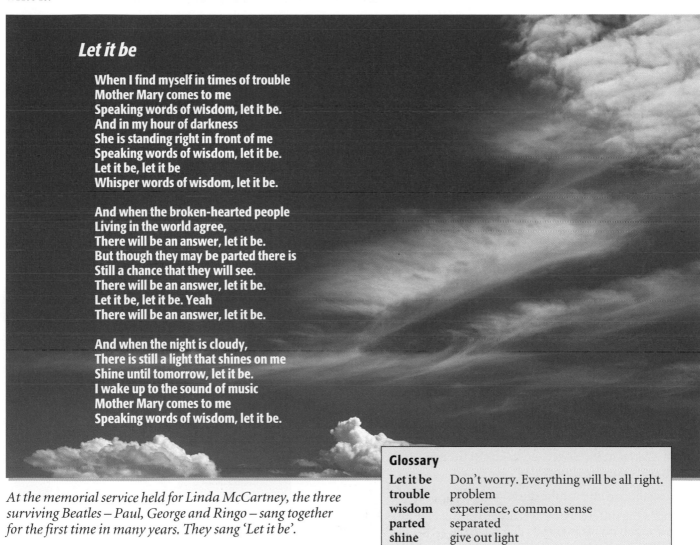

Let it be

When I find myself in times of trouble
Mother Mary comes to me
Speaking words of wisdom, let it be.
And in my hour of darkness
She is standing right in front of me
Speaking words of wisdom, let it be.
Let it be, let it be
Whisper words of wisdom, let it be.

And when the broken-hearted people
Living in the world agree,
There will be an answer, let it be.
But though they may be parted there is
Still a chance that they will see.
There will be an answer, let it be.
Let it be, let it be. Yeah
There will be an answer, let it be.

And when the night is cloudy,
There is still a light that shines on me
Shine until tomorrow, let it be.
I wake up to the sound of music
Mother Mary comes to me
Speaking words of wisdom, let it be.

At the memorial service held for Linda McCartney, the three surviving Beatles – Paul, George and Ringo – sang together for the first time in many years. They sang 'Let it be'.

Glossary

Let it be	Don't worry. Everything will be all right.
trouble	problem
wisdom	experience, common sense
parted	separated
shine	give out light

▶ Go to **Check your progress 6**, *p.119.*

Going out

1 ARRANGING TO MEET

a | T6.11 | Listen to Pieter and Anya arranging
to go out. Answer the questions.

1 When are they going to go out? *Saturday*
2 What are they going to do? ~~watch~~ *watch a show*
3 What's Pieter going to pay for? *tickets*
4 What's Anya going to pay for? *diner*
5 Where are they going to meet? *outside the theatre*
6 What time are they going to meet? *7:00*

b Listen again. Complete the questions and responses in the box.

Inviting/suggesting	Responding
Are you _*doing*_ anything (tonight)?	Nothing _*special*_.
Do you _*want*_ to (come)?	Yes, great./I'd love to.
Would you like to (see a show)?	Sorry, I can't (tonight).
Do you fancy _*seeing*_ (*Cats*)?	That's a good idea.
How _*about*_ (*Miss Saigon*)?	

Arranging to meet	
Where _*shall*_ we meet?	_*What*_ about (outside the station)?
What time shall we meet?	How about (7 o'clock)?
*Let's* meet (outside the theatre).	OK. Fine.

BETTER PRONUNCIATION
Intonation

a | T6.12 | Listen to the questions in the box above.
Underline the stressed words.

b Listen again and repeat. Copy the intonation.

c Think of something to do on Saturday night.
Invite your partner. Arrange a time and place to meet.

2 LISTEN BETTER

a | T6.13 | Listen to Pieter getting tickets at the box office.
Which seats does he choose?

b Listen again and answer the questions.
1 What's the difference between *stalls* and *circle*? *nearer the stage*
2 How much do his two seats cost? *£130*. *① upstairs*
3 Which seats are the most expensive? *circle*
   Which are the cheapest? *stalls*
4 How does he pay? *visa card. credit*

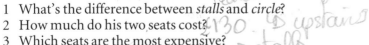

3 UNDERSTANDING INFORMATION

Signs

1 TONIGHT'S PERFORMANCE SOLD OUT

2 LATECOMERS WILL NOT BE ADMITTED UNTIL THE INTERVAL

3 YOU CAN ORDER YOUR INTERVAL DRINKS IN THE BAR BEFORE THE PERFORMANCE

a In pairs, explain what each sign means.

b Quickly read the information about four musicals on in London. Answer the questions with LM (*Les Misérables*), MS (*Miss Saigon*), C (*Cats*) or PO (*Phantom of the Opera*).

Palace Theatre
0171 434 0909
Shaftesbury Ave. London W1.

Les Misérables "Stands out as the greatest musical of this half century" *International Herald Tribune*
Victor Hugo's great novel about the French revolution brought to the stage by the outstanding talent of Boublil and Schönberg, sweeps its audience through an epic tale of love, passion and destruction, set against the backdrop of a nation in the grip of revolutionary turmoil. Indisputably the world's most popular musical, *Les Misérables* has earned itself a unique place in musical history. Evenings 7.30pm, Matinées Thu and Sat at 2.30pm.

Theatre Royal Drury Lane
0171 494 5000
Catherine St. WC2.

Miss Saigon "The musical is already a legend" *Newsweek*
Miss Saigon is the classical musical love story of our time. Set against the terror and chaos of the last days of Vietnam, *Miss Saigon* tells of the love between a young Vietnamese girl and an American soldier. Written by Boublil and Schönberg, its spectacular staging and powerful music have made *Miss Saigon* a worldwide triumph. Evenings 7.45pm, Matinées Wed and Sat at 3.00pm.

New London 0171 405 0072
Drury Lane WC2

Cats
THE MEMORY WILL LIVE FOREVER
London and Broadway's longest-running musical has enchanted audiences ever since it first opened in 1981. An intoxicating blend of fantasy and drama combine with some of the most exciting dance ever seen on stage, and of course the wonderful music of Andrew Lloyd Webber. Evenings 7.45pm, Matinées Tues and Sat at 3.00pm.

Her Majesty's 0171 494 5400
Haymarket, London SW1.

Phantom of the Opera
"Magic, memorable and so spectacular" *Sunday Express*
With some of the most spectacular sets, costumes and special effects ever to have been created for the stage, this haunting musical tells the tragic story of a beautiful opera singer and a young composer, shamed by his physical appearance into living a shadowy existence beneath the majestic Paris Opera House. Evenings 7.45pm, Matinées Wed and Sat at 3.00pm.

1 Which two musicals are set in France?
2 Which two are based on real historical events?
3 Which one is not a love story?
4 Which one can you see on a Thursday afternoon?
5 Which one has spectacular costumes?
6 Which one has been on the longest?
7 Which one starts earliest in the evening?
8 Which one does not use a newspaper quote in its advertisement?

c Imagine you're in London. Choose the show you would most like to go to. Decide when you'd like to see it.

d Talk to other students and find someone who'd like to go to the same show on the same day.

4 SONG 🎵

T6.14 *Memory* (from *Cats*)

5 WRITE BETTER
A note

Write a note to a friend suggesting that you go to one of the four shows together. Include the following information:
● which show you'd like to see.
● what day and time you'd like to go.
● suggest a place to meet.

Use expressions from the box in **1b**.

! Begin a note just with your friend's name, NOT ~~Dear...~~ Finish with your name, NOT ~~Best wishes~~.

1 PRESENTATION

a Match sentences 1–6 with the people in the picture.

d 1 He's speaking in Spanish.
e 2 She looks very elegant.
a 3 They've got enormous backpacks.
f 4 He's wearing a cowboy hat.
b 5 They don't look very happy.
c 6 She's much too young for him.

a They must be travelling round Europe.
b They might be having an argument.
c She can't be his wife.
d He could be South American.
e She can't be English.
f He must be American.

b Match sentences 1–6 with a–f.

c **T7.1** Listen to two tourists speaking and check your answers.

2 GRAMMAR ANALYSIS

Modals of deduction

He	**might/could**	be South American.	(+ adjective)
They	**must**	be travelling round Europe.	(+ verb + *ing*)
She	**can't**	be his wife.	(+ noun)

a Look at the sentences in the box and answer the questions.

1 Which verb means *it's impossible*? can't
2 Which verbs mean *it's possible*? might/could
3 Which verb means *I'm sure it's true*? must

b Look at the grammar rules.

Use *might/could, must,* or *can't*:
● to make guesses or logical deductions about people or things.

   You can also use *may* instead of *could* and *might* when something is possible.
   He may be South American.

! Don't use *can* for deductions. NOT ~~He can be South American.~~

PRACTICE

a Complete with *might/could/must/can't + be*.

1 **A** What nationality do you think that man over there is?
   B Well, he _might be_ Italian or Spanish, but I'm not sure. ✓

2 She plays basketball for the national team so she _must be_ a ✓
   good player.

3 **A** I don't want to go out. I'm tired.
   B You _can't be_ tired! You went to bed at 10.30 and you got up at ✓
   11 o'clock this morning!

4 **A** Did you know that Jill and Greg have broken up?
   B That _can't be_ true. I saw them together yesterday and they looked ✓
   very happy.

5 **A** How old do you think he is?
   B Well, his children are at university so he _~~might be~~_ *must be* at least forty. ·

6 **A** Do you know where Diana is? I've been phoning her all evening.
   B I'm not sure but she _could be_ playing tennis. She sometimes ✓
   plays on Wednesdays. *might / may*

b Look at the picture and answer the questions about the man sitting at the table.
   Use *might/could/must/can't + be*.

> **A** *It might be Brazil or it might be Greece.*
> **B** *Yes. It can't be England. The weather's too good!*

1 What country do you think he is in?   Brazil? (Greece?) England?
2 What nationality is he?   Italian? British? Swedish?
3 Why do you think he's there?   on holiday? working?
4 What do you think his job is?   a model? a journalist? a teacher?
5 What time of year is it?   winter? spring? summer?
6 What's he drinking?   tea? coffee? vodka?

3 LISTEN BETTER

a T7.2 Listen to the man talking to the waiter.
   Did you guess correctly in **PRACTICE b**?

b Listen again for more detail. Use the information
   you hear to fill in the form.

TOURIST OFFICE
Visitors' Survey

City visited	1	
Month	2	August
First visit	3 Yes ☐ No ☒	
Purpose of visit	4	travel article (journalist)
Nationality	5	british
Marital Status	6	married
Occupation	7	(drinking a coffee) / journalist
Employer	8	x times
	Sunday	

4 READ BETTER

a Read the three texts. In pairs, discuss where you think the people might be. Answer the other competition questions.

Where am I?

Win a week for two in Hawaii with our travel competition.
All you have to do is read the description of three popular tourist
destinations and answer the questions about each place.

A

I'm sitting on a park bench near a river, looking at a modern building which was built in the sixties, and which is one of the
5   most famous theatres in this country. Although this is only a small town, it's crowded with tourists who come here all year round, especially to visit a small
10 sixteenth-century house where one of the best-known writers in the world was born. Some people feel that the town has been ruined by all the souvenir shops and
15 cafés. On the other hand, many people who live here depend on the tourist trade, and without it there wouldn't be much work. Personally, I still find it attractive
20 and full of charm. If you want to avoid the rather expensive restaurants, you can always have a drink and something to eat at a pub, some of which are over a
25 hundred years old.

1   What country am I in?
2   Where am I?
3   What's the first name of the famous writer?

B

30 **It's** February, but I am sitting on a beautiful beach watching four young people playing beach volleyball. Behind me is one of the biggest cities in the country, though it is not the
35 capital. New hotels are being built all around me, and in general the city is much cleaner and safer than it used to be. However, the noise in the city centre is deafening – there are six
40 million inhabitants. I can speak a little Spanish so I can communicate a bit with the local people, as their language is similar. Today the only topic of conversation on the beach is
45 the victory of the local football team at the huge stadium last night. When I get tired of the beach, I'm going to take a train up the nearby mountain and see the enormous statue close
50 up, whose presence dominates the city. Tonight I'm going to explore the nightlife and try the local speciality *cachaça* which, according to the guidebook, is a kind of liqueur made
55 from sugar cane.

1   What country am I in?
2   Where am I?
3   Who is the big statue of?

C

Most people think of this place as one
60 city, but in fact it was originally two, on either side of one of the most romantic rivers in Europe. The name it is called today is simply the two old city names put together. I am sitting high up in the
65 square opposite the wonderful castle, from where you can probably get the best view of the city. I am feeling quite full, having just finished an enormous plate of *gulyás*, the well-known local
70 dish, made of beef and hot red peppers. It's delicious, and very cheap as well. This city is also famous for its bridges which join the two parts. If you want to have a look round the older parts, it's a
75 good idea to get a guidebook so that you don't miss any of the sights. At night the centre is very lively and there's a great atmosphere, especially in July and August, which is when most
80 tourists visit. If you're not in a hurry, you are only a few hours away from Prague or Vienna, which you may also want to see.

1   What country am I in?
85 2   Where am I?
3   What's the name of the river which separates the two parts of the city?

b Read the texts again and underline any words you don't know. In pairs, try to guess their meaning from the context. Check with the teacher or with a dictionary.

5 BUILD YOUR VOCABULARY

Describing a tourist town

a 🖊 Complete **Vocabulary Builder 11A** *Tourism*, *p.139*.

b In your town …

what's the local speciality?
what's the best area to have a look round?
what's the most famous monument?

where is there most atmosphere at night?
what are the typical souvenirs?
where's the best place, nearby, to go for a day trip?

Is your town lively/crowded/romantic/historic/a tourist town?

6 GRAMMAR ANALYSIS
Connectors

Look at how the highlighted words on *p.94* connect two sentences or parts of sentences. Write them in the correct column.

additional information	contrast
_____	*Although/though*
_____	_____
	_____

- *also/as well* have the same meaning, but *as well* (like *too*) usually goes at the end of a phrase or sentence. *Also* usually goes before the main verb, but after the verb *be*.
- *although/though* mean the same. *Although* goes at the beginning or in the middle of a sentence. *Though* usually goes in the middle.
- *on the other hand/however* can *only* be used to introduce an opposite idea. NOT *The town was very crowded.* ~~On the other hand it was very dirty.~~ They are often used at the beginning of a sentence.

PRACTICE

a Complete 1–6 with a suitable ending from a–f.

1 Bangkok is a fascinating city. However, …
2 Although Tokyo is very expensive, …
3 Food is good and cheap. On the other hand, …
4 You can relax on the beach and …
5 The buses are quite cheap, though …
6 The old town has lovely cafés and also …

a do some water sports as well.
b drinks are very expensive.
c it's definitely worth visiting.
d it's extremely polluted.
e some excellent souvenir shops.
f they are usually very crowded.

b Complete these sentences in your own words.

1 Although the weather was awful, _____.
2 You can go sightseeing and _____ as well.
3 The museum was very interesting. However, _____ _____.
4 The city is very lively in the summer. On the other hand, in the winter _____.

BETTER PRONUNCIATION
Silent letters

a In English many words have 'silent' letters which are written but not pronounced, e.g. *wrong* (the 'w' is silent). Cross out one silent letter in each of these words.

1 building   2 know   3 castle   4 climb   5 mountain
6 scenery   7 half   8 hour   9 island   10 walk

b T7.3 Listen and check.

c T7.4 Listen and repeat the sentences. Practise saying them.

1 I know it takes half an hour to climb the mountain.
2 The island has lovely scenery and an old castle.
3 If you walk past this building, you'll see the fountain.

7 MAKING CONVERSATION
For or against?

a In pairs, look at the topics in the box. **A** make a list of the advantages, **B** of the disadvantages.

> a holiday with the family
> a sightseeing holiday
> a holiday in your country
> a holiday abroad
> living in a tourist town

b Discuss the topics together and decide if there are more advantages or disadvantages.

> A *Well, I think one advantage/disadvantage is that …*
> B *Yes, but on the other hand …*
> A *That's true but …*
> B *I agree/disagree because …*

8 WRITE BETTER

a Imagine you are on holiday in a place you have been to before. Write a paragraph similar to the texts on *p.94* describing it but without saying the name. Begin *I am sitting …*. Include information about:

- what you can see from where you're sitting.
- the good things and bad things about the place.
- what you can do there during the day and at night.

Use *although, on the other hand, as well*, etc. to link your ideas.

b Give your paragraph to the teacher or another student to read. See if they can identify the place.

I love New York!

1 BUILD YOUR VOCABULARY
Travelling

a Ask a partner about his/her last holiday. Was there anything he/she wasn't satisfied with?

b ✎ Complete **Vocabulary Builder 11B** *Travelling*, *p.139*.

c What is the difference between…?
1 a cruise and a tour
2 journey, trip, and travel
3 a flight and a voyage
4 a hotel and a youth hostel
5 camping and a campsite

2 READ BETTER

a Do you ever listen to or read American English? What differences have you noticed in vocabulary, spelling, and pronunciation?

b Read the brochure information about New York quickly. Write **T** (true) or **F** (false) next to 1–7.
1 On the first day you will visit the Statue of Liberty.
2 Central Park is outside Manhattan.
3 On the second day there is nothing organized for you.
4 On the third day you will visit a historic part of New York.
5 The Chrysler Building has over seventy floors.
6 You have to walk up to the top of the Empire State Building.
7 From the Tavern-on-the-Green restaurant you can see Central Park.

c Read the text again. Underline words or phrases which mean:

Day 1
1 a wonderful and extraordinary thing _____

Day 2
2 very tall buildings, typical of New York _____
3 objects or buildings that can be seen easily from a distance _____

Day 3
4 *floors of a building* in US English _____
5 *lifts* in US English _____
6 with a view of _____

d In the description of Day 1, underline three examples of American spelling.

SUN TOURS:
Short breaks in New York

DAY 1: TIMES SQUARE AND THE LINCOLN CENTER

Welcome to New York – the Big Apple! Here in New York the wonders of the Big Apple exceed all expectations – the fantastic skyline, marvelous restaurants, theaters, museums, shops and attractions. On your first day you will visit the famous Lincoln and Rockefeller Centers, and drive down Fifth Avenue. You will drive through Times Square, the 'Crossroads of the World'. You will then travel to Central Park, a miracle in the center of Manhattan. Lunch is on your own, but this evening you will have dinner at the famous Jekyll and Hyde club, where the waiters are all dressed as vampires, and at some point in the evening Frankenstein comes to life!

DAY 2: EXPLORING THE CITY

The entire day is yours for sightseeing and shopping. Explore the captivating city of New York with its skyscrapers, bridges, historic landmarks and Broadway theaters.

DAY 3: DOWNTOWN AND SOUTH STREET SEAPORT

Today you will visit Greenwich Village, Wall Street and the Chrysler Building, at 77 stories one of the tallest buildings in New York. You will visit South Street Seaport, a 19th-century seaport with narrow streets, hundreds of shops, an international food pavilion and street entertainment. This afternoon you will visit Chinatown, and finally the Empire State Building Observatory, which towers 1,250 feet above New York City. You will use the high-speed elevators to get to the top, unlike King Kong who climbed up the outside of the building. This evening, you will have dinner at the prestigious Tavern-on-the-Green restaurant overlooking Central Park.

3 PRESENTATION

ARRIVING IN NEW YORK

A Sun Tours representative will meet you at JFK airport and take you to your hotel, which is in the center of the city. When you check in, you will receive further information about this evening's 'Getting-to-know-each-other' party at the Manhattan Restaurant.

YOUR HOTEL

Often called New York's 'friendliest hotel', the *New York Park* hotel has 300 rooms, most of which have a wonderful view of Central Park and the New York skyline. All rooms were completely redecorated in 1997. Ideally located for Broadway theaters and Fifth Avenue, it's a favorite with many guests, who return again and again for the friendly service, excellent rooms and central location. It has one of New York's finest restaurants, the Manhattan, offering superb food. All rooms include private bath, phone, TV and full security services.

a Read the brochure extract above. Tick (✓) the things in the list which the brochure promises.

Promises
1 Somebody will take you to the hotel. ☐
2 There's a party in the evening. ☐
3 Everybody will have a view of Central Park. ☐
4 It's very near Broadway. ☐
5 All the rooms were redecorated recently. ☐
6 The hotel has an excellent restaurant. ☐

b **T7.5** Listen to Stella and Jack, two British tourists, complaining to Sun Tours about their holiday. Which of the six things in **3a** *didn't* they complain about? What do they ask the travel agent for?

c Listen again. Complete the sentences.

Complaints
1 You _____ us that we _____ a wonderful view of Central Park.
2 You _____ that the hotel _____ near Broadway and Fifth Avenue.
3 You _____ that they _____ 'completely redecorated'.
4 The brochure _____ that it _____ one of New York's finest restaurants.

d Compare the promises in **a** and the complaints in **c**. In pairs, answer the questions.

1 How have the verbs changed?
2 When do you use *say*? When do you use *tell*?
3 Do you have to use *that* after *said* or *told*?

4 GRAMMAR ANALYSIS

Reported speech: statements

Direct speech	Reported speech
'The hotel **is** near Broadway.'	You told us (that) the hotel **was** near Broadway.
'**You will have** a wonderful view.'	You said (that) **we would have** a wonderful view.
'The rooms **were** redecorated.'	The brochure said (that) the rooms **had been** redecorated.

a Look at how the words in **bold** have changed in the examples of reported speech above. Complete the chart.

Direct speech	Reported speech
'I don't like New York.'	She said she _____ like New York.
'I'm staying in the Hilton.'	He told me he _____ staying in the Hilton.
'You'll have a wonderful time.'	They said I _____ have a wonderful time.
'I'm going to buy some jeans.'	She said she _____ going to buy some jeans.
'I've been to Chicago twice.'	He told me he _____ been to Chicago twice.
'I saw a Broadway show.'	She said she _____ seen a Broadway show.

b Now complete the rules for the tense changes.

Direct speech	Reported speech
present simple	_past simple_
present continuous	_____
will + infinitive	_____
is/are going to	_____
present perfect	_____
past simple	_____

Use reported speech:
- when you talk about what somebody said or what you read.
  1 *might, could, would, should,* and *ought to* stay the same.
  2 The past simple does not have to change to the past perfect. It can stay the same.
  3 You can use *said,* or *told* + person.
     He said it was a good hotel. or *He told me it was a good hotel.* NOT ~~He said me it was a good hotel.~~
  4 *that* after *said/told me* is optional.
  5 Certain time expressions often change:

direct	→	reported
today	→	that day
tomorrow	→	the next day
next (week)	→	the following (week)
last (week)	→	(the week) before
this	→	that
here	→	there

PRACTICE

a Write the sentences in reported speech.

1 'The plane takes off at 14.30.'
   She said _____.
2 'We won't be able to pay until next week.'
   They said _____.
3 'She left the hotel at ten twenty.'
   The receptionist said _____.
4 'I'm taking my holidays in August.'
   Kate said _____.
5 'I've never seen anything like it.'
   He said _____.
6 'You can't take photos here.'
   The guide told them _____.
7 'The lift doesn't go to the top floor.'
   The receptionist said _____.
8 'You should get to the airport early.'
   The travel agent told them _____.

b Complete with the correct form of *say* or *tell.*

1 'Come here,' she _____ angrily.
2 They _____ us that it was time to leave.
3 Please _____ Mr Hopkins that there's a message for him.
4 Excuse me, but this notice _____ that you can't smoke.
5 Could you _____ me the way to Fifth Avenue, please?
6 Sorry, what did you _____?

5 MAKING CONVERSATION

Go to **Communication** *But you told me…,*
A *p.124,* **B** *p.128.* Roleplay: **A** is a travel agent, **B** is a tourist who has had a bad holiday and wants to complain.

BETTER PRONUNCIATION
American and British pronunciation
There are many differences between American and British pronunciation.

a **T7.6** Listen to a British speaker and an American speaker saying five sentences. Which is the US speaker: a or b?

1 ____ 2 ____ 3 ____ 4 ____ 5 ____

b Listen again. Which words change the most?

6 PRESENTATION

a **T7.7** Listen to an American woman talking to Stella and Jack. Number the questions in the order she asks them.

- ☐ She asked them how long they were staying.
- ☐ She asked them if they liked the food.
- ☐ She asked them if they were British.
- ☐ She asked them if they'd been to New York before.
- ☐ She asked them what they thought of the 'Big Apple'.
- ☐ She asked them where they were from.

b Listen again. Write the questions the woman asked.

1 *'Are you British?'*
2 _____
3 _____
4 _____
5 _____
6 _____

7 GRAMMAR ANALYSIS
Reported speech: questions

Direct question	Reported question
'Are you tired?'	He asked me if/whether I was tired.
'Where do you live?'	He asked me where I lived.
'What's the time?'	He asked me what the time was.

Look at how the questions change from direct speech to reported speech above.
Remember that in reported questions:

- **!** you don't use auxiliary verbs *do/does/did*. NOT ~~He asked me where did I live.~~
- you have to use *if* or *whether* when the direct question begins with a verb.
- the word order is subject + verb.
- tenses change as in reported statements, e.g. present → past.

PRACTICE

a Write questions 1–6 in reported speech. Begin *She asked him…*

1 Do you know New York well?
2 Where's the nearest bank?
3 Can you show me the way?
4 How much is a subway ticket?
5 What time do the banks open?
6 Is it far to Fifth Avenue?

b **T7.8** Listen to six more questions and write them in reported speech.

1 *He asked me…*

c Write six questions to ask your partner. They **must** be questions to which you really don't know the answer.

What…? How long have you…? Can you…?
Did you…? Where do you…? Are you…?

d Interview your partner and make a note of his/her answers.

e Change pairs. Tell your new partner about your previous interview.

A *I asked Juan what his girlfriend looked like and he told me she was very tall and very attractive.*

8 SONG 🎵
T7.9 *Daniel*

1 PRESENTATION

a Read the story. Complete with an infinitive verb from the list.

~~to get~~   to come   to change   to give   to tell   to follow   not to worry

Welcome to Britain!

*Read what happened
to one of our readers, and
be warned!*

It was eight o'clock in the evening. I'd just arrived at Heathrow Airport with my family and we were exhausted after the long flight. We were going to stay in London for a couple of days before travelling to Dublin. Some friends of ours had told us ___*to get*___ a taxi to our hotel, so we went to look for one. The airport was extremely bright and modern, but as soon as we came out, we found ourselves in a dark depressing area of car parks and bus stations. We couldn't see the taxi rank anywhere, so we asked someone ¹_____ us the way, but he didn't speak English. Suddenly a big, friendly-looking man came up to us and said, 'Give me your cases. I'll take them to the taxi rank for you.' I told him ²_____ because our cases weren't heavy, but he just picked up my wife's case and told us ³_____ him. I told him ⁴_____ back but he didn't stop.

When we reached the taxi rank, he put the cases down and asked me ⁵_____ him ten pounds. I couldn't believe it. Ten pounds seemed ridiculous for just walking a hundred yards with one not very heavy case, but I was too tired to argue, so I took out my wallet. However, I only had a fifty-pound note. I said, 'I'm sorry, I haven't got any change.' 'No problem,' he said. 'Wait here and I'll ask one of the taxi drivers ⁶_____ it.' He disappeared round the corner. He never came back, of course.

b Read the story again. Number these sentences in the order in which they were said.

- ☐ 'Excuse me, could you tell us where the taxis are?'
- ☐ 'Follow me!'
- ☐ *1* 'I think you should get a taxi to your hotel.'
- ☐ 'Right, that's £10.'
- ☐ 'Sorry, I don't speak English.'
- ☐ 'Look, I've only got a £50-note.'

2 GRAMMAR ANALYSIS

Reported speech: imperatives, requests

a Look at the three sentences on the right in the box. When you report an imperative or a request, you use *told/asked* + the person + *to* + infinitive.

Direct speech	Reported speech
'Follow me!'	He **told us to follow** him.
'Don't worry.'	I **told him not to worry**.
'Could you tell us the way?'	We **asked someone to tell** us the way.

b *He told me that the hotel was nice.* (reported statement)
He told me to come back. (reported imperative)

Translate the two sentences into your language. Is the grammar the same or different?

To report an imperative, use:
tell (NOT ~~said~~) + person + *to* + infinitive
He told us to wait. NOT ~~He told us that we waited.~~

To report a request, use:
asked + person + *to* + infinitive
I asked him to tell us the way. NOT ~~I asked him that he told us the way.~~

! Remember that the negative infinitive is *not to* (+ verb). '*To be or not to be, that is the question.*'

PRACTICE

Rewrite the following sentences in reported speech.

1 'Don't leave your luggage unattended.'   They told us _____.
2 'Could you open the window, please?'   He asked me _____.
3 'Fasten your seat belts.'   The flight attendant told passengers _____.
4 'Would you mind not smoking?'   He asked us _____.
5 'Take the lift to the second floor.'   The receptionist told us _____.
6 'Don't go there in July or August.'   He told us _____.

3 LISTEN BETTER

a **T7.10** Listen to two people talking about bad travel experiences. The first
time you listen, number each set of pictures in the order of the story.

Story 1

Story 2

b Listen again for more detail. Complete the sentences.

Story 1

1 First he told me not to _____ _____.
2 Then he told me not to _____ a word, and to _____ him my _____ and my _____.
3 Then he told me not to _____ and to _____ to 20.

Story 2

1 I shouted at the receptionist to _____ _____.
2 He told me to _____ my room.
3 I told him to _____ it.

c In pairs, cover the sentences in **b** and use the pictures to retell the two stories. **A** tell story 1, **B** tell story 2.

4 BUILD YOUR VOCABULARY
-ed/-ing adjectives

> We were **exhausted** after the long flight.
> The long flight was **exhausting**.

a Look at the two sentences. What's the difference between *exhausted* and *exhausting*?

b Look at the two columns of adjectives. In pairs, for the -ed adjectives think of a situation in which you *feel*, e.g. *exhausted*. For the -ing adjectives think of something that *is*, e.g. *exhausting*.

frightened	frightening
bored	boring
surprised	surprising
tired	tiring
depressed	depressing
terrified	terrifying
annoyed	annoying
excited	exciting
embarrassed	embarrassing
fascinated	fascinating

I feel frightened when I see a spider.
I think horror films are frightening.

c Add two more pairs of adjectives to the columns.

5 MAKING CONVERSATION
Travel problems

In pairs, ask each other the questions. If the answer is *yes*, ask what happened, what you did and how you felt.

Have you ever …

got lost in a foreign city?
been ill on holiday?
been robbed while you were on holiday?
had a problem with your luggage?
been delayed (at an airport or station)?
left something important at home when you were travelling?

6 PRESENTATION

Match the two parts of eight top travel tips.

Travel wisely travel well

These are some of our experienced travellers' top tips for a trouble-free holiday:

1 Always make a list of what you need to take …

2 Carry identification and a contact phone number …

3 Don't carry too much cash on you …

4 Don't drink tap water …

5 Make sure you know about visa regulations …

6 Take out medical insurance before you leave …

7 Write down the numbers of your credit cards/travellers cheques …

8 Talk to your doctor before you go …

- ☐ in case you need one.
- ☐ in case you get ill while you're on holiday.
- ☐ in case you have an accident.
- ☐ in case it's not safe.
- ☐ in case you need any injections.
- ☐ in case you get robbed.
- ☐ in case you forget something important.
- ☐ in case they're stolen.

7 GRAMMAR ANALYSIS
in case

> 1 Don't carry too much cash on you **in case** you get robbed.
> 2 Take an umbrella **in case** it rains.

Look at sentences 1 and 2. Does **in case** mean *if* or *because there's a possibility*? Check with the grammar rules.

Use *in case*:
- to say what *might* happen.
  Take a map in case you get lost. = Take a map because you might get lost.
  1 Use the present tense after *in case* to talk about the future, NOT ~~in case you will get lost.~~
  2 You can also use the past after *in case* if the main verb is in the past.
  *She **took** her passport in case she **needed** it.*

PRACTICE

a Complete the sentences with *if* or *in case*.

1 I'll take some sandwiches _____ I get hungry.
2 Can you buy me some bread _____ you pass a supermarket?
3 Close the windows before you leave _____ it rains later.
4 You'll need some warm clothes _____ you go in November.
5 Could you give her a message _____ you see her?
6 You ought to take extra batteries _____ you can't buy the ones you need.

b A friend of yours is going on holiday to India. Look at the pictures. For each one, write a sentence to explain why it might be useful to take it with him/her. Begin *Take _____ in case…*

> *Take a phrasebook in case nobody understands you.*

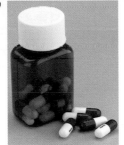

1 phrasebook
2 insect repellent
3 suntan lotion
4 driving licence
5 raincoat
6 comfortable shoes
7 local currency
8 extra bag
9 medicine

BETTER PRONUNCIATION

a **T7.11** Say which word is different. Listen and check.

1 abroad, goal, coast, road, coat
2 clothes, love, wrote, hole, close
3 won't, photo, local, lost, both

b **T7.12** Listen and repeat. Try to make the /əʊ/ sound correctly.

1 He told me to go home.
2 Although it wasn't cold, I took a coat.
3 I don't know if the old road is open.
4 I won't go to the show.
5 We took some photos of the coast from our boat.

8 WRITE BETTER

Some English friends tell you that they are going to spend a week in your town/city in the summer. Unfortunately you won't be there. Write them a letter to give them some advice. Begin the letter like this:

> Your address
>
> date
>
> Dear _____,
>
> Thanks for your letter. I'm really pleased that you are coming to _____ in August. Unfortunately I won't be here then! But here's some advice about what to bring with you and what to see.

Continue the letter by telling them:

Paragraph 2
● what they should bring with them and why.

Paragraph 3
● what they should do/what they must do (sightseeing, beach, etc.).

Paragraph 4
● what they should eat/drink (local speciality, etc.).
● what they should buy (typical souvenirs, etc.).

Use **Vocabulary Builder 11**, *p.139* and the **Writing Bank** *A letter to a friend*, *p.143* to help you.

> *Don't forget to bring… in case…*
> *You must (see)…*
> *I think you should (go to)…*

▶ Go to **Check your progress 7**, *p.120*.

Any complaints?

1 BUILD YOUR VOCABULARY
Complaints

a Look at the pictures and complete problems 1–8 with a word or phrase from the list.

are broken   are missing   broken   button missing
doesn't work   in the sleeve   on the collar   shrunk

1   2   3

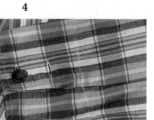 

4   5

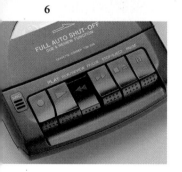 

6   7

8

Problems with clothes

1   There's a hole   _____.
2   There's a stain   _____.
3   The zip's   _____.
4   There's a   _____.
5   This sweater has   _____.

Problems with machines (e.g. a hi-fi system)

6   The rewind button   _____.
7   The headphones   _____.
8   The instructions   _____.

b Cover the sentences. Look at the pictures. Try to remember the problems.

2 COMPLAINING IN A SHOP

a **T7.13** Listen to two conversations in shops. Complete the chart.

	Customer 1	Customer 2
What did they buy?		
When?		
What's their complaint?		
What happens?		

b Listen again and complete the expressions in the box.

> **Complaining in a shop**
> I _____ (*this sweater two weeks ago…*)
> Have you got the _____?
> I'm not _____ with it.
> I'd _____ my money _____.
> I'd like to speak to the _____.

c Go to **Communication** *Any complaints?* **A** *p.124*, **B** *p.128*. **A** is a customer who complains to **B**, a shop assistant. Swap roles.

3 UNDERSTANDING INFORMATION

1   **100%** C O T T O N MACHINE WASH COLD

2   **DRY CLEAN ONLY.** Warm iron.

3   **10% service included in the bill**

4   ★★★ *CHILDREN'S PORTIONS SERVED* ★★★

a Look at the signs. Where might you see this information?

b In pairs, explain what they mean.

4 BUILD YOUR VOCABULARY

Restaurant language

Do the 'Restaurant' quiz.

1 What are the three usual sections on a menu (apart from drinks)?
2 What do you normally find on a restaurant table?
3 Name three jobs related to a restaurant.
4 What do you call the extra money you leave for good service?
5 What do you say when
   a you want a table?
   b you order your food?
   c you want to pay?
6 If the waiter says, *How would you like your steak/ hamburger cooked?* what are the three possible answers?
7 What are the two kinds of mineral water?
8 What's *dressing*, and what could you eat it with?

5 COMPLAINING IN A RESTAURANT

a Have you ever complained in a restaurant? What about? What happened? What kinds of things can you complain about in a restaurant?

b **T7.14** You're going to hear two people complaining in a restaurant. Listen once and answer the questions.

1 What did they order?
2 What did they complain about?

c Listen again. Complete the sentences in the box below.

Complaining in a restaurant

I'm sorry, but I _____ a chicken burger, not a special burger.

Excuse me. My cheeseburger isn't _____
_____.

I _____ for medium. This is _____.

I ordered _____ mineral water. This is sparkling.

Excuse me. There's a _____ in the _____.

BETTER PRONUNCIATION

Intonation, contrastive stress

a **T7.15** Listen and underline the stressed words in the sentences above.

b Which words are stressed extra strongly? Why?

c Listen again and repeat. Copy the stress and intonation.

6 WRITE BETTER

A letter of complaint

Imagine you are one of the people who went to the restaurant in **5**. After the meal you filled in this form, and you expected to receive a reply from the manager of Sunset Boulevard. You haven't had one, so you decide to write him/her a letter.

SUNSET BOULEVARD

Charing Cross Road
London W1
Tel: 0171 5857764

CUSTOMERS' COMMENTS

We would be very grateful if you could complete this form and hand it to one of the restaurant staff. Your comments will help us to improve the quality of food and service.
Any serious complaints will receive a personal reply from the manager.

DATE 1st April   **TIME OF ARRIVAL** 20.15

DISHES ORDERED
A cheeseburger, I chicken burger, I onion soup and I tropical salad.

	EXCELLENT	GOOD	OK	BAD
Food	☐	☐	☐	☑
Atmosphere	☐	☑	☐	☐
Service	☐	☐	☐	☑

NAME _____

ADDRESS _____

_____

_____

Read the form and look at your comments.
Write the letter, including the following information:

Paragraph 1
Explain why you are writing, and give the date you had your meal.
Explain that you filled in the form but haven't had a reply yet.

Paragraph 2
Explain your complaints.

Check with the **Writing Bank**, *p.144* on how to start and finish a formal letter to a person you don't know.

The true story of the Titanic

1 LISTEN BETTER

a Do the quiz in pairs.

What do you know about the *Titanic*?

1 When did the *Titanic* sink?
  a January 1910   b April 1912   c March 1914
2 Where was the ship sailing to?
  a America   b England   c Canada
3 How many people were there on board (passengers and crew)?
  a 2,207   b 4,532   c 1,263
4 How many lifeboats were there?
  a enough for everybody   b enough for most people
  c enough for half the people
5 What was the name of the ship that went to help them?
  a The *Olympic*   b The *Carpathia*   c The *Californian*
6 What happened to Bruce Ismay, the director of the company?
  a He drowned.   b He survived.   c He killed himself.
7 When did the rescue ship arrive?
  a about an hour too late   b four hours too late   c a day too late
8 How many people survived?
  a about 1,500   b about 1,200   c about 700

---

b **T8.1** Listen to a radio programme called *The sinking of the Titanic* and check your answers.

c Listen again for more detail. In pairs, answer the questions.
1 What was the weather like on the night of the tragedy?
2 What were the passengers doing at 11.40 when the ship hit the iceberg?
3 How big was the hole it made?
4 What radio message did they send?
5 What did the orchestra do? Why?
6 Who did the Captain tell to leave the ship first?
7 What time did the ship sink?
8 Did the rescue ship find anybody alive in the water?

2 READ BETTER

a Read the text and match the questions below to paragraphs 1–6.

Did the orchestra really play until the end?
Was Captain Smith to blame?
What happened to Bruce Ismay after the disaster?
Why weren't there enough lifeboats?
*Was there **another** ship which could have helped the Titanic?*
Why didn't the lifeboats go back to rescue survivors?

b Read the text again and underline any words or expressions you don't know. In pairs, try to guess their meaning.

c In pairs, cover the text and answer the questions in **a** from memory.

The truth about the *Titanic*

The sinking of the *Titanic* on its first voyage has fascinated people all over the world for nearly a hundred years. It is a story surrounded by mystery and speculation.
5 Here we answer the questions most often asked about the most famous of ships.

1 _____

The regulations controlling the number of lifeboats that a ship should carry were
10 terribly out of date. The *Titanic* only had to have 16 lifeboats, enough for 962 people, which was ridiculous as the ship could carry 3,511 people. Nobody would have died on April 14th 1912 if the *Titanic* had had enough
15 lifeboats for all the passengers.

Bruce Ismay   *Captain Smith*

2 _____

A small ship called the *Californian* was only
20 kilometres away from the *Titanic*. It had
stopped for the night because of the
icebergs. It was so near that the two ships
could see each other's lights. The radio
operator had just gone to bed so he didn't
hear the *Titanic*'s S.O.S message. Later,
sailors saw the *Titanic*'s eight white rockets
in the sky. They woke up their captain but he
didn't do anything as he didn't think the
rockets were important. If the *Californian*
had known the *Titanic* was sinking, it would
have rescued everybody. The captain of the
Californian was later blamed for not going to
help the *Titanic* and his reputation was
destroyed.

3 _____

Although they had received several
warnings of icebergs from other ships in the
area, the *Titanic* was going at top speed.
The captain of the *Titanic*, like other
captains, was under great commercial
pressure to make the Atlantic crossing as
quickly as possible. Also Bruce Ismay, the
director of the White Star Line which owned
the *Titanic*, was on board and he wanted his
ship to beat the company record for the
fastest crossing. Another criticism of

Captain Smith is that he was not on the
bridge at the time of the collision. Perhaps if
he had been there, his ship would not have
hit the iceberg. Captain Smith and the ship's
designer Thomas Andrews both drowned.

4 _____

In the confusion of the evacuation, many
lifeboats left the *Titanic* half empty. This was
partly because Captain Smith and his crew
found it difficult to persuade people to leave
the 'unsinkable' *Titanic*. Many were terrified
at the idea of being lowered down into the
sea in a tiny lifeboat. When the *Titanic* finally
sank, some of the passengers in the
lifeboats wanted to go back and rescue
some of the people swimming in the
freezing water. If they had gone back, many
more people might have been saved. But
other people in the lifeboats argued that they
had to put their own lives first and that if too
many people in the water tried to get into the
lifeboats, they would overturn and
everybody would drown. Finally, only one of
the sixteen lifeboats went back to pick up
survivors. They only managed to rescue five
people. Everyone else was dead.

5 _____

After the collision, the little group of
musicians started playing in the first-class
lounge to keep the passengers calm, but
later they moved up onto the deck. Some
survivors in the lifeboats said they could still
hear the musicians playing a waltz called
Autumn until just before the ship finally
sank. If they hadn't continued playing until
the end, there would have been much more
panic on the ship. Not one of the orchestra
survived.

6 _____

The public were extremely suspicious about
any of the 58 men who survived the
disaster, especially as about 150 women
and children died (mostly from Second and
Third class). But Bruce Ismay received the
most criticism. When his beautiful ship
sank, Ismay, in one of the lifeboats, turned
his head so as not to see it. Later, numerous
articles were written in newspapers
attacking him for saving his own life. Ismay
had to retire from the company and from
public life. Nobody was ever allowed to
mention the *Titanic* in his presence.

3 BUILD YOUR VOCABULARY

Ships and disasters

a Cover the phonetics. Can you remember the words for these definitions?

1	sailors and officers on a ship	_____ /kruː/
2	go down in water	_____ /sɪŋk/
3	save someone from danger	_____ /ˈreskjuː/
4	die in water	_____ /draʊn/
5	a small boat used in emergencies	_____ /ˈlaɪfbəʊt/
6	person who doesn't die in an accident	_____ /səˈvaɪvə/
7	a journey by sea	_____ /ˈvɔɪdʒ/
8	the floor of a ship	_____ /dek/
9	people who travel on a ship, plane, etc.	_____ /ˈpæsɪndʒəz/
10	two things hitting each other	_____ /kəˈlɪʒən/
11	something telling you about possible danger	_____ /ˈwɔːnɪŋ/
12	leave a ship (because it's sinking)	_____ /əˈbændən/

b Look at the phonetics. How are the words pronounced?

c Cover the words and look at the definitions. Can you remember them?

4 MAKING CONVERSATION

The *Titanic*

a Go to **Communication** *The Spanish couple* and *The French children*, **A** *p.124*, **B** *p.128*.

b In pairs or groups, discuss these questions.

1 Who do you think was most responsible for the disaster – the government, the company which owned the ship, or the captain?

2 Have you seen the film *Titanic*? Did you enjoy it? Did it tell the true story?

5 GRAMMAR ANALYSIS

Third conditional

> 1 If the *Californian* **had known** the *Titanic* was sinking, it **would have rescued** everybody.
> 2 Nobody **would have died** if the *Titanic* **had had** enough lifeboats.

a Look at the sentences above. Answer the questions and complete the rules.

1 Did the *Californian* know the *Titanic* was sinking? Did it rescue anybody?

2 Did the *Titanic* have enough lifeboats? Was everybody saved?

Make the third conditional with:

if + _____
would _____ + _____

! You can't use *would have* after *if*.
If he had seen her… NOT ~~If he would have seen her.~~

● You can use *could/might* instead of *would* (= less sure).
If the *Californian* had known the *Titanic* was sinking, it **could** have rescued everybody.

Use the third conditional:

● to speculate about something that happened in the past and how it could have been different.
Facts There weren't enough lifeboats. Many people died.
Speculation If there had been enough lifeboats, nobody would have died.

b Find and write down three more examples in the text of the third conditional. For each example, say who it refers to and what really happened.

BETTER PRONUNCIATION
Sentence stress and weak forms

a **T8.2** Listen and repeat. Emphasize the stressed syllables, not the weak ones.
How do you pronounce *had* and *have* in these sentences?

1 If the *Titanic* had <u>gone</u> slower, it <u>would</u>n't have <u>hit</u> the iceberg.
2 If the *Californian* had <u>heard</u> the <u>S.O.S.</u>, it would have <u>helped</u> the *Titanic*.
3 They would have <u>rescued</u> <u>everybody</u> if they'd ar<u>rived</u> <u>ear</u>lier.

b **T8.3** Listen and write six phrases.

PRACTICE

a Match 1–6 with a–f.

1 If you hadn't played so badly,   a I would have gone to see him.
2 If my car hadn't broken down,   b we would have had a picnic.
3 If Jane had applied for the job,   c we wouldn't have lost.
4 If you'd told me earlier,   d I wouldn't have been late.
5 If Tom had told me he was ill,   e I would have been able to help.
6 If the weather had been better,   f she would have got it.

b Put the verbs in the correct tense to make third conditional sentences.

1 If I'd known the exam was today, I _____ last night. (not go out)
2 You would have had a great time if you _____ with us. (come)
3 You wouldn't have been late if you _____ earlier. (leave)
4 I would have phoned you if I _____ your number. (have)
5 If it hadn't been so windy, they _____ tennis. (play)
6 She wouldn't have got the job if she _____ the boss's daughter. (not know)
7 If I'd had more time, I _____ something special. (cook)
8 If you hadn't reminded me, I _____. (forget)

6 GAME: TELEPATHY

a In pairs or small groups, complete the sentences
below. Your teacher is going to do the same.
Try to 'telepathize' and write exactly the same
sentence as your teacher.

You get **two** points for exactly the same sentence.
  one point for a different but correct sentence.
  no points for an incorrect sentence.

1 If you'd told me it was your birthday,…
_____
2 If she'd known what he was really like, she…
_____
3 I would have written to you if I…
_____
4 If he hadn't insulted the boss, he…
_____
5 They wouldn't have got lost if they…
_____
6 We would have missed the plane if…
_____

b Read out your sentences. How many were the same?

An incredible coincidence?

In 1898, fourteen years before the *Titanic* sank, a
little known novelist Morgan Robertson wrote a
novel about an imaginary ship. It was the newest,
biggest, most luxurious ship in the world and was
'unsinkable'. It was travelling across the Atlantic to
New York on its first voyage and was carrying some
of the richest people in the world. On a freezing cold
night in April it hit an iceberg and sank. There weren't
enough lifeboats for everyone so most of the
passengers and crew drowned.
The name of the ship?
…The *Titan*.

8 B

Looking back

1 REVISE YOUR GRAMMAR

a In pairs or small groups, look at the 24 sentences. Some are correct and some are not. Tick (✓) the sentences that are correct. Don't look back at previous lessons.

1 How long do you know him? ☐

2 They've been studying English since three years. ☐

3 She looks like her mother, but she's got her father's personality. ☐

4 Both of them has curly hair. ☐

5 Are you doing anything next weekend? ☐

6 I don't think there are enough onions to make the soup. ☐

7 I don't like get up early. ☐

8 She didn't use to drink beer. ☐

9 My parents don't let me to go out during the week. ☐

10 Do you think you will be able finish the exercise? ☐

11 I'm going to visit my grandmother next weekend. ☐

12 I'll tell her the news as soon as she'll arrive. ☐

13 If I didn't have so much work, I'd go to the cinema tonight. ☐

14 You don't have to drink and drive. It's against the law. ☐

15 When she got home, her husband had already made the dinner. ☐

16 I met a girl whose father is a pilot. ☐

17 Have you seen the letter he wrote? ☐

18 A new road is been built between the two towns. ☐

19 Basketball is one of the more popular sports in the world. ☐

20 I might go to the party but I'm not sure. ☐

21 She asked him where the station was. ☐

22 He said me that he didn't know. ☐

23 They asked the waiter that he brought some more coffee. ☐

24 If you'd seen the film, you would have loved it. ☐

b Correct the mistakes.

2 REVISE YOUR VOCABULARY

a WORD GROUPS

Cross out the word which doesn't belong. Explain why.

1 mean jealous tidy bossy moody

2 fresh frozen spicy salt tinned

3 heart lungs knee kidneys liver

4 subject research degree term overtime

5 employee boss manager employer director

6 inherit lend resign waste invest

7 van coach scooter lorry sports car

8 single cast plot script soundtrack

9 track pitch pool racket court

10 cruise fly trip voyage journey

b WORD PAIR RACE

In five minutes, write as many correct pairs of verb + noun phrases as possible.

book crash
do fail win
wear
VERBS earn
take go look like
inherit shoot
put on

into a tree
weight a salary
a holiday sightseeing
a film
a seat-belt **NOUNS** an exam
a photo research
a match a fortune
your father

3 PRONUNCIATION

Which word is different?

1 said, sent, paid, felt

2 food, cook, good, book

3 since, science, resign, private

4 manager, goal, message, job

5 subject, student, study, money

6 court, bald, work, caught

7 earn, journey, research, wear

8 steak, season, seat, meal

9 sociable, pollution, sugar, coach

10 thriller, although, wealthy, maths

11 ages, ago, allow, annoy

12 coast, photo, lose, won't

4 PRACTISE SPEAKING

Talk in pairs. Choose two photos, e.g. 1a and 1b. Describe one photo each, then answer the questions together.

1a

- Describe the photo (the place, the people, what's happening).
- What kind of food do you have at home?
- Do you think your diet is healthy? Why (not)?
- Who does the cooking? What kind of things can you cook?

1b

- Describe the photo (the place, the people, what's happening).
- Do you often eat at fast food restaurants? Why (not)?
- What kind of food do you usually have when you eat out?
- What other places (not restaurants) do you go to with your friends?

2a

- Describe the photo (the place, the people, what's happening).
- What kind of games did you use to play when you were a child?
- Do you look like either of your parents? How?
- Who are you most like in personality?

2b

- Describe the photo (the place, the people, what's happening).
- What kind of school do you/did you go to?
- What clothes do you/did you wear to school?
- Do you think single-sex schools are a good idea?

3a

- Describe the photo (the place, the people, what's happening).
- Do you do any sport or exercise? Why (not)?
- Which sports do you like watching on TV?
- What do you think is the best kind of exercise to keep fit?

3b

- Describe the photo (the place, the person, what's happening).
- How much TV do you watch during the week/at weekends?
- What kind of programmes do you like? Why?
- What do you think of the TV in your country?

4a

- Describe the photo (the place, the people, what's happening).
- Have you ever been on this kind of holiday? When?
- What do you think are the advantages/disadvantages of this kind of holiday?
- Where would you most like to travel to in the world? Why?

4b

- Describe the photo (the place, the people, what's happening).
- What was the last city you visited?
- Which do you think is the most beautiful city in your country? Why?
- What do you like to do when you're on holiday?

GRAMMAR

1 Past simple and present perfect

Correct the sentences. *I have lived*

1 I live in this street since I ~~was~~ a child. *have been*
2 We ~~have~~ sold our flat last month. *have*
3 How long ~~do~~ you know Andy? *have*
4 We're ~~waiting~~ for the bus for nearly half an hour. *have waited*
5 He's been breaking his leg. *He broke*
6 When has the plane arrived?
"arrived the plane? *did the plane arrive?*

/6

2 Time expressions

Complete with the correct word.

for   since   yet   already   just

1 I wrote to him three weeks ago but he hasn't answered my letter _*yet*_.
2 A How long have you been sharing a flat?
  B _*For*_ six months.
3 A Do you want a cigarette?
  B No thanks, I've ~~just~~ had one.
4 He's had his car _*since*_ last April.
5 A *Indiana Jones* is on TV tonight.
  B Oh no! I've _*already*_ seen it about five times.

/5

3 Reflexive pronouns (*myself*, etc.), *each other*

Complete with the correct word(s).

1 We really enjoyed ~~ourselves~~ at the party.
2 David cut _*himself*_.
3 They see ~~themselves~~ *each other* at least once a week.
4 Nobody helped me. I did it all by _*myself*_.
5 We can write to _*each other*_ when you're away.

/5

4 both, either, neither

Complete with the correct word.

1 _____ my brother nor I like sport.
2 A Would you like tea or coffee?
  B _____. I don't mind.
3 My parents are _____ very tall.
4 A Are you coming to the party tonight?
  B No, _____ of us can come. We _____ have to work.

/5

5 Question forms

Match the questions and answers.

d 1 What does she look like?   a Fine.
c 2 What does she like doing?   b Friendly, but a bit shy.
a 3 How is she?   c Reading and skiing.
b 4 What's she like?   d She's tall and fair.

/4

VOCABULARY

6 Verb phrases

Complete with a verb.

get   keep   share   have   do

1 _*Do*_ the housework   4 _*keep*_ in touch
2 _*get*_ to know somebody   5 _*share*_ a flat
3 _*have*_ an argument

/5

7 Irregular verbs

Complete the chart.

INFINITIVE	PAST SIMPLE	PAST PARTICIPLE
to break	broke	*broken*
to catch	*caught*	caught
fall	*fell*	*fallen*
to give	gave	*given*
to go	*went*	gone
to hurt	hurt	*hurt*
to keep	*kept*	kept
know	*knew*	*known*
to steal	stole	*stolen*
write	*wrote*	*written*

/10

8 Vocabulary groups

a the family

Write the female forms.

1 uncle _*aunt*_   4 husband _*wife*_
2 son _*daughter*_   5 brother-in-law _*sister-in-law*_
3 nephew _*niece*_

b descriptions

Which one is different?

1 blond, curly, straight, (medium height)
2 fat, overweight, ~~slim~~, well-built
3 beard, fringe, ~~bald~~, moustache
4 ~~mean~~, selfish, jealous, (affectionate)
5 (lazy), sociable, ~~sensible~~, self-confident

/5

9 Phrasal verbs

Write the correct definition next to each phrasal verb.

discover   wash the plates, etc.   end a relationship
return something   have a (good) relationship with

1 I've **broken up** with my girlfriend. *end a relationship*
2 Could you **find out** what's happened? *discover*
3 I **get on well with** my sister. *have a good +*
4 **Give** me **back** my book! *return something*
5 I hate **washing up**. *wash the plates*

/5

TOTAL MARKS **/50**

GRAMMAR

1 Gerund or infinitive?

Put the verbs into the correct form.

1 John and Sue are planning _to get married_ soon. (get married)
2 Carol left without _saying_ goodbye. (say)
3 _Travelling_ by plane is quite expensive. (travel)
4 I'm trying _to find_ a new flatmate. (find)
5 It's difficult _to sleep_ when you're worried. (sleep)
6 I went to the supermarket _to get_ some vegetables. (get)
7 She doesn't mind _cooking_ but she hates _shopping_. (cook, shop)
8 Mark's good at _drawing_. He'd like _to be_ an architect. (draw, be)

/10

2 Present simple or continuous?

Put the verbs into the correct form.

1 A Where ~~do~~ you usually _go_ for your holidays? (go)
  B To the mountains. We _have_ a house there. (have)
2 A I _'m going_ to the shops. _Do_ you _need_ anything? (go, need)
3 A What time _does_ the film _start_? (start)
  B At 7.30. _Do_ you _want_ to come? (want)
4 A _Are_ you _doing_ anything this weekend? (do)
  B Yes, I _'m going_ to the cinema with a friend. (go)
5 A What _does_ your sister _do_? (do)
  B She's an architect. She _works_ for a French company. (work)

/10

3 Adverbs and expressions of frequency

Reorder the words to make correct sentences.

1 always at have home I lunch. _I always have lunch at home._
2 a go holiday on once we year. _We go on holiday once a year._
3 do each how other often see you? _How often do u see each other._
4 ever hardly I take vitamins. _I ever hardly take vitamins._
5 is ill never she. _She is never ill._

/5

4 Quantifiers (*much, many, a few,* etc.)

Choose the correct word(s). _few_

1 We've only got _a little_ potatoes. a little/~~a few~~
2 I don't like curry. It's _too_ spicy. too/~~too much~~
3 Do you eat _many_ eggs? ~~much~~/many
4 We haven't got _enough food_ enough food/~~food enough~~
5 I drink _a lot of_ fruit juice. ~~a lot~~/a lot of

/5

VOCABULARY

5 Body, health, and diet

Which one is different? Why?

1 (blood) heart, liver, kidneys → plural
2 flu, hurt, toothache, a sore throat not at ill
3 fattening, unhealthy, wholemeal, junk good meal
4 protein, fat, carbohydrate, (diet) not sthg for a diet
5 cod, salmon, lentils, mussels not a fish

/5

6 What's the word?

Write the words for the definitions.

1 open your mouth when you're tired y_awn_
2 make a noise when you sleep s_nore_
3 where you put your head when you sleep p_illow_
4 what you use to wake up in the morning a_larm_ c_lock_
5 a bad dream n_ightmare_
6 what you use to move your arms and legs m_uscles_
7 keep yourself in good physical condition k_eep_ f_it_
8 another way to say *fat* o_verweight_
9 adjective for hot food, e.g. curry s_picy_
10 adjective for below 0°C f_rozen_

/10 (adj)

7 Phrasal verbs

Complete with a preposition.

down   on   off   ~~up~~ (×2)

1 I **woke** _up_ in the middle of the night. (stop sleeping)
2 He's **put** _on_ weight recently. He's quite fat. (get fatter)
3 What time do you **get** _up_ in the morning? (leave your bed)
4 I've **put** _off_ my birthday party until next week. (postpone)
5 Fantastic! The price of petrol is **going** _down_ next month. (become lower)

/5

TOTAL MARKS /50

a little → uncountable
a few → countable

GRAMMAR

were used to (handwritten annotation)

1 used to

Complete with *used to* (+, –, or ?) and one of the verbs.

argue be do like sleep take talk to get on

1 Before TV was invented, people _were_ *used to talk to* each other more.
2 When I was a child, my parents _used to take_ me on holiday every summer.
3 _Did_ they _used to argue_ so much before they got married?
4 I _used to sleep_ well but now I often suffer from insomnia.
5 I _didn't used to like_ opera but now I love it.
6 He _wasn't do_ any sport, but now he goes to the gym once a week.
7 She _was used to be_ very overweight but now she's slim.
8 _Would_ you _used to get on_ with your brother when you were a child?

/8

2 make, let, be allowed to, any more

Complete the second sentence so that it means the same as the first.

1 I used to smoke.
   I don't _smoke anymore_.
2 I'm not allowed to go out in the week.
   My parents don't let _me go out_.
3 I have to do homework every night.
   They make _me do my homework_.
4 They don't let me go out on Saturday night.
   I'm not allowed _to go out_.
5 We used to see each other.
   We don't _see any more_.

/5

3 Definite article: the or no article

Complete with *the* or – (= no article).

1 In general _____ girls do better at _____ school than _____ boys.
2 We went to _the_ cinema in _the_ city centre.
3 I'm going to _the_ university _____ next year.
4 I love playing _the_ guitar, and _____ rock music.
5 _–_ education is very important.

/10

4 can / could / be able to

Complete with the correct form.

1 I _can't_ swim. I'm frightened of the water.
2 If you buy a car, you _'ll be able to_ drive to work next year.
3 I'd like _to be able to_ speak a foreign language perfectly.
4 I _couldn't_ talk until I was three years old.
5 I've been looking for a flat for ages but I haven't _be able to_ find what I want.
6 I used to _be able to_ play chess very well but now I can't.
7 I love _being able to_ stay in bed on Sunday mornings.

/7

VOCABULARY

5 Extreme adjectives (furious, etc.)

Write one word for each definition.

1 very small   t_iny_
2 very big   e_normous_
3 very interested f_ascinating_
4 very cold   f_reezing_ _freezing_
5 very surprised   a_mazed_

/5

6 Vocabulary groups: education

Write the words for the definitions.

1 a school for children under four years old   n_ursery_ s_chool_
2 the school year is divided into three …   t_erms_
3 a university qualification   d_egree_
4 a government school. You don't pay.   s_tate_ s_chool_
5 for example *geography, history, maths*   s_ubjects_
6 what scientists do to discover new things   r_esearch_
7 the opposite of *pass* (an exam)   _fail_
8 the most important teacher in a school   h_ead teacher_
9 a school for boys and girls   m_ixed school_
10 the most important teachers at university   p_rofessor_

/10

7 Phrasal verbs

Complete with a phrasal verb.

give up   lie down   look up   look for   set off

1 Could you _look up_ this word for me?   (find in a dictionary)
2 We're going to _set off_ at 8 a.m.   (start a journey)
3 I think you should _give up_ smoking.   (stop)
4 Please help me to _look for_ my keys.   (try to find)
5 Why don't you go to your room and _lie down_?   (put yourself in a horizontal position)

/5

TOTAL MARKS **/50**

GRAMMAR

1 Future tense

Complete with the correct form of the future.

I may see I might go I'll go I'll see I'm going to go
I'm seeing Shall I go

1 _I might go_ to France this summer but I'm not sure.
2 _I'm seeing_ some friends tonight. We're going out for dinner.
3 A Have you got any plans for your holiday?
   B Yes, _I'm going to go_ to the South of France.
4 A I'm really thirsty.
   B _Shall I go_ and make some tea?
5 If I have time, _I'll go_ to the bank.
6 _I'll see_ you tomorrow. Bye!
7 _I may see_ Susana tonight. I'm not sure.

/7

2 if, unless, as soon as, etc.

Match the two halves of the sentences.

1 If you don't like spicy food,
2 As soon as we get home,
3 I'll do it
4 Will you buy a car
5 If they don't pay us more,
6 I won't start
7 We won't catch the train
8 What will you do
9 You'll get sacked
10 Unless you help me,

a I won't be able to do it.
b we'll go on strike.
c unless we hurry up.
d when you retire?
e if you pass your test?
f if you're late again.
g we'll have dinner.
h until everybody stops talking.
i as soon as I can.
j you won't like this curry.

/10

3 First and second conditionals

Complete with the correct conditional form.

1 If he wasn't so mean, he _would pay_ us a better salary. (pay)
2 She won't be able to buy it unless you _lend_ her some money. (lend)
3 If you _spoke_ to your parents, I'm sure they'd understand. (speak)
4 If he _found_ a better job, he'd be happier. (find)
5 Don't buy it if you _don't like_ it. (not like)
6 What _will_ she _do_ if she finds out? (do)
7 If we don't book early, we _won't be able to_ get tickets. (not be able to)
8 If I inherited a fortune, I _wouldn't work_. (not work)

/8

VOCABULARY

4 Verb phrases

Complete with a verb.

earn inherit owe retire sign win work

1 _work_ part time
2 _inherit_ a fortune (from your grandfather)
3 _sign_ a contract
4 _owe_ someone money
5 _earn_ a salary
6 _win_ money on the football pools
7 _retire_ because you're 65

/7

5 Prepositions

Complete with a preposition.

1 John has applied _for_ the director's job.
2 Who paid _for_ the drinks?
3 State-school teachers are going to go _on_ strike next week.
4 She works _as_ a secretary.
5 They work _at_ General Motors. /for
6 He spends a lot of money _on_ holidays abroad.
7 Don't worry _about_ the money you lent me.
8 I had to borrow a lot of money _from_ the bank.

/8

6 Definitions

Write the word for the definitions.

1 speak very quietly — w_hisper_
2 lose your job — be _sacked_
3 speak very loudly — sh_outed_
4 don't have enough money to pay for something — can't a_fford_
5 a piece of paper money — n_otes_

/5

7 Phrasal verbs

Complete with the right verb in the correct tense.

go on look after hold on give away pay back

1 I always _give away_ my old clothes. (give and not want back)
2 I'll _pay_ you _back_ tomorrow. (return money you owe)
3 The meeting _went on_ until 8.00 last night. (continue)
4 Au pairs usually _look after_ children. (be responsible for)
5 _Hold on_ a moment! (wait)

/5

TOTAL MARKS /50

GRAMMAR

1 must, have to, should

Rewrite the sentences using the correct form.

1 It's not necessary to leave a tip in a restaurant.
   You _haven't to leave_ .
2 It's not a good idea for you to eat so much junk food.
   You _shouldn't eat_ .
3 It's important that you remember to check the oil and water!
   You _must remember to_ .
4 You aren't allowed to take photos in the museum.
   You _mustn't take_ .
5 I advise you to stop for coffee on the motorway.
   You _should stop for_ .
6 Driving on the left is compulsory in Britain.
   You _have to drive on the_ .

/6

2 Past perfect or past simple?

Put the verbs into the correct form.

1 When we _opened_ the door, we _saw_ that somebody _has stolen_ our TV. (open, see, steal)
2 The police _arrived_ after the thieves _had gone_ . (arrive, go)
3 I _don't want_ to go to the show because I _saw_ it before. (not want, see)
4 Just after she _closed_ the front door she _realized_ that she _has left_ the keys inside. (close, realize, leave)
5 We _got_ to the cinema late. The film _had started_ . (get, start)

/12

3 Relative clauses

Complete with who, which, where, whose or – (= not necessary).

1 My mother, _who_ is eighty, is still very fit.
2 Is he the man _whose_ burglar alarm is always ringing?
3 Is that the shop _∅_ you bought that dress?
4 The girl _who_ was sitting opposite you was the manager's daughter.
5 That's the restaurant _which_ I told you about.
6 The car, _which_ has automatic gears, only costs £5,000.
7 He's going to marry a girl _who_ works at his office.
8 What's the name of the boy _∅_ you met on holiday?

/8

VOCABULARY

4 Vehicles and driving

Put the words into the correct columns.

boot brake coach tram crash gear stick handbrake
overtake reverse scooter seat-belt steering wheel
tyres van wheels windscreen

vehicles	inside the car	outside/ body of car	verbs
coach	brake	crash	overtake
tram	gear stick	tyres	reverse
scooter	handbrake	wheels	brake
van	seat-belt	windscreen	boot
	steering wheel		

/8

5 Compound nouns

Write the words for the definitions.

1 a place to park cars   c_ar_ p_ark_
2 a lot of cars which can't move   tr_affic_ j_am_
3 a fast car   s_port_ c_ar_
4 maximum speed on a road   s_peed_ l_imit_
5 time of day when there's a lot of traffic   r_ush_ h_our_
6 what you get for parking badly   p____ t____
7 lights which control the traffic   tr_affic_ l_ights_
8 place where you can cycle   c_ycle_ l_ine_

/8

6 Phrasal verbs

Complete with the correct preposition.

down around off ~~on~~ (×2) ~~out~~ over up

1 When the film is _over_ , we'll have dinner. (finish)
2 The best way to get _around_ in London is by tube. (travel)
3 His car's very old. It often breaks _~~up~~ down_ (stop working)
4 I wouldn't like to run _out_ of petrol on the motorway. (be without)
5 She put _~~up~~_ a coat and went out. (get dressed in)
6 To drive a car, first you need to switch _on_ the engine. (start)
7 Please switch _off_ the lights before you go out. (disconnect)
8 Can you fill _on_ the car with petrol? (fill completely)

/8

TOTAL MARKS /50

GRAMMAR

1 The passive

Rewrite the sentences.

1 Hitchcock directed *Psycho*.
Psycho _was directed by Hitchcock_.

2 In Spain they dub most foreign films.
In Spain most foreign films _are dubbed_.

3 They will shoot the film in three months.
The film _will be shot in 3 months_.

4 They are making the film in Budapest.
The film _is made in Budapest_.

5 They have already chosen the cast.
The cast _is already chosen_.

6 Andrew Lloyd Webber wrote the music for *Evita*.
The music for *Evita* _was written by ALW_

/6

2 Comparatives and superlatives

Right (✓) or wrong (✗)? Correct the wrong sentences.

1 Skiing isn't as dangerous ~~than~~ as surfing. ✗
2 He's the faster runner in the world at the moment. ✓
3 They played worst yesterday than last week. ✓
4 I think cycling is the ~~more~~ most boring sport that exists. ✗
5 Swimming is better ~~exercise~~ more than jogging. ✗
6 The new sports centre is moderner than the old one. ✗
7 My tracksuit is the same as yours. ✓

/7

3 Narrative tenses

Put the verbs into the past simple, past continuous, or past perfect.

The first record I 1 *bought* was | buy
Satisfaction by The Rolling Stones.
I was 12 years old, and until then my
father 2 _had never let_ me buy any pop records. | never let
But then one day in an act of rebellion
my sister and I 3 _went_ and 4 _bought_ it. | go, buy
When we got home, we immediately
5 _put_ it on the record player, but | put
while we 6 _were listening_ to it my father | listen
suddenly 7 _came_ in and 8 _shouted_ 'Where | come, shout
9 _did_ you _get_ that from?' We | get
10 _heard_ (hadn't) him come into the room, | not hear
because we 11 _were singing_ at the top of our | sing
voices. He 12 _took_ the record off the | take
record player, and 13 _broke_ it in two. | break
We were furious.

/12

VOCABULARY

4 Word groups: cinema, music, sport

a Write the missing words.

EXAMPLE
tennis / court | football / _pitch_

1 film / actors | match / _players_
2 sport / crowd | cinema /
3 football / nil | tennis / _net_ 0
4 3–1 / win | 2–2 / _nil_
5 basketball / play | karate / _fight_
6 song / lyrics | film / _dialogue_ _script_

b Write the missing words.

1 h_orror_ — a kind of film which makes you feel frightened
2 p_____ — the story of a film
3 _famous_ — people who like a singer or group
4 n_et_ — the thing which separates the two halves of a tennis court
5 m_edal_ — the prize you win at the Olympics
6 t_____ — the circuit where athletes run
7 _referee_ — the person who controls a (football) match

/13

5 Verb phrases

Complete with a verb from the list.

beat   go   play   record   win   shoot   star

1 _record_ a soundtrack
2 _play_ a part in a film
3 _shoot_ a film
4 _star_ in a film
5 _go_ cycling
6 _win_ a match
7 _beat_ your opponent

/7

6 Phrasal verbs

Complete with the right verb in the correct tense.

fall over   be on   throw away   run over   hurry up

1 _Hurry up_! We'll be late for the match. (be quick)
2 I'm going to _throw away_ this old tennis racket. (put in the rubbish)
3 He was _running over_ by a car and taken to hospital. (hit by a vehicle)
4 What _'s on_ at the ABC cinema? (be showing – TV, cinema)
5 The runner _fell over_ in the middle of the race. (fall to the ground)

/5

TOTAL MARKS **/50**

GRAMMAR

1 can't / must / might be

Complete with the correct form.

1 You've been sightseeing all day? You *might be* exhausted.
2 I'm not sure what her nationality is. She *might be* Portuguese or Brazilian.
3 She ~~must't~~ *can't be* very ill. I saw her on the beach this morning.
4 They've got three houses – they *must be* millionaires!
5 I don't know where Jack is but he *might be* playing golf. He sometimes plays on Friday afternoons.

/10

2 Reported statements, commands, and questions

Rewrite the sentences.

1 'It's a three-star hotel.'
She said (that) *it was a 3-star hotel*.
2 'What's the time?'
The tourist asked us *what time it was*.
3 'Open your case, please!'
The customs officer asked me *to open my case*.
4 'I've just come back from Rome.'
She told me (that) *she had just come back from Rome*.
5 'Don't move!'
The man told us *to not move*.
6 'Do you want a double room?'
She asked us *if we wanted a double room*.
7 'I'll do it immediately'.
The receptionist said he *will be do it immediately*.
8 'Where have you been?'
He asked me *where I had been*.
9 'Please help me.'
She asked me *to help her*.
10 'Do you smoke?'
He asked me *if I smoke*.

/10

3 Connectors

bien que

Complete with *although, as well, in case, on the other hand, however*.

1 Take the map *in case* you get lost.
2 You can sunbathe and go swimming *as well*.
3 *Although* it's a tourist town, it isn't too crowded.
4 A cruise would be very relaxing. ~~However~~ *on the other hand*, it's expensive.
5 The hotel was quite old. *However*, our room was very nice.

/5

VOCABULARY

4 Tourism and travelling

Which one is different?

1 castle, cathedral, ~~statue,~~ museum
2 ~~romantic,~~ crowded, lively, scenery
3 trip, journey, flight, ~~travel~~
4 ~~a port,~~ a cruise, a hotel, a voyage
5 guidebook, guide, brochure, ~~magazine~~

/5

5 Verb phrases

Complete with a verb.

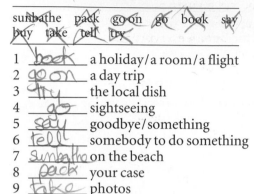

sunbathe ~~pack~~ go on ~~go~~ book say
buy take tell ~~try~~

1 *book* a holiday / a room / a flight
2 *go on* a day trip
3 *try* the local dish
4 *go* sightseeing
5 *say* goodbye / something
6 *tell* somebody to do something
7 *sunbathe* on the beach
8 *pack* your case
9 *take* photos
10 *buy* souvenirs

/10

6 -ed or -ing adjectives

Cross out the wrong word.

1 I'm bored / ~~boring~~. I haven't got anything to do.
2 My job is very ~~tired~~ / tiring.
3 Our trip to New York was really ~~excited~~ / exciting.
4 The film lasted four hours. It was very ~~bored~~ / boring.
5 I crashed into my boss's car. I was very embarrassed / ~~embarrassing~~.

/5

7 Phrasal verbs

Complete with a phrasal verb.

go away ~~go out~~ pick up take off ~~take out~~

1 I don't want to *go out* tonight. I think I'll stay in. (leave the house)
2 The plane won't *take off* before 10.00. (go into the air)
3 Are you going to *go away* this weekend? (leave your town / city)
4 I need to *take out* some money from the bank. (take from somewhere)
5 Please *pick up* the paper and throw it away. (lift something from the ground)

/5

TOTAL MARKS /50

STUDENT A

Introduction *All about you* Ⓐ

Read your instructions and write the answers in the correct place on *p.7*.

- In the rectangle at the top on the left, write your first name and surname.
- Next to numbers 1 and 2, write two things you love doing in your free time, e.g. *reading, swimming*.
- In the square, write the number of people who live in your house.
- In the triangle, write the number of the month when you were born, e.g. June = 6.
- Next to number 3, write the name of the most beautiful city you have ever visited.
- Next to number 4, write the name of a film you really liked or really hated.
- In the circle, write the name of a person you admire.
- In the oval, write the names of two sports which you think are really boring to watch.
- Next to number 5, write the name of your favourite subject at school.
- Next to number 6, write the name of a group or singer that you like very much.
- In the rectangle at the bottom on the right, write the name of your ideal job or occupation.

1 A *Truth or lie?* Ⓐ

a Ask **B** the questions below. **B** *must* answer *Yes, I have.* Decide if **B**'s telling the truth by asking more questions. When you have decided, write **T** (true) or **F** (false). Don't show **B** what you've written.

Have you ever…
- (do) a very dangerous sport?
- (buy) some very expensive clothes which you've never worn?
- (see) a famous singer or group live?
- (write) graffiti on a wall?
- (make) friends with someone on the Internet?
- (leave) a bar or restaurant without paying?
- (speak) to a very well-known person?

b **B** will ask *you* some questions. You *must* answer *Yes, I have.* If you have really done it, tell the truth. If you *haven't* really done it, *invent* the details.

c When you've both finished, compare what you've written. Who was the best 'liar'?

1 International English *Introductions* Ⓐ

You're going to study in Britain. You have just arrived at your host family's house. **B** is the father/mother of the family. Introduce yourself to **B**.
Say *hello* to the people he/she introduces you to. Answer his/her questions.
You begin *Hello. I'm …*
Swap roles.

2 A *Usually or now?* Ⓐ

a Ask **B** these questions. When he/she answers, ask for more information.

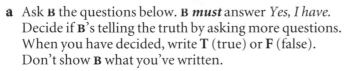

How often do you…?
argue with your family   do exams   eat out in a restaurant
go away at the weekend   miss classes
play computer games
What time do you…?
get up every day   go to bed at weekends
When do you usually…?
have a snack   feel stressed

Are you…?
learning anything (apart from English) at the moment
teaching somebody to do something at the moment
meeting anybody tonight
going anywhere on Saturday night

b Answer **B**'s questions.

2 C *Gerunds and infinitives* Ⓐ

a Ask **B** to tell you the following things. Ask for more information.

Tell me about…
- something you**'d like to do** in the summer.
- something you **need to do** this week.
- something you are **afraid of doing**.
- something you **enjoy doing** on Saturdays.
- something you **hate watching** on TV.
- something you **forgot to do** this week.
- something you're **hoping to do** in the future.

b Respond to what **B** says. Try to use a gerund or infinitive in your answer.

2 `International English` *I know you, don't I?* **Ⓐ**

You're at a language school and you meet **B** in the coffee bar. You met in class for the first time yesterday.

You *think* (but you aren't completely sure)…

- his name's Paul/her name's Paula.
- he/she's Swiss.
- he/she's from Zurich.
- he/she speaks German.
- he/she doesn't smoke.
- he/she went to the party last night.
- he/she hasn't been to England before.
- he/she's staying for a month.

Check the information using question tags.

Your name's Paul(a), isn't it?
You're Swiss,…?

3 **B** *Test your memory* **Ⓐ**

a Ask **B** these questions, and see if he/she can remember the answers.

1 What time does Jie Sun get up?
   (*At 6.30 a.m.*)
2 How much does her school bag weigh?
   (*Six and a half kilos.*)
3 Where's her school?
   (*Just outside Seoul.*)
4 What time does she go to bed?
   (*At midnight.*)
5 Why do South Korean children study so much?
   (*Because there's a lot of competition to get into university, and going to university is the only way to get a good job.*)
6 What's the teaching like in South Korean schools?
   (*Traditional.*)
7 What are the teachers like?
   (*Strict, hardly ever give pupils individual attention.*)
8 What kind of social life does Jie Sun have?
   (*Very little – she hasn't got a boyfriend. Her studies come first.*)

b Now answer **B**'s questions. Who has the best memory?

3 `International English` *Choosing a hotel* **Ⓐ** and **Ⓑ**

A Mr Wright has to spend three days in Edinburgh on business. He's a non-smoker, and he wants to have dinner at the hotel every night, preferably local food, at about 9.00 p.m. as his meetings may go on until late.

B Mr and Mrs Fenton and their children, Mark and Alice, want to spend a week in Edinburgh. They'd like somewhere that's friendly, reasonably cheap and small. They would prefer to all sleep in the same room. ③

C Françoise wants to stay somewhere not too expensive (not more than £100 for a single room). She's a smoker, and wants to be able to have dinner at the hotel, but she doesn't like British food. ④

4 **A** *Clairvoyant* **Ⓐ**

a **B** is going to tell you your fortune. Choose six numbers (between 1 and 10) and **B** will tell you which pictures you've chosen and what they mean.

b Now, look at the 10 pictures below. **B** is going to choose **six** of them. Use the six pictures to tell your partner's fortune.

A *Right, so what's your first picture?*
B *Number 5.*
A *In this picture I can see a plane. You're going to travel. It might be a very long journey, perhaps to…*

4B As soon as possible   Ⓐ

a Ask **B** your questions. Write down **B**'s answers.

When are you going to ...   *As soon as ...*
- do your homework?   _____
- phone Kevin?   _____
- buy my birthday present? _____
- ask your boss for more
  money?   _____
- move to a new flat?   _____
- retire?   _____

b Answer **B**'s questions with *As soon as* + one of the expressions below.

> (meet) the right person
> (see) her
> (think) I'll pass it
> (finish) reading it
> (sell) my old one
> (stop) raining

c Ask **B** your questions again. **B** must answer from memory.

d Answer **B**'s questions from memory.

4C Quiz answers   Ⓐ and Ⓑ

Give yourself the following points. Find your total.

1 a) 3 b) 0 c) 1
2 a) 3 b) 0 c) 2
3 a) 3 b) 0 c) 2
4 a) 3 b) 0 c) 1
5 a) 3 b) 0 c) 1

HOW IMPORTANT IS MONEY TO **YOU**...?

10–15
Money is obviously very important to you – you would do almost anything to get it, and you definitely don't like giving it away. Your ambition in life is to be as wealthy as possible. Your attitude to money is not very healthy – there are other things in life which are more important.

6–9
You are careful with money – this is not necessarily a bad thing, but make sure you're not *too* careful, or some people might think you're mean. You are probably good at saving money, and don't like owing it to other people.

0–5
You know that money is not the most important thing in life. If you have money, you are happy to share it with others. But make sure you are not *too* generous or you could find yourself broke!

4C What would you do if ...?   Ⓐ

a Ask **B** your questions.

What would you do ...
- if you thought that your best friend's partner was falling in love with you?
- if you had an exam the next day and somebody offered to sell you the answers?
- if you found a gold necklace in the street?
- if you came home one night and saw that somebody was in your home?
- if a company offered you a job in Australia?
- if somebody wanted to pay you to talk about your private life on TV?
- if a friend asked you if you liked her new dress, and you thought it was horrible?

b Answer **B**'s questions.

4 International English   Explaining what you want   Ⓐ

a You're a shop assistant at a chemist's. **B** is going to describe four things he/she wants to buy. **Wait until B has finished each description**, and then tell him/her what it is in English. Say *Ah, you mean a ...*

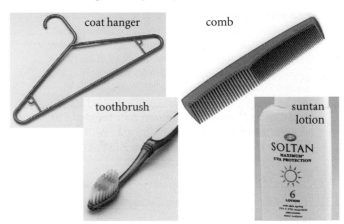

coat hanger

comb

toothbrush

suntan lotion

b Now you are a customer at a department store. You want to buy the following four things, but you don't know how to say them in English. Try to describe them to **B**, who is the shop assistant.

Begin *Excuse me, I'm looking for something, but I don't know what it's called in English. It's ...*

corkscrew

thread

socket

candle

5 C The defining game

a Define the first word in your list to **B**. You mustn't say the word(s). **B** must write it down and show it to you. If it's wrong, try again.

1 the handbrake   2 a motorway   3 a state school
4 junk food   5 a (university) degree   6 lungs
7 an employer   8 selfish   9 a cash-point
10 an au pair

A *Are you ready? Here's my first word. It's part of a car. It's the thing which…*

b Listen to **B**'s definition, and write it down. ***Don't say it***. Show it to **B**.

c Continue until you have both finished your lists. The pair that finish first are the winners.

6 C How the Beatles broke up

a Read another extract from Paul McCartney's biography. Try to remember the story.

> 'Things had already got difficult when we were recording the album *Abbey Road*. We were all getting on very badly with each other, and there were a lot of arguments about money and contracts. John and his wife Yoko Ono had had a car accident and the doctors had told her that she had to stay in bed. So John bought a double bed and put it in the studio, just where we were working, with a microphone in case she wanted to say anything. I and the other members of the Beatles (George Harrison and Ringo Starr) found that really hard to accept – before, it had always been the four of us alone. When we had finished the album, we went to a meeting to sign a new contract and John suddenly said, "I'm leaving the group." And that was the end.'

b Tell **B** what you remember of your story from memory.

Begin *I'm going to tell you about how the Beatles broke up. They were recording the album 'Abbey Road'.*

c Listen to **B**'s story.

7 B But you told me …

You are a travel agent. **B** is going to come to you with some complaints about a holiday he/she booked with you.

This is the holiday he/she went on:

TWO UNFORGETTABLE WEEKS IN THE BAHAMAS

- direct flights + transport from airport to hotel
- luxury hotel with swimming pool, gym and disco
- all rooms have balcony and sea view
- water sports and a trip round the island included in price
- sunshine guaranteed

Listen to **B**'s complaints. Apologize and try to explain why the problems happened. (It wasn't your fault!)

Offer **B** a discount on a future holiday. You ***cannot*** offer to refund the price of the holiday.

You begin the conversation: *Hello. Did you have a good holiday?*

I'm terribly sorry.
It wasn't my fault.
I can explain.

7 International English Any complaints?

You're a customer. You bought an item of clothing (**decide what**) last week and there's a problem (**decide what**).

Go back to the shop. **B** is the shop assistant. You'd like to change it for another identical one. If you can't, you'd like your money back.

8 A The Spanish couple

a Read your story and try to remember it.

> A YOUNG SPANISH COUPLE, Victor and Josefa, aged 24 and 22, had just got married. They were from two of the richest families in Spain. They wanted to spend part of their honeymoon travelling to New York on the *Titanic*. They got on board the ship when it stopped in France.
>
> But Victor's mother didn't want them to travel on the *Titanic* because she had had a dream that it was going to sink. So Victor left one of his servants in Paris with a lot of postcards, already written. He told the servant to send one postcard every day to his mother in Madrid, so that she would think that they were in Paris on holiday.
>
> When the *Titanic* hit the iceberg, Josefa was in bed and her husband was getting ready for bed. Victor went up to see what had happened. When he came back, he told Josefa to get dressed.
>
> They both went up on deck, and Josefa got into a lifeboat. Victor stayed on the ship.
>
> When the *Titanic* sank, Josefa and the other people in the lifeboat heard the terrible cries of the people in the water. Josefa shouted the name of her husband Victor again and again.
>
> Josefa arrived safely in New York on the *Carpathia*. At first Victor's mother refused to believe that her son was dead. 'But he's in Paris!' she said. 'I've just had a postcard from him today.'
>
> Josefa married again six years later and had three children. She died in 1972, aged 83.

b Tell **B** what you remember of your story from memory.

Begin *I'm going to tell you about the Spanish couple…*

c Then, listen to **B**'s story.

STUDENT B

F.C.N.A

Introduction *All about you* Ⓑ

Read your instructions and write the answers in the correct place on *p.7*.

- In the rectangle at the top on the left, write your first name and surname.
- Next to numbers 1 and 2, write two things you *don't* like doing at the weekends, e.g. *studying, ironing*.
- In the square, write the year when you started studying English.
- In the triangle, write the number of the house or flat where you live.
- Next to number 3, write the name of the place where you spent your last holiday.
- Next to number 4, write the name of an animal you have or would like to have as a pet.
- In the circle, write the name of your favourite person in your family.
- In the oval, write the names of two sports which you think are really exciting to watch.
- Next to number 5, write the name of a subject you hate/hated at school.
- Next to number 6, write the name of a kind of music you hate.
- In the rectangle at the bottom on the right, write the number which you think is the ideal age to get married.

1 A *Truth or lie?* Ⓑ

a A will ask *you* some questions. You *must* answer *Yes, I have*. If you have really done it, tell the truth. If you *haven't* really done it, *invent* the details.

b Ask A the questions below. A *must* answer *Yes, I have*.

Decide if A's telling the truth by asking more questions. When you have decided, write **T** (true) or **F** (false). Don't show A what you've written.

Have you ever…
- (see) a film more than three times?
- (be) trapped in a lift?
- (win) a medal or trophy?
- (stay) in a five-star hotel?
- (phone) a radio or TV programme?
- (lose) something important on a computer?
- (sing) karaoke?

c When you've both finished, compare what you've written. Who was the best 'liar'?

1 International English *Introductions* Ⓑ

You're Chris Smith, the father/mother of an English family. A is a foreign student who has come to stay with you for a month.
Say *hello* to A when he/she arrives and introduce yourself. Introduce your wife/husband and the rest of your family. Ask A these questions and have a conversation.

- Did you have a good journey?
- Are you tired?
- Would you like a cup of tea or coffee?
- Where are you from?
- Have you been to Britain before?
- What do you do? (job/studies)
- Have you got any brothers and sisters? What do they do?
- Is there any food that you don't like?

A begins *Hello. I'm…*
Swap roles.

2 A *Usually or now?* Ⓑ

a Answer A's questions.

b Ask A these questions. When he/she answers, ask for more information.

How often do you…?
do housework   do sport or exercise   get angry
go out during the week   go shopping for clothes   take taxis

What time do you…?
get up at weekends   start work or school

When do you usually…?
drink coffee   read for pleasure

Are you…?
reading a good book at the moment
studying for exams at the moment
going anywhere after class today
doing anything special next weekend

2 C *Gerunds and infinitives* Ⓑ

a Ask A to tell you the following things. Ask for more information.

Tell me about…
- something you're **thinking of doing** next weekend.
- something you **need to do** tomorrow.
- something you are **very bad at doing**.
- something you **love doing** when you're on holiday.
- a job you **don't mind doing** in the house.
- something you **must remember to do** this week.
- a foreign language you**'d like to learn** to speak well.

b Respond to what A says. Try to use a gerund or infinitive in your answer.

2 International English | *I know you, don't I?* **B**

You're at a language school and you meet **A** in the coffee bar. You met in class for the first time yesterday.

- Your name's Paul/Paula.
- You're Swiss.
- You're from Geneva.
- You speak French.
- You don't smoke.
- You didn't go to the party last night.
- You haven't been to England before.
- You're staying for a month.

Listen and respond to **A**.
If what he/she says about you is right, say *That's right* or use a short answer (e.g. *Yes, I am.*).
If what **A** says is wrong, give him/her the right information.

3 **B** *Test your memory* **B**

a Answer **A**'s questions.

b Now ask **A** your questions, and see if he/she can remember the answers. Who has the best memory?

1. What's the first thing she does when she gets out of bed?
   (*She goes to the kitchen.*)
2. What time does she leave home?
   (*7 o'clock.*)
3. Where does she study after dinner?
   (*At a private academy.*)
4. How many hours a day do South Korean secondary school pupils study?
   (*Up to 17.*)
5. Do students have to go to extra classes after school?
   (*No, but most parents make them.*)
6. How many pupils are there sometimes in a class?
   (*50.*)
7. Why don't the teachers give pupils individual attention?
   (*Because they haven't got time.*)
8. What happens to many British teenagers when they leave school?
   (*They can't find jobs because they haven't got any qualifications.*)

4 **A** *Clairvoyant* **B**

a Look at the 10 pictures. **A** is going to choose **six** of them. Use the six pictures to tell your partner's fortune.

B *Right, so what's your first picture?*
A *Number 7.*
B *In this picture I can see a man with a beard and glasses. He might be…*

b Now **A** is going to tell you *your* fortune. Choose six numbers (between 1 and 10) and **A** will tell you which pictures you've chosen and what they mean.

4 **B** *As soon as possible* **B**

a Answer **A**'s questions with *As soon as* + one of the expressions below.

```
(be) 65
(can) find his phone number
(find) one I like
(finish) watching this programme
(get) to work tomorrow
(tell) me what you want
```

b Ask **A** your questions. Write down **A**'s answers.

When are you going to…	As soon as…
• give me back the book I lent you?	_____
• take the dog for a walk?	_____
• tell Susan about the party?	_____
• buy a new car?	_____
• take your driving test?	_____
• get married?	_____

c Answer **A**'s questions from memory.

d Ask **A** your questions again. **A** must answer from memory.

4 C *What would you do if…?* Ⓑ

a Ask **A** your questions.

What would you do…
- if a cat or dog came into your house from the street and wanted to stay?
- if you found a friend's personal diary open on the table?
- if your neighbours were having a noisy birthday party and you had to study?
- if your boss asked you to work at his/her house at the weekend?
- if you borrowed your father's new car and you broke one of the lights?
- if you were invited to dinner at a friend's house but you really didn't like the food they'd cooked?
- if a friend gave you an expensive shirt that you thought was awful?

b Answer **A**'s questions.

4 International English *Explaining what you want* Ⓑ

a You are a customer at a chemist's. You want to buy the following four things, but you don't know how to say them in English. Try to describe them to **A**, who is the shop assistant.

Begin *Excuse me, I'm looking for something but I don't know what it's called in English. It's…*

b Now you're a shop assistant at a department store. **A** is going to describe four things he/she wants to buy. *Wait until **A** has finished each description*, and then tell him/her what it is in English. Say *Ah, you mean a…*

black thread   adaptor

candle

corkscrew

5 A *Who arrived first?* Ⓐ and Ⓑ

They all left at 8.36 a.m.

Linda arrived first, at exactly 9.03 a.m. She was a bit hot, but quite relaxed.
Nick arrived on the bike three minutes later. He was feeling fit, but had to have a shower and change his clothes 'because if not, nobody would have wanted to sit next to me.'
Alan, in his Audi A8, arrived in third place at 9.13 a.m.
Dalya came in last at 9.25, stressed and tired. Her tube journey had taken almost double the time of Linda's on the scooter.

So, our conclusions are:
Use a scooter if you want to get around London quickly. Use a bike if you want to keep fit. A car is comfortable but slow and unless the government invests some more money in the London Underground, don't take 'the tube'!

How long did their journeys take?

Linda (scooter)	_24_	minutes
Nick (bike)	_30_	minutes
Alan (car)	_37_	minutes.
Dalya (underground)	_49_	minutes

5 C *The defining game* Ⓑ

a Listen to **A** defining a word to you. When you think you know it, write it down. ***Don't say it***. Show it to **A**, who will tell you if it's correct.

b Define the first word in your list to **A**. You mustn't say the word(s). **A** must write it down and show it to you. If it's wrong, try again.

1 the boot (of a car)	2 a nursery school	3 the pavement
4 biology	5 heart	6 spicy food	7 a teenager	8 jealous
9 a coin	10 a lawyer	

B *Are you ready? Here's my first word. It's part of a car. It's the place where…*

c Continue until you have both finished your lists. The pair that finish first are the winners.

6 C How Paul McCartney wrote 'Yesterday' B

a Read another extract from his biography. Try to remember the story.

> 'I woke up one morning in May 1965 with a lovely tune in my head which I had dreamt. I got out of bed, sat down at the piano and started to try to play it. I didn't have any words at first, I used to sing, 'Scrambled eggs*, oh my baby how I love your legs'. A few weeks later I was on holiday in Portugal, and we were driving somewhere. It was a long, boring car journey and I started to write the lyrics: 'Yesterday, all my troubles seemed so far away...'. When I'd finished, I played it to the other Beatles, and they said, "Lovely, nice song", but they told me to record it myself, so in fact I was the only Beatle who played on that song. But it became one of our biggest hits.'
>
> * eggs mixed with milk and cooked in a pan

b Listen to **A**'s story.

c Tell **A** what you remember of your story from memory. Begin *I'm going to tell you about how Paul McCartney wrote 'Yesterday'. He woke up one morning...*

7 B But you told me ... B

You booked this holiday at your local travel agent's:

> **TWO UNFORGETTABLE WEEKS IN THE BAHAMAS**
> ● direct flights + transport from airport to hotel
> ● luxury hotel with swimming pool, gym and disco
> ● all rooms have balcony and sea view
> ● water sports and a trip round the island included in price
> ● sunshine guaranteed

You have just come back. The holiday was a disaster, for the following reasons:

1 Nobody met you at the airport.
2 The hotel was quite old and not very clean.
3 Your room didn't have a sea view.
4 You had to pay for the water sports.
5 The weather was terrible.

A is the travel agent who sold you the holiday. Complain to him/her. You want a complete refund of the price of the holiday.

The information in your brochure wasn't true. You told me that..., but...

7 International English Any complaints? B

You're a shop assistant in a clothes shop. **A** is going to come to you with a problem with something he/she bought. You can't change it for an identical one because there are no more in his/her size.

Try to persuade **A** to change it for something else, because your manager doesn't like you to give customers their money back unless it's really necessary.

Begin *Can I help you?*

8 A The French children B

a Read your story and try to remember it.

> A FRENCH MAN called Louis Hoffman was travelling on the *Titanic* with his two young sons, Michel and Edmond, aged four and two. He told the other passengers that his wife was dead. But this wasn't true.
>
> The true story was that his name was Michel Navratil. He had just separated from his wife Marcelle. He had decided to run away with his children. He was going to take them to New York to start a new life there.
>
> When the *Titanic* was sinking, Michel dressed the two little boys and put them into the last lifeboat. He stayed on the ship when it sank and he drowned. The two boys were rescued by the *Carpathia*.
>
> When the two little boys arrived in New York on the *Carpathia*, they were the only children who didn't have a mother or father. Newspapers all around the world put their photograph on the front page. Their mother, Marcelle, in France saw the newspaper and recognized her children. She immediately travelled to New York to get them.
>
> Her older child, Michel, had a message for her from her ex-husband. On the deck of the sinking ship he had told his son, 'when you see your mother, tell her that I loved her and that I still love her.'

b Listen to **A**'s story.

c Tell **A** what you remember of your story from memory.

Begin *I'm going to tell you about the French children...*

COMMON VERB PHRASES

a Complete the boxes with these verbs.

catch do go have keep know lose
make meet miss play spend take

1 _____	the housework (the ironing, etc.), the shopping, a course, homework, an exam/a test, research, military service, somebody a favour, sport/exercise, yoga
2 _____	a pizza, a mistake, friends, a noise, the beds, a phone call
3 _____	breakfast/lunch/dinner, something in common, time (to do something), a shower, a good time, a good weekend, a rest, a meeting, a party, a sandwich, a coffee
4 _____	home, to the cinema, to bed/work/ school/university, for a walk, by car/ bus, shopping, sightseeing, cycling, abroad
5 _____	your money in the bank, a promise, doing something (= continue), fit, in touch
6 _____	your car to the garage, somebody to (the cinema) an exam, a photo, a bus/train/ plane/taxi, medicine
7 _____	somebody (who's not there), a bus/ train/plane, a lesson
8 _____	your job, your keys, a (football) match
9 _____	(somebody) for the first time, (somebody) outside the cinema, (somebody) by chance
10 _____	something, somebody for a long time
11 _____	a bus/train/plane (NOT ~~taxi~~), a cold, a ball
12 _____	with your friends, tennis, cards, the guitar, a CD
13 _____	time, money (on something), your holidays somewhere

❗ **make** usually means *create* something *(make a pizza)*. **do** is usually for *obligations (do an exam, do the ironing)*.

b Match the meanings of *get* to groups 1–6.

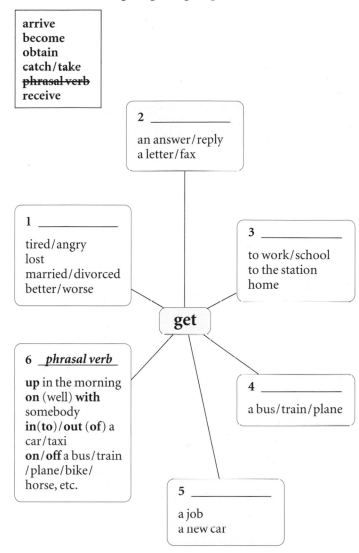

arrive
become
obtain
catch/take
~~phrasal verb~~
receive

2 _____
an answer/reply
a letter/fax

1 _____
tired/angry
lost
married/divorced
better/worse

3 _____
to work/school
to the station
home

get

6 *phrasal verb*
up in the morning
on (well) **with** somebody
in(to)/out (of) a car/taxi
on/off a bus/train /plane/bike/ horse, etc.

4 _____
a bus/train/plane

5 _____
a job
a new car

c What's the meaning of *get* in these sentences?
1 *Get* ready!
2 I wrote to IBM but I didn't *get* an answer.
3 Did you *get* any potatoes at the supermarket?
4 I forgot my umbrella so I *got* wet.
5 We *got* the plane to Paris.
6 When we *got* to the hotel, it was full.
7 I *got* a phone call from my sister.
8 We *got* off the plane.

Add other new **verb phrases** to this page or write them in your vocabulary book.

DESCRIBING PEOPLE

A Appearance

Match the descriptions and pictures.

> A He's **in his twenties**. He's tall and **well built** /wel'bɪlt/ with **curly** /'kɜːlɪ/ **brown hair**. He's got a **beard** /'bɪəd/ and a **moustache** /mə'staːʃ/.
>
> B He **looks about fifty**. He's short and **a bit overweight** /əʊvə'weɪt/. He's **bald** /bɔːld/.
>
> C She's a **teenager**. She's **slim** and **medium height** /haɪt/. She's got **shoulder-length fair** (or **blond**) **hair** and a **fringe**.
>
> D She's **in her forties**. She's quite tall and slim. She's got **grey** hair, and it's short and **straight**. She wears glasses.

Look at the words in **bold**. How do you pronounce them? Underline the stress.

B Personality

a Match the adjectives and definitions. Underline the stress.

affectionate	co-operative	lazy /'leɪzɪ/	sensible
aggressive	charming	moody	sensitive
ambitious	insecure	self-confident	jealous /'dʒeləs/
bossy	shy	selfish	sociable /'səʊʃəbl/

1 She feels very sure of herself. _____
2 He only thinks about himself. _____
3 She's always telling other people what to do. _____
4 He's always ready for a fight. _____
5 She's good at working with other people. _____
6 He likes being with other people. _____
7 She wants what another person has. _____
8 He's happy one moment and sad the next. _____
9 She's not sure of herself. _____
10 He's good at making people like him. _____
11 She doesn't like working. _____
12 He's very loving. _____
13 She has a lot of common sense. _____
14 He feels things quickly and deeply. _____
15 She finds it difficult to talk to new people. _____
16 He wants to do well in life. _____

Cover the words. Read the definitions and try to remember the adjectives.

b Write the opposite adjectives. Underline the stress.

quiet	hard-working	disorganized	unimaginative
generous	impatient	unfriendly	untidy

1 friendly / nice _____
2 imaginative _____
3 lazy _____
4 mean _____
5 organized _____
6 patient /'peɪʃnt/ _____
7 talkative _____
8 tidy _____

Jane's very untidy.

Add other **appearance** and **personality** adjectives to this page or write them in your vocabulary book.

BODY AND HEALTH

THE BODY

Match the words and pictures.
How do you pronounce them?

blood /blʌd/
bone
brain /breɪn/
heart /haːt/
kidneys /ˈkɪdniːs/
liver /ˈlɪvə/
lungs /lʌŋz/
muscle /ˈmʌsl/
skin

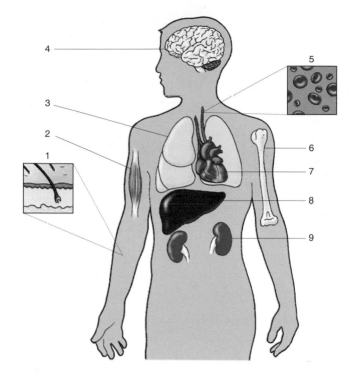

STRESS AND FITNESS

Complete the text. Underline the stress in the words
below. What do the words/phrases in **bold** mean?

cold	headaches /ˈhedeiks/	hurt /hɜːt/	illnesses	
keep fit	pains	pull a muscle	relax	stressed
stressful				

Nowadays many people have very ¹ _____
lives. Doctors say that **stress** can cause many
² _____, and in some cases even **heart
attacks**. If you are feeling ³ _____ you are
also more likely to get a ⁴ _____ or **flu**, or
suffer from ⁵ _____. You should try to **rest**
and ⁶ _____, and **do exercise** to ⁷ _____.
But be careful! You should start slowly, or you
could ⁸ _____ your back or ⁹ _____. If
you notice any ¹⁰ _____ after doing exercise,
see a doctor.

SYMPTOMS OF ILLNESS

a Look at the list of symptoms. Translate them. Do you have any
at the moment?

- I've got **a cold**
  a cough /cɒf/
  a sore throat /sɔːˈθrəʊt/
  a temperature.
- I've got **a headache**
  an earache
  a toothache
  a stomach-ache /ˈstʌməkeɪk/
- My back **hurts**.
- I've got a **pain** in my leg.
- I've **hurt myself**.

b What's the matter with these people?

FOOD AND DIET

FOOD ADJECTIVES

Match the adjectives and definitions. Underline the stress. Write an example food for each one.

junk   fresh   hot/spicy   tinned   fattening   frozen   take-away   wholemeal /ˈhəʊlmiːl/

	ADJECTIVE	DEFINITION	EXAMPLE
1	_____	makes you put on weight	_chocolate_
2	_____	with a strong flavour, often from a spice, e.g. paprika	_____
3	_____	recently picked, not old	_____
4	_____	made from unrefined flour	_____
5	_____	bought at a restaurant but not eaten there	_____
6	_____	kept below 0°C	_____
7	_____	kept in a tin or can	_____
8	_____	not healthy, bad for you	_____

YOUR DIET

Complete the text. Underline the stress.

balanced   carbohydrates   healthy   overweight   unhealthy
calories   fast   lose   put   vegetarians

What you eat is very important for your health. Many people today have an ¹_____ **diet**. They eat too much ²_____ **food** (especially take-away food) and **processed** food (tinned or frozen). A healthy, ³_____ **diet** should include **proteins**, ⁴_____, **fats**, and fresh fruit and vegetables. You should control the amount of fat and carbohydrates you eat if you don't want to ⁵_____ **on weight**. If you are ⁶_____ you can **go on a diet** to ⁷_____ **weight**, for example avoiding food with too many ⁸_____. Many people today are ⁹_____ and don't eat any meat. This is a ¹⁰_____ diet if you make sure you eat enough protein from pulses (beans, etc.), eggs and cheese.

TYPES OF FOOD

Put the foods in the correct columns. Underline the stress. Add more **food** words.

apricots   asparagus   aubergines /ˈəʊbəʒiːnz/   beans   beef   cod   cream   cherries
lentils   margarine   mussels   olive oil   pasta   rice   turkey   yoghurt /ˈjɒgət/

meat	fish/seafood	eggs/milk products	pulses	fruit	vegetables	carbo-hydrates	fats

EDUCATION

TYPES OF SCHOOL

Complete the text. Underline the stress.

university /juːnɪ'vɜːsətɪ/	uniforms /'juːnɪfɔːmz/
secondary school	mixed
primary school	nursery school
boarding /'bɔːdɪŋ/ schools	nuns
private /'praɪvət/ schools	pupils /'pjuːplz/
state schools	priests /priːsts/
head	

1 _____ (ages 2–4)

2 _____ (ages 4–11)

3 _____ (ages 11–18)

4 _____ (ages 18+)

In a typical school system in many countries, there are two kinds of schools: 5_____, which are run by the government, and 6_____. Private schools are often stricter than state schools, and in many of them the 7_____ (schoolchildren) have to wear 8_____.

Both state and private schools are often 9_____ (for boys and girls) or are for boys only or girls only. There are also some schools, usually private, where the pupils sleep at school, which are called 10_____.

The 'boss' of a school is called the 11_____ (teacher). In some religious schools there are also 12_____ (women) and 13_____ (men) who work as teachers.

HIGHER EDUCATION

arts science /'saɪəns/	courses
subjects /'sʌbdʒɪkts/	degree /dɪ'griː/
do research /rɪ'sɜːtʃ/	professors

Complete the text. Underline the stress.

At university you can do 1_____ in many different 2_____ (e.g. law). Some students prefer to do an 3_____ course (e.g. languages) and others prefer a 4_____ course (e.g. engineering). In Britain, it usually takes three or four years to get a university 5_____. When they finish their course, some people stay at university and 6_____. The most important teachers at a university are called 7_____.

SUBJECTS AND EXAMS

a Look at the subjects and underline the stress. Translate them. What other school subjects do you know?

biology	maths
foreign languages	economics
chemistry	P.E. (physical education)
history	geography
computer studies	physics

b Complete the text.

take/do   marks (n.)   fail /feɪl/   terms   pass

The school year is divided into three 1_____. Most children at secondary school have to 2_____ exams at the end of the summer term. Copying in exams is strictly forbidden. Of course all pupils hope to get good/high 3_____ and to 4_____ their exams, not to 5_____ them!

Add other **education** words to this page or write them in your vocabulary book.

I'm at school. I'm in my fourth year of secondary school. What about you?

WORK

GETTING A JOB

a Read the text. Number the pictures A–I below in order 1–9. What do the words / phrases in **bold** mean? Underline the stress.

Michael was **unemployed** and was **looking for a job**. He saw an advertisement for a job **as** a computer programmer. He decided to **apply** /ə'plaɪ/ **for** it, and sent his **CV** and an **application form**. A week later he **had an interview** and a few days later the boss phoned to say that he had **got the job**. He went to **sign the contract**, and the next day he started work. He had to work very hard and **do overtime**, but he was happy because he **earned a good salary**. At first everything went well, and after six months he **got promoted**. But unfortunately a few months later he had an argument with the boss and **was sacked**. Michael was unemployed again.

b Cover the text. Look at the pictures and tell the story.

PEOPLE AND WHAT THEY DO

Match the words and definitions. Underline the stresss.

retire /rɪ'taɪə/   **company   manager   employee** /emplɔɪ'iː/
resign /rɪ'zaɪn/   **employer   trade union   (go on) strike**

1 _employer_   someone who pays other people to do work
2 _employee_   someone who is paid to work
3 _company_   an organization or group of people who work together in business
4 _resign_   leave your job (because you want to go)
5 _retire_   leave your job (because you are old, e.g. 65)
6 _(go on) strike (to)_ stop work because you want better working conditions
7 _trade union_ group of people who represent workers
8 _manager_   someone who controls an organization

Cover the words. Read the definitions and try to remember the words.

JOBS / PROFESSIONS

Complete the text. Underline the stress.

**conditions   hours   part time   temporary   experience   job
qualifications   work**

Nowadays in many countries, there is not enough
¹ _work_ for everybody, and many people are looking for a
² _job_. If they are lucky enough to find one, it is often ³ _a part-time_, (only a few hours a day) not **full time**, or it is a ⁴ _temporary_ job _(3 syllables)_ (only for a few months), not a **permanent** one. Many jobs involve working **long**
⁵ _hours_, and often the **working** ⁶ _conditions_ (e.g. **salary**, holidays) are not good. To get a good job, it's important to have
⁷ _qualifications_ (e.g. a university degree) and some
⁸ _experience_.

> I'm **a** civil servant.

> I work **for** the government.

> I used to work **as** a lawyer.

> I've got a degree **in** law.

Add more **jobs**. Underline the stress.

-er	-or	-ist	-ian	others
lawyer	inspector	scientist	librarian	accountant
				cook
teacher	inventor	journalist	optician	kitchen porter
film maker	creator	chemist	&	
trader	animator		politician	

MONEY

TYPES OF MONEY

1
2
3
4
5

Match the words and pictures.

a coin	5	foreign currency	2
a credit card	3	a note	4
a cheque-book	1		

BANKS AND OTHER EXPRESSIONS

Match the words and definitions. Underline the stress.

a cash-point   income   a bank loan   the cost of living
the exchange rate   a bank account   a safe   tax

1 _a bank loan_ — money which is lent to you by the bank
2 _a bank account_ — way of keeping your money in the bank
3 _income_ — the money you receive each year from work, investments, etc.
4 _tax_ — money that the government takes from your salary
5 _a cash-point_ — a machine in the wall of a bank where you can take money out
6 _a safe_ — a metal box for keeping money
7 _the exchange rate_ — the value of one country's money against another
8 _The cost of living_ — what it costs to live in a country

Cover the words. Read the definitions and try to remember the words.

WHAT YOU CAN DO WITH MONEY

a Complete with a preposition where necessary.

1 Peter paid _for_ the meal last night.
2 When can you pay me _back_ the money I lent you?
3 Would you like to pay _in_ cash or _by_ cheque?
4 I paid _∅_ 50 dollars _for_ that sweater.
5 Did you pay _∅_ the waiter?

In cash
+ by cheque

b Complete the text. Put the verbs into the past tense in the first part and the present in the second part.

buy   cost   give away   inherit   invest   lose   save
sell   spend   wealthy (*adj.*) /'welθi:/

Derek used to be very [1] _wealthy_. When he was a young man, he [2] _inherited_ a fortune from his uncle. He [3] _invested_ most of it in the stock market, and [4] _bought_ an enormous house which [5] _cost_ £2,000,000. He also had a good job, and he [6] _saved_ his salary (put it in the bank), so he got richer and richer. He [7] _spent_ a lot of money on cars and holidays, but he was also very generous, and [8] _gave away_ a lot of his money to charities (e.g. the Red Cross). But one day he started going to the casino with a friend, and that was the beginning of the end. He soon [9] _lost_ everything, and after a few months he [10] _sold_ his house and his cars.

borrow   broke (*adj.*)   can't afford   lend   owe /əʊ/
waste   win

Now he's [11] _broke_. He rents a small flat – he [12] _can't afford_ (hasn't got enough money) to buy one. He's unemployed. His parents [13] _lend_ him money, and he also [14] _borrows_ money from friends so he [15] _owes_ (has to give back) money to lots of people. But he still [16] _wastes_ (spends badly) the little money he has on the lottery and the football pools. He thinks his only hope of getting rich again is to [17] _win_ a big prize. Perhaps one day he will.

c Look at the pictures. Remember Derek's story.

Add other **money** words to this page or write them in your vocabulary book.

TRANSPORT AND DRIVING

A Vehicles and traffic

VEHICLES

Match the words and pictures. Underline the stress.

a bus — 2
a coach /kəʊtʃ/ — 9
a lorry — 7
a motorbike — 6
a scooter — 4

a sports car — 3
a tram — 5
the underground — 8
a van — 1

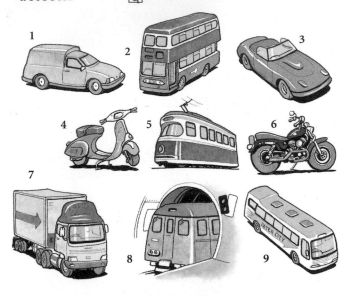

Look at the pictures. Try to remember the words.

TRAFFIC

Match the words and definitions. Underline the stress.

(cycle) lane   parking ticket   rush hour   pavement
speed limit   fine (*n.* and *v.*)   public transport   traffic jam
motorway   road sign

1	Public transport	buses, underground, etc.
2	a a lane	single part of a motorway or main road
3	a parking ticket	piece of paper put by the police on badly-parked cars
4	a traffic jam	a lot of cars which can't move
5	the pavement	the side of the road where pedestrians walk
6	a road sign	words or symbols which give traffic information
7	a fine	money you have to pay for driving too fast or parking badly
8	the rush hour	time of day when there is a lot of traffic
9	the speed limit	maximum speed permitted, e.g. 120 km per hour
10	a motorway	fast road between cities

Cover the words. Read the definitions and remember the words.

B Cars and driving

PARTS OF A CAR

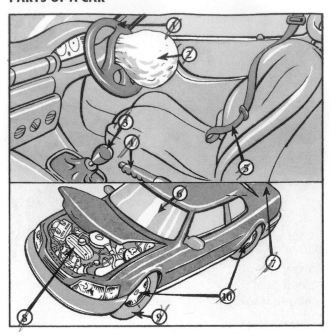

Match the words and pictures. Underline the stress.

airbag — 9
boot — 7
engine — 8
gear stick — 3

handbrake — 4
seat-belt — 5
steering wheel — 1
tyre — 2

wheels — 10
windscreen — 6

Look at the picture. Try to remember the words.

DRIVING

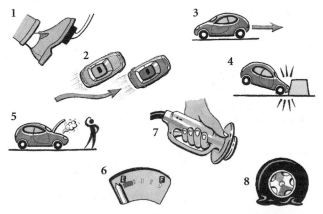

a Match the verbs and pictures. Underline the stress.

brake — ☐
break down — ☐
crash into — ☐
fill up (with petrol) — ☐

get a puncture — ☐
overtake — ☐
reverse — ☐
run out of petrol — ☐

b Look at the pictures. Remember the words. What's the past tense of each verb?

Add other **transport and driving** words to this page or write them in your vocabulary book.

THE CINEMA

MAKING A FILM

Match the words and definitions. Underline the stress.

audience /'ɔːdɪəns/ extras cast script stars screenplay
director plot producer scene /siːn/ sequel /'siːkwəl/
soundtrack special effects

1	the _____	the person who makes the film
2	the _____	the most famous actors in a film
3	the _____	all the actors and actresses in a film
4	the _____	the person who finds the money and actors to make a film
5	the _____	the people who watch a film
6	the _____	the people (not actors) who appear in the film, e.g. in crowd scenes
7	the _____	the actions and dialogue of a film
8	the _____	the dialogue of a film
9	a _____	part of a film happening in one place
10	the _____	the music of a film
11	the _____	the story, what happens
12	the _____	images created often by computer
13	a _____	a film (or book) that continues the story of the previous one

VERBS RELATED TO FILMS

a Read the definitions and complete the text.

dubbed	= not in the original language
played the part of	= acted the role of
set	= situated in a particular time and place
shot (**shoot**)	= filmed
starred	= had as its main actors
subtitled	= with translation at the bottom of the screen

I'm Italian, but I like watching English and American films to improve my English. Last night I went to see a western. It was ¹_____ in the Wild West in the 1890s but in fact I know it was ²_____ in Spain. It ³_____ several well-known actors and Clint Eastwood ⁴_____ the bandit. It was ⁵_____, which is important for me so that I can practise understanding English. I don't like films which are ⁶_____ into Italian – the voices are always the same.

b Think of the last film you saw and answer these questions:

Who was in it? Were they good?
Who was the director?
Where and when was it set?
Was there a good plot and script?
Were there any special effects?
What was the soundtrack like?
Was it dubbed or subtitled?

TYPES OF FILM

Write the names of different types of films in the space below, e.g. *western*.

Add other **cinema** words to this page or write them in your vocabulary book.

SPORT

PLACES AND EQUIPMENT

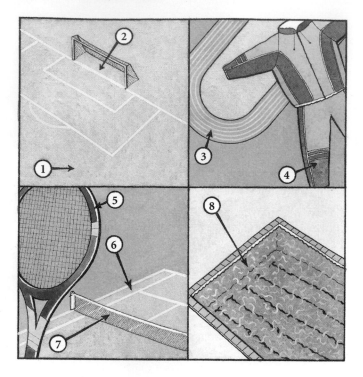

Match the words and pictures.

an athletics track	☐	**a racket**	☐
a football pitch	☐	**a tennis court**	☐
a goal	☐	**a track suit**	☐
a net	☐	**a swimming pool**	☐

> **!** **pitch** is for outdoor ball sports, e.g. rugby, football, hockey.
> **court** is for racket sports and indoor ball sports,
> e.g. basketball, squash, tennis.

PEOPLE IN SPORT

Match the people and definitions. Underline the stress.

---
captain   players   coach   referee /refəˈriː/
crowd /kraʊd/   spectator   goalkeeper   team
---

1 the _____ people who play a sport, e.g. basketball, tennis
2 the _____ the head of a team
3 the _____ the person who controls a sports match
4 a _____ a person who trains a team or a player
5 a _____ a person who watches a sport
6 the _____ the big group of people who watch a sport
7 a _____ people who play a sport together on one side
8 the _____ the player who defends the goal, e.g. in football

Cover the definitions. Explain who the people are.

WHAT'S THE SCORE?

Complete with **all**, **love**, **nil** or **deuce** /djuːs/.

Most sports	**Tennis**
3–3 = three _____	15–15 = fifteen _____
1–0 = one _____	40–0 = forty _____
	40–40 = _____

WINNING AND LOSING

a Write the past tense and past participles of these verbs:

beat	_____ _____	Charlton *beat* Liverpool 4–0.
win	_____ _____	Charlton *won* 4–0.
lose	_____ _____	Chelsea *lost to* Arsenal 2–1.
draw	_____ _____	Everton *drew with* Leeds 0–0.

> **!** You **win** a match or a competition. You can't win a person.
> You **beat** another team or person. *Charlton beat Liverpool*
> NOT ~~Charlton won Liverpool~~.

b Complete the text with words from the list.

---
a draw   fan   drew   injured (*adj.*) /ˈɪndʒəd/   beat
the score   lose   season   win   the stadium   lost

I'm a football ¹_____ and my team is
Arsenal. I go to ²_____ at Highbury on
Saturdays to watch them play. I love it when Arsenal
³_____ and I hate it when they
⁴_____.
Last week they ⁵_____ with Coventry, 2–2.
I don't like it when a match ends in ⁶_____.
It's boring. The best match last ⁷_____
was when they ⁸_____ Manchester United
at home. ⁹_____ was 3–2. Their worst
match was when they ¹⁰_____ to PAOK
Salonika in the UEFA cup, but that was only because one
of their best players was ¹¹_____ and
couldn't play. Arsenal for ever!

SPORTS

Add some more **sports** to each column.

> **!** **play** for racket and ball sports (*play tennis*, *volleyball*)
> **do** for exercise (*do yoga*) and martial arts (*do karate*)
> **go** + verb + *-ing* (*go swimming*)

INDOOR SPORTS	OUTDOOR SPORTS	WATER SPORTS
play handball do karate	play rugby go cycling	go sailing go swimming

TOURISM AND TRAVELLING
A Tourism
WHAT TO SEE ON HOLIDAY

Match the words and pictures. How do you pronounce them?

a castle /ˈkɑːsl/ ☐
a cathedral /kəˈθiːdrəl/ ☐
a fountain /ˈfaʊntɪn/ ☐
a monument /ˈmɒnjʊmənt/ ☐
a museum /mjuːˈzɪəm/ ☐
a port/harbour /ˈhɑːbə/ ☐
a square /skweə/ ☐
a statue /ˈstætʃuː/ ☐
an art gallery /ˈgæləri/ ☐
the scenery /ˈsiːnəri/ ☐

Look at the pictures. Remember the words.

VERBS RELATED TO HOLIDAYS
Complete the phrases with the verbs.

book	buy	go	go on	have	pack	read
see	sunbathe	take	take out	try		

BEFORE YOU GO
1 _____ a holiday, a flight, a hotel
2 _____ holiday brochures /ˈbrəʊʃəz/, guidebooks
3 _____ travel insurance
4 _____ your (suit)case

WHEN YOU'RE THERE
5 _____ a look round a town
6 _____ camping, sightseeing, shopping
7 _____ day trips, excursions
8 _____ monuments, the scenery
9 _____ photos
10 _____ local dishes, the local speciality
11 _____ on the beach, by the pool
12 _____ souvenirs

Look only at the verbs. Remember the phrases.

B Travelling
TYPES OF JOURNEY

cruise /kruːz/ **flight** **journey** /ˈdʒɜːni/ **tour** /tʊə/ **trip**
voyage /ˈvɔɪdʒ/

Match the nouns and definitions.

1 a _____ when you travel from one place to another by road, rail, etc.
2 a _____ when you travel by plane
3 a _____ when you go somewhere, stay there and come back (on business or on holiday)
4 a _____ when you travel by ship (to a place far away)
5 a _____ when you travel by ship and stop at several places
6 a _____ when you visit several different places following an organized plan

> **!** **travel** is usually used as a verb, e.g. *I travel a lot.*
> You can't say **a** *travel* NOT ~~I had a good travel~~.

HOLIDAY ACCOMMODATION

a Match the words and symbols. Underline the stress.

a bed and breakfast ☐ **a hotel** ☐
a campsite ☐ **a youth hostel** ☐
a farmhouse ☐

b Answer the questions.
1 Which one is the most expensive and most comfortable?
2 Which one offers cheap accommodation in shared rooms, usually for young people?
3 Which one offers you a place to put up your tent?
4 Which one usually provides a room in a private house?
5 Which one often allows you to live with a family and help them with their work?

Add other **tourism and travelling** words to this page or write them in your vocabulary book.

PHRASAL VERBS

Look at the phrasal verbs and example sentences. Write a translation in your language.

> **!** 1 With the verbs marked *, the object can go between the verb and the particle or after the particle.
> *He put on his coat.* OR *He put his coat on.*
> But if the object is a pronoun, it always goes between the verb and the particle. *Turn it off.* NOT ~~Turn off it.~~
> 2 Some phrasal verbs have more than one meaning, e.g. *take off* (see below).

PHRASAL VERB	EXAMPLE	EXPLANATION	TRANSLATION
be on	There's a good film on (TV).	be shown (TV, cinema)	
be over	The match is over.	finish	
break down	My car has broken down.	stop working (cars)	
break up	He broke up with his girlfriend.	end a relationship	
fall over	He fell over and broke his leg.	fall to the ground	
fill in*	Fill in the form, please.	complete	
find out*	Find out what it means.	discover	
get around	The best way to get around is by car.	travel in a place	
get in(to)/out (of)	Get into the car. We're leaving.	enter/leave a car	
get on/off	Get off the bus at the next stop.	enter/leave a bus, train	
get on with	I get on (well) with my sister.	have a (good) relationship with	
get up	She gets up at 7 every morning.	leave (your) bed	
give away*	He gave away all his money.	give and not want back	
give back*	Give me back my ball!	return something	
give up*	I've decided to give up smoking.	stop	
go away	We went away for the weekend.	leave the town	
go out	We went out last night.	leave your house	
go back	He went back to work.	return	
go down	The temperature has gone down.	become lower	
go/carry on	He went on speaking for two hours.	continue	
go up	Prices are going up.	become higher	
hold on	Please hold on a moment.	wait	
hurry up	Hurry up. We're late.	be quick	
lie down	He lay down on the bed.	put yourself in a horizontal position	
look after	He's looking after the children.	be responsible for	
look for	I'm looking for a job.	try to find	
look forward to	I look forward to seeing you.	wait for something nice to happen	
look up*	Can you look up this word in the dictionary?	find in a book	
pay back*	I'll pay you back tomorrow.	return money you owe	
pick up*	I'll pick you up at your house at 7.	collect, lift from the ground	
put on*	Put on your coat. It's cold.	get dressed in	
put off*	Let's put off the meeting until Monday.	postpone	
run out of	Oh no! We're running out of petrol.	be without	
run over*	He was run over by a bus.	be hit by a vehicle	
set off	They set off early in the morning.	start a journey	
switch/turn off*	Please switch/turn off the lights.	disconnect	
switch/turn on*	First switch/turn on the engine.	connect	
take back*	I'm going to take this sweater back.	return to (a shop)	
take off	The plane took off at 6 o'clock.	go into the air	
	He was hot so he took off* his jacket.	remove	
take out*	She took some money out of the bank.	take from somewhere	
throw away*	He threw the shoes away.	put in the rubbish	
try on*	Can I try on these jeans?	put on to see if something fits	
turn up/down*	Can you turn up the TV? I can't hear it.	make louder/quieter	
wake up*	I wake up at 8 every morning.	stop sleeping	
wash up*	I'll cook if you wash up.	wash the plates, etc.	

Add other **phrasal verbs** to this page or write them in your vocabulary book.
Write an example sentence and a translation.

REGULAR AND IRREGULAR VERBS

Regular verbs

Remember how to spell and pronounce regular verbs in the past tense and past participles.

SPELLING

work	work**ed**
smoke	smok**ed**
carry	carri**ed**
stop	stop**ped**

PRONUNCIATION

/d/	/t/	/ɪd/
Verbs ending in voiced sounds	**Verbs ending in unvoiced sounds**	**verbs ending in /t/ or /d/ sounds**
played	watched	wanted
studied	liked	needed
called	kissed	invited

Irregular verbs

INFINITIVE	PAST	PAST PARTICIPLE	INFINITIVE	PAST	PAST PARTICIPLE
be	was/were	been	lend	lent	lent
beat	beat	beaten	let	let	let
become	became	become	lie /laɪ/	lay /leɪ/	lain /leɪn/
begin	began	begun	light	lit	lit
bite	bit	bitten	lose /luːz/	lost	lost
break	broke	broken	make	made	made
bring	brought /brɔːt/	brought	mean	meant /ment/	meant
build	built /bɪlt/	built	meet	met	met
buy	bought	bought	pay	paid /peɪd/	paid
can	could /kʊd/		put	put	put
catch	caught	caught	read	read /red/	read
choose /tʃuːz/	chose /tʃəʊz/	chosen	ride	rode	ridden
come	came	come	ring	rang	rung
cost	cost	cost	run	ran	run
cut	cut	cut	say	said /sed/	said
do	did	done	see	saw	seen
draw /drɔː/	drew /druː/	drawn	sell	sold	sold
drink	drank	drunk	send	sent	sent
drive	drove	driven	shoot	shot	shot
eat	ate	eaten	shut	shut	shut
fall	fell	fallen	sing	sang	sung
feel	felt	felt	sink	sank	sunk
fight	fought	fought	sit	sat	sat
find	found	found	sleep	slept	slept
fly	flew	flown	speak	spoke	spoken
forget	forgot	forgotten	spend	spent	spent
get	got	got	stand	stood	stood
give	gave	given	steal	stole	stolen
go	went	gone	swim	swam	swum
grow	grew	grown	take	took	taken
have	had	had	teach	taught	taught
hear	heard /hɜːd/	heard	tell	told	told
hide	hid	hidden	think	thought	thought
hit	hit	hit	throw	threw	thrown
hold	held	held	understand	understood	understood
hurt /hɜːt/	hurt	hurt	wake	woke	woken
keep	kept	kept	wear	wore	worn
know	knew	known	win	won /wʌn/	won
leave	left	left	write	wrote	written

ENGLISH SOUNDS

Vowels

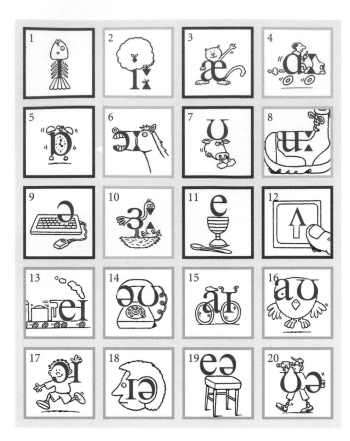

Consonants

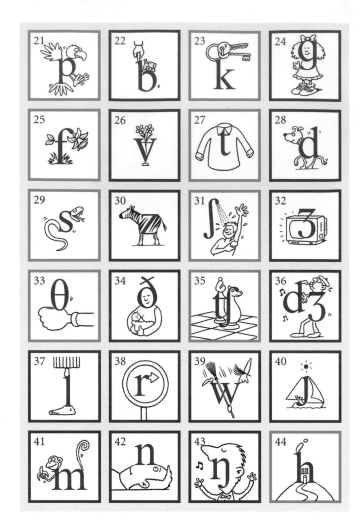

■ short vowels

ɪ long vowels

■ diphthongs

■ voiced

■ unvoiced

Key to vowels

1 fish /fɪʃ/
2 tree /triː/
3 cat /kæt/
4 car /kɑː/
5 clock /klɒk/
6 horse /hɔːs/
7 bull /bʊl/
8 boot /buːt/

9 computer
/kəmp'juːtə/
10 bird /bɜːd/
11 egg /eg/
12 up /ʌp/
13 train /treɪn/
14 phone /fəʊn/
15 bike /baɪk/

16 owl /aʊl/
17 boy /bɔɪ/
18 ear /ɪə/
19 chair /tʃeə/
20 tourist
/'tʊərɪst/

Key to consonants

21 parrot /'pærət/
22 bag /bæg/
23 key /kiː/
24 girl /gɜːl/
25 flower /'flaʊə/
26 vase /vɑːz/
27 tie /taɪ/
28 dog /dɒg/
29 snake /sneɪk/

30 zebra /'zebrə/
31 shower /'ʃaʊə/
32 television
/'telɪvɪʒn/
33 thumb /θʌm/
34 mother /'mʌðə/
35 chess /tʃes/
36 jazz /dʒæz/
37 leg /leg/

38 right /raɪt/
39 witch /wɪtʃ/
40 yacht /jɒt/
41 monkey
/'mʌŋkɪ/
42 nose /nəʊz/
43 singer /'sɪŋə/
44 house /haʊs/

A LETTER TO A FRIEND

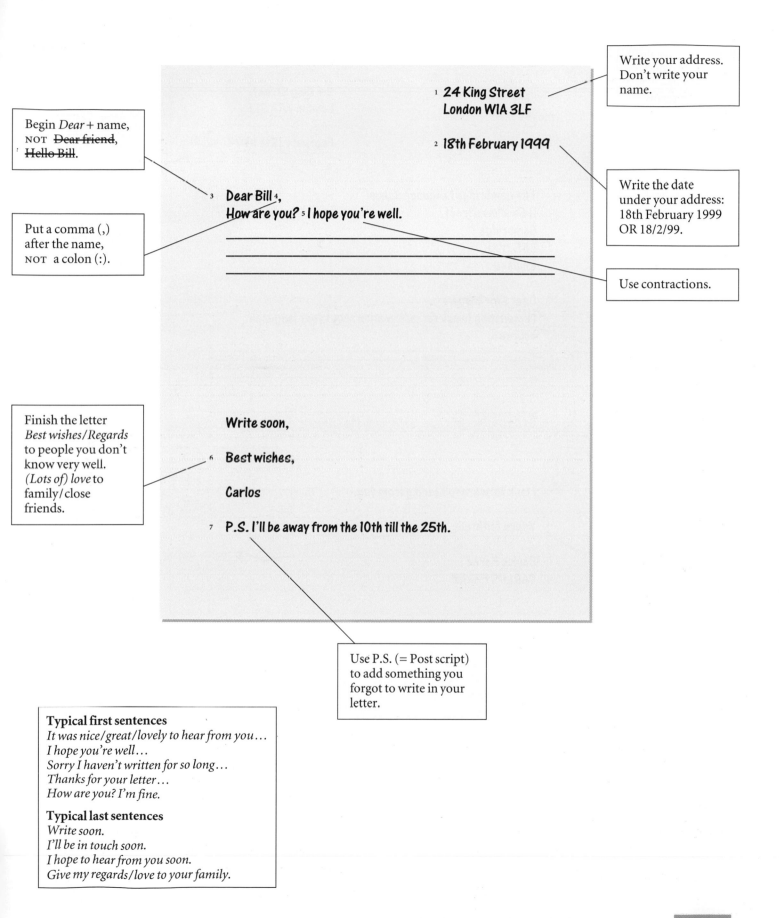

Write your address. Don't write your name.

¹ **24 King Street London W1A 3LF**

² **18th February 1999**

Write the date under your address: 18th February 1999 OR 18/2/99.

Begin *Dear* + name, NOT Dear friend, Hello Bill.

³ **Dear Bill** ⁴**,**
How are you? ⁵ **I hope you're well.**

Put a comma (,) after the name, NOT a colon (:).

Use contractions.

Finish the letter *Best wishes/Regards* to people you don't know very well. *(Lots of) love* to family/close friends.

Write soon,

⁶ **Best wishes,**

Carlos

⁷ **P.S. I'll be away from the 10th till the 25th.**

Use P.S. (= Post script) to add something you forgot to write in your letter.

Typical first sentences
It was nice/great/lovely to hear from you…
I hope you're well…
Sorry I haven't written for so long…
Thanks for your letter…
How are you? I'm fine.

Typical last sentences
Write soon.
I'll be in touch soon.
I hope to hear from you soon.
Give my regards/love to your family.

A FORMAL LETTER

Write the name of the person (if you know it) and the address of the person/company you are writing to.

Write your address. Don't write your name.

Begin *Dear Sir/ Madam,* if you **don't** know the name of the person you're writing to. Begin *Dear Mr Green/ Ms Black* if you know the name, NOT ~~Dear Mr John Green~~.

Write the date under your address or above the address you are writing to: *February 18th, 1999* OR *18th February 1999*.

Don't use contractions.

Put a comma (,) after the name, NOT a colon (:).

If you want to receive a reply, write as a final sentence: *I look forward to hearing from you.*

Finish the letter *Yours faithfully* (if you started with *Dear Sir/ Madam*) or *Yours sincerely* (if you started with *Dear + name*).

Sign your name.

Write your name in capital letters.

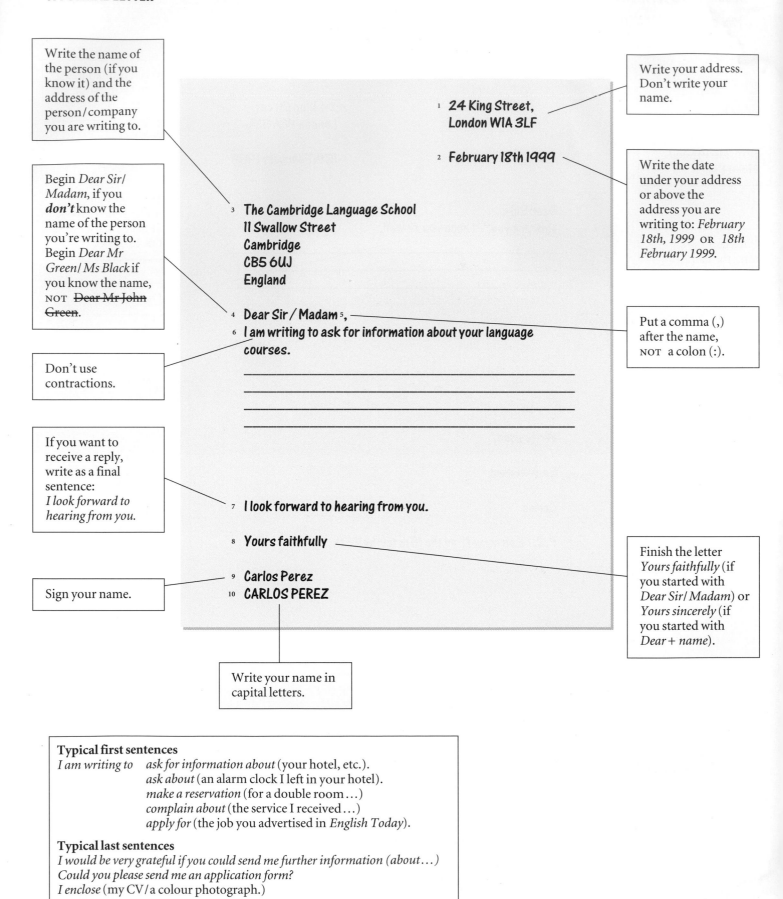

1 **24 King Street,
London W1A 3LF**

2 **February 18th 1999**

3 **The Cambridge Language School
11 Swallow Street
Cambridge
CB5 6UJ
England**

4 **Dear Sir / Madam** 5 **,**
6 **I am writing to ask for information about your language courses.**

_____
_____
_____
_____

7 **I look forward to hearing from you.**

8 **Yours faithfully**

9 **Carlos Perez**
10 **CARLOS PEREZ**

Typical first sentences

I am writing to   *ask for information about* (your hotel, etc.).
     ask about (an alarm clock I left in your hotel).
     make a reservation (for a double room…)
     complain about (the service I received…)
     apply for (the job you advertised in *English Today*).

Typical last sentences

I would be very grateful if you could send me further information (about…)
Could you please send me an application form?
I enclose (my CV/a colour photograph.)

A FAX

Begin a fax like this:

To: (full name of person you're writing to)	**Number of pages:**
From: (your name)	
Tel: (your phone number)	**Date:**
Fax: (your fax number)	

Continue as for a formal letter: *Dear Sir*, etc.

TELLING A STORY

We had a fantastic time in London yesterday. First (of all) we went to the British Museum to see the Egyptian rooms. Then / After that / Afterwards we went for a walk in Hyde Park and had lunch in a pub. But unfortunately as soon as / when we got to Hyde Park, it started to rain.

After lunch we went shopping in Oxford Street and bought some clothes. As / When / While we were walking down Oxford Street, we met some friends. Finally, we decided it was time to go home. We got completely lost looking for the station, but eventually / in the end* we found it, and we caught the last train.

*=finally, after some problems or difficulty

COMPOSITION: WRITING ABOUT ADVANTAGES AND DISADVANTAGES

Sharing a flat

PARAGRAPH 1: ADVANTAGES
Sharing a flat has several advantages. Firstly, ...
Secondly ... Above all, (most important advantage)

PARAGRAPH 2: DISADVANTAGES
On the other hand, there are also disadvantages.
For instance / For example ...
Also ... But the biggest disadvantage is ...

PARAGRAPH 3: CONCLUSION
To sum up / In conclusion, there are both advantages and disadvantages. If you get on well with your flatmates, you will probably enjoy flat-sharing very much, but ...

Grammar Summary

FILE 1

Past simple: *went, played*, etc.

Use	Example	Notes/Problems
For **finished actions in the past** when you say, ask, or know **when** they happened.	*I lost my car keys yesterday.* *When did they arrive?* *I lived in Egypt ten years ago.*	NOT ~~I've lost …~~ ~~When have you arrived?~~

Present perfect simple: *have / has* + past participle

Use	Examples	Notes/Problems
1 For **past experiences** (we don't say **when**).	*I've been to London.* *Have you ever seen a snake?* *I've never met his wife.*	NOT ~~I've been to London last year.~~
2 For **unfinished actions** which started in the past and are **still true now**, especially with *be*, *have* (possession), and *know*.	*We've had this car for six months.* *I've known her for two years.* *How long have you been married? Since 1996.*	❗ Don't use the present simple: NOT ~~We have this car …~~ ~~I know her …~~ ~~How long are you …~~ ❗ To answer *How long …?* use *for* + a period of time, e.g. *for two months*. *since* + a point of time, e.g. *since 1985, since April*. NOT ~~during two months.~~
3 For **an action in the past which has recently finished**. (You can often see the results of the action when you speak.)	*They've painted the walls.* *Look. I've cut myself!*	
4 With *just*, *already*, and *yet*.	*He's just arrived.* *They've already arrived.* *Have you finished yet?*	*just* and *already* go before the main verb or after *be*. *yet* goes at the end of the sentence with (−) and (?).

Present perfect continuous: *have / has* + *been* + (verb + *-ing*)

Use	Examples	Notes/Problems
1 For **unfinished actions** which started in the past and are **still true now**.	*I've been learning English for three years.* *How long has he been working here?*	❗ Don't use the present continuous: NOT ~~I am learning English …~~ ~~How long is he working here?~~ ❗ Use the present perfect simple (NOT continuous) with verbs like *know, be, have*. *I've known him for years.* NOT ~~I've been knowing him …~~
2 For a **continuous action in the past which has recently finished**. (You can often see the results of the action when you speak.)	*You're wet. What have you been doing?* *I've been washing the car.*	

Reflexive pronouns: *myself, yourself, himself, herself, itself, ourselves, yourselves, themselves*

Use	Example	Notes/Problems
1 When the **object** of a verb is the **same** as the **subject**.	*He hurt himself.* *They enjoyed themselves very much.*	*enjoy* always needs a reflexive pronoun or an object, e.g. *They enjoyed the party very much.*
2 For **emphasis**.	*Do it yourself!* *I wrote it myself.*	
3 After *by* = alone.	*She went out by herself.*	

each other

Use	Example	Notes/Problems
With *we*, *you*, and *they*, when **A does something to B and B does the same to A**.	*Kevin and Gemma help each other with the housework.* *We don't speak to each other.*	Compare: *They looked at each other.* (**A** looked at **B** and **B** looked at **A**) *They looked at themselves in the mirror.* (**A** looked at **A** and **B** looked at **B**)

both, either, neither

Use	Example	Notes/Problems
For **A** <u>and</u> **B** use: *Both ... and ...* *Both of us/ you/ them* *... both ...*	*Both Ana and I can come.* *Both of us can come.* *We can both come.*	Use a plural (+) verb after *both*. *both* goes before the main verb or after *be*.
For <u>not</u> **A** and <u>not</u> **B** use: *Neither ... nor ...* *Neither of us/ you/ them ...*	*Neither my brother nor my sister can drive.* *Neither of us like(s) tea.*	Use a (+) verb after *neither*. The verb can be singular or plural, e.g. *Neither of us speak/speaks French.*
For **A** <u>or</u> **B** use: *Either ... or ...* *Either of us/ you/ them ...*	*Either Ana or I can do it.* *Either of us can help you.*	After *either ... or ...* the verb must be singular. With *either of*, the verb can be singular or plural, e.g. *Do/ Does either of you want to come?*

FILE 2

Present simple: *play, lives, studies*, etc.

Use	Example	Notes/Problems
1 For **permanent actions**.	*They work in a bank.* *Where do you live?* *How much does it cost?*	❗ Don't forget the 's' in the third person singular. *She works/ studies*, etc. *Does he ...? No, he doesn't.*
2 For **habitual actions**, (often with an adverb of frequency, e.g. *always* or a frequency expression, e.g. *once a week*).	*He often watches TV.* *She's never late.* *We come to class twice a week.*	Adverbs of frequency go <u>before</u> the main verb and <u>after</u> *be*. Frequency expressions usually go at the end of the sentence or at the beginning.

Present continuous: *be* + (verb + *-ing*)

Use	Example	Notes/Problems
1 For actions happening **now/ at the moment**.	*We can't go out. It's raining.* *What are you doing here?* *I'm waiting for a friend.*	❗ Don't use the present simple: NOT ~~What do you do here?~~ ~~I wait for a friend.~~ ❗ Remember the spelling rules for the *-ing* form: *write → writing sit → sitting study → studying*
2 For **future arrangements** (+ time expression, e.g *tonight/ tomorrow*).	*What are you doing tonight?* *I'm going to the cinema.*	NOT ~~What do you do tonight?~~ ~~I go to the cinema.~~ ❗ Some verbs, e.g. *be, like, want, know, need, have* (possession) are NOT normally used in the present continuous, e.g. *I need a holiday.* NOT ~~I'm needing a holiday.~~

The gerund (verb + *-ing*), *to* + infinitive

Use	Example	Notes/Problems
Use **the gerund**: 1 after **prepositions**.	*She left without saying goodbye.* *I'm thinking of buying a flat.*	
2 after **certain verbs**.	*I love cooking but I hate cleaning.* *I don't mind driving you to the airport.*	The most common verbs followed by the gerund are: *like, love, hate, enjoy, mind, finish, stop.*
3 as the **subject** of a sentence.	*Eating in restaurants is expensive.* *Swimming is good exercise.*	
Use *to* + **infinitive**: 1 to answer the question *Why?* (**reason/ purpose**)	*Why did you to go to Mexico?* *To see my aunt and uncle.*	NOT ~~For see .../ For to see ...~~
2 after **adjectives**.	*It's difficult to learn a language.*	
3 after **certain verbs**.	*Would you like to come?* *I'm hoping to get a better job soon.*	The most common verbs followed by the infinitive (+ *to*) are: *would like, want, need, decide, hope, expect, plan, forget, seem, try, promise, offer, refuse, learn, manage.* ❗ *begin* and *start* can be followed by either the gerund or the infinitive.

Grammar Summary

Expressions of quantity

Use	Example	Notes/Problems
1 With **plural countable nouns** (e.g. *chips*) use: *How many ...?*	How many chips do you want?	
For big quantities: *a lot of/lots of* in (+) sentences *(not) many* in (−) and (?)	I eat a lot of vegetables. Do you eat many potatoes?	But *I eat a lot.* NOT ~~I eat a lot of/lots of.~~ ❗ You can use *a lot (of)* in (?) and (−) in informal English.
For small quantities: *a few*	I only want a few strawberries.	You can also use *very few* (= less than a few).
For zero quantity: *not ... any* (*none* in short answers)	I don't want any potatoes. How many potatoes do you want? None, thanks.	
2 With **uncountable nouns** (e.g. *bread*) use: *How much ...?*	How much bread do you eat?	
For big quantities: *a lot of/lots of* (+) *(not) much* (−) and (?)	I eat a lot of fish. I don't eat much rice. Do you drink much coffee?	
For small quantities: *a little*	I only want a little ice cream.	You can also use *very little* (= less than a little)
For zero quantity: *not ... any* (*none* in short answers)	I don't eat any meat. Would you like some wine? No, none for me, thanks.	

too, too much, too many, (not) enough

Use	Example	Notes/Problems
To say something is more than you need/want use: *too* + adjective *too much* + uncountable noun *too many* + countable noun	Ugh! It's too sweet. I've made too much pasta. You eat too many burgers.	NOT ~~It's too much sweet.~~
To say something is (not) sufficient use: *enough* + noun adjective + *enough*	Have we got enough eggs? This soup isn't hot enough for me.	NOT ~~eggs enough~~ ~~enough hot~~

FILE 3

used to / didn't use to (+ infinitive)

Use	Example	Notes/Problems
1 For **past habits**.	I used to play basketball (but I don't now).	❗ *used to* does not exist in the present tense. To talk about a present habit, use *usually* + present simple, e.g. *I usually get up at 8.00.* NOT ~~I use to get up ...~~
2 For **past situations or states** that have changed.	She used to be a nurse (but now she's a teacher). He used to have long hair (but now it's short).	❗ Don't confuse *I used to* + infinitive with *I'm used to* + gerund. *I used to drive all day* = I drove all day in the past but now I don't. *I'm used to driving all day* = I'm accustomed to driving all day. It's not a problem for me.

make, let (+ person + infinitive), be allowed to (+ infinitive)

Use	Example	Notes/Problems
Use *let* to talk about giving permission.	*Our teachers let us wear what we like.*	NOT ~~Our teachers let us to wear...~~
Use *make* to say what **A** obliges **B** to do.	*Our boss makes us work late.* *Does your teacher make you speak English in class?*	NOT ~~Our boss makes us to work late.~~
Use *be allowed to* to say what you can/can't do.	*We aren't allowed to smoke in the office.*	

can, could, be able to (+ infinitive)

Use	Example	Notes/Problems
Use *can/could* to say that something is possible or that someone has the ability to do something.	*I can speak German.* *They can come at 7 o'clock.* *She couldn't help me.*	Don't use *to* after *can/could*, e.g. NOT ~~I can to speak...~~
Use *be able to* when there is no form of *can*, e.g. in the present perfect or infinitive.	*I'll be able to drive next year.* *She's never been able to park.* *I'd like to be able to dance well.*	❗ Compare *could* and *was/were able to*: Use *could* to talk about a general ability, e.g. *My grandfather could play the violin.* Use *was/were able to* (NOT ~~could~~) when someone did something on <u>one particular occasion</u>, e.g. *Although the restaurant was very full, we were able to get a table.*

any more

Use	Example	Notes/Problems
Use *any more* at the end of a sentence with a (−) verb to say that a past situation doesn't exist now.	*I don't see her any more.* *He doesn't work here any more.* *He left last year.*	(= I used to see her but now I don't.) *any longer/no longer* means the same as *any more* but is more formal, e.g. *This ticket isn't valid any longer.* or *This ticket is no longer valid.*

The definite article: *the*

Use	Example	Notes/Problems
Use *the*: 1 when you talk about a **specific** person, thing or place.	*I asked the teacher about the date of the exam.*	
2 when there's only one of something or it's clear what you're talking about.	*We looked at the moon.* *He opened the door and came into the classroom.*	(= There's only one moon)
3 with musical instruments.	*I can play the piano but not the violin.*	
Don't use *the*: 1 when you're talking about things or people **in general**.	*Men/women are selfish.* *Footballers earn a lot of money.* *Love is more important than money.*	NOT ~~The men...~~ ~~The footballers...~~ ~~The love...~~, etc.
2 with *school, university, work, bed, hospital, church, prison* when you're talking about the place in general (and after the verbs *be in/at, go to, get to, start, finish, leave*)	*She's at school.* *I start work at 8.00.* *How often do you go to church?*	NOT ~~She's at the school.~~ ~~I start the work...~~
3 with *next/last + week/month/year/ summer/Monday*, etc.	*I went to Amsterdam last month.* *What are you doing next weekend?*	NOT ~~the last month~~, etc.
4 with sports, meals, and school subjects.	*I hate football but I love cycling.* *We always have lunch together.* *I'm terrible at maths.*	NOT ~~the football~~, etc.

FILE 4

Future forms: *will*, *going to*, present continuous

Use	Example	Notes/Problems
1 For **plans** (something which you have already decided to do) use *going to*.	*I'm going to look for a job.* *What are you going to do when you finish university?*	(= I've already decided.) (= What are your plans?) ❗ With *go* you can leave out the infinitive, e.g. *I'm going (to go) out tonight.*
2 For **unplanned decisions/offers** (when you make a decision at the moment of speaking) use *will/won't* + infinitive.	*I'll answer the phone!* A *This case is heavy.* B *I'll help you.* or *Shall I help you?*	NOT ~~I answer …~~ NOT ~~I help you.~~ ❗ If the offer is a question, use *shall* with *I* or *we*, NOT ~~will~~.
3 For **predictions** use either *will* or *going to*.	*I think Brazil will win/are going to win.*	(= it's my opinion.)
4 For **future arrangements** we often use the present continuous, especially with the verbs *go, come, see, meet, leave, have* (*dinner*, etc.)	*I'm having dinner with Ann tomorrow.* *We're meeting some friends tonight.*	(= We've already booked the restaurant.) *going to* is also possible here, e.g. *I'm going to have dinner with Ann tomorrow.*

may (not), *might (not)*, (+ infinitive)

Use	Example	Notes/Problems
To say what is possibly going to happen (but you aren't sure).	*Take your umbrella. It might rain.*	(= it's a possibility.) NOT ~~It's possible that it rains.~~
	Jane may not come tomorrow.	(= maybe she won't come.)
		may and *might* are the same, but *might* is more common in spoken English.

Future time clauses: *when …*, *as soon as …*, *until …*

Use	Example	Notes/Problems
Use *when*, *as soon as*, and *until* + the present tense to talk about the future.	*Turn off the TV when you go to bed.* *Come and see us as soon as you have time.* *We'll stay here until she comes.*	NOT ~~when you'll go to bed.~~ ~~as soon as you'll have time.~~ ~~until she'll come.~~

First conditional: *if* + present simple, *will/won't* + infinitive

Use	Example	Notes/Problems
To talk about a **future possibility** and its **consequence**.	*If I see her, I'll tell her.* *Phone me if you get home before 6.00.* *She won't wear it if she doesn't like it.*	*unless* can be used with a (+) verb instead of *if … not*, e.g. *She won't wear it unless she likes it.*

Second conditional: *if* + past simple, *would/wouldn't* + infinitive

Use	Example	Notes/Problems
To talk about an **imaginary present or future situation** and its consequence.	*If I had a lot of money, I'd buy a big house.*	(= but I'm poor so I can't.) *I'd = I would*
	If he was richer, he'd be happier.	❗ With the verb *be*, you can use *was* or *were* for *I* and *he/she/it*, e.g. *If I/he **was** rich …* or *If I/he **were** rich …*

FILE 5

Modal verbs of obligation: *must / mustn't, have to / don't have to, should / shouldn't* + infinitive

Use	Examples	Notes/Problems
Use **must**: 1 for obligation. 2 for strong recommendation.	*I must remember her birthday.* *You <u>must</u> see that film*	*must* is especially used when the obligation comes from the speaker. It is always stressed for strong recommendation.
Use **mustn't**: 1 when you want to say 'not allowed', 'you can't'. 2 for strong recommendation.	*You mustn't park here.* *You <u>mustn't</u> miss the concert.*	
Use **have to**: for obligation.	*You have to drive on the left.* *I have to work on Saturdays.*	*have to* is especially used for laws, or a general / external obligation.
Use **don't have to**: for no obligation / necessity.	*I don't have to work on Saturdays.* *It's free. You don't have to pay.*	(− it's not necessary) NOT ~~I mustn't go to work …~~
Use **should / shouldn't**: for recommendation, advice.	*You should drive more slowly.* *You shouldn't eat so much.*	You can also use *ought to*, e.g. *You ought to drive more slowly.*

Past perfect simple: *had / hadn't* + past participle

Use	Examples	Notes/Problems
To say that **one past action** happened **earlier** than another.	*We arrived too late. They'd already gone.*	(= they went **before** we arrived.) **!** Don't confuse: *'d* + past participle (= *had*) with *'d* + infinitive (= *would*)

Defining relative clauses: *a person who …, a thing which …,* etc.

Use	Examples	Notes/Problems

To give **essential information** about a person, place, or thing.
Use **who** for people.
    which for things / animals.
    where for places.
    whose to say *of who / of which*.
	She's the woman who works with me.
	It's a book which tells you how to relax.
	That's the flat where Alice lives.
	That's the girl whose father is a film director.
		You can use *that* instead of *who* or *which*, especially when speaking, e.g. *She's the woman that works with me.*

who / which are often omitted when the verb after the relative pronoun has a different subject.	*She's the girl (who) I met last night.*	The subject of *met* is I. *whose* and *where* can never be omitted.

Non-defining relative clauses: *John, who's 23, is …,* etc.

Use	Examples	Notes/Problems
To give **extra information** about a person, place or thing. Use *who, which, where,* and *whose*.	*Chester, where my parents live, is a beautiful town.* *Last week I saw my aunt, who's nearly 80 years old.* *This picture, which was painted in 1923, is worth millions of pounds.*	Always put commas (or a comma and a full stop) before and after the clause. In these clauses *who, which, where,* and *whose* can't be omitted. **!** You can't use *that* instead of *who / which*.

FILE 6

The passive: *be* + past participle

Use	Example	Notes/Problems
1 When you are **not especially interested in the person or people** who did an action.	*The book was written in 1990. Rice is grown in Japan. In Britain, films for cameras are sold in chemist's.*	(= we are interested in the book, not the writer.) The passive is often used in English where other languages use an impersonal verb.
2 When you <u>also</u> **want to mention the person or people that did the action** use *by*.	*The new building was opened by the Prime Minister.*	

Narrative tenses: past simple, past perfect, past continuous

Use	Example	Notes/Problems
Use the **past simple** to talk about consecutive actions in the past.	*She bought a newspaper and then she had a coffee in a small café.*	(= she had a coffee <u>after</u> she bought the paper.)
Use the **past perfect** to talk about something which happened <u>before</u> the time we are talking about.	*When she went to pay, she saw that they had made a mistake in the bill.*	(= they made the mistake <u>before</u> she paid.)
Use the **past continuous** (*was/were* + verb + *-ing*) to describe a longer continuous past action.	*The sun was shining when she left the café.*	*The sun was shining* = a longer continuous action; *she left* = a shorter action which happens in the middle of the continuous one.

Comparative and superlative adjectives and adverbs: *better, more slowly, the biggest,* etc.

Use	Example	Notes/Problems
To compare two people, things or actions use a **comparative adjective** or **adverb** + *than*.	*Your steak is bigger than mine. I can speak English better than my sister.*	NOT ~~Your steak is more big than mine~~.
To express maximums or minimums use *the* + a **superlative adjective** or **adverb**.	*She's the youngest in the class. Skiing is the most exciting sport. She plays the best.*	NOT ~~of the class~~. ~~the more exciting~~.

(not) as + adjective/adverb + *as*

Use	Example	Notes/Problems
To say that two things are the same use: 1 *as* + adjective/adverb + *as*. 2 *the same as*.	*My book's as good as yours. Her dress is the same as mine.*	NOT ~~as good than~~ ~~the same than~~
To say that two things are different use *not* + *as* + adjective/adverb + *as*.	*London isn't as noisy as Tokyo. I can't cook as well as you.*	

FILE 7

Modals of deduction: *must, might/could, can't* (+ infinitive)

Use	Example	Notes/Problems
Use *must* to say that you're sure that something is (logically) true.	*He must be out. All the lights are off. They must be Italian. They're speaking Italian.*	! Don't confuse with *must* for obligation. The opposite of *must be* is **can't be**, NOT ~~mustn't be~~.
Use *might/could* to say that something is possibly true.	*She might be working. I'm not sure.* *He might be at home or he might be at the gym.*	You can also use *may* instead of *could*. It is more formal. ! Don't use *can* for possibilities. NOT ~~He can be at home~~.
Use *can't* to say that something is impossible.	*It can't be true! I don't believe it. They can't be in New York! I saw them this morning.*	NOT ~~couldn't be~~

Reported speech: statements and questions

Use	Example	Notes/Problems
Use **reported speech** when you talk in the past about what somebody said, asked, or wrote.	*I asked him where he lived.* *He said (that) he lived in Milan.* *The brochure said (that) the hotel was new.*	In reported speech the verb tense changes, e.g. present → past. *might, could, would, should,* and *ought* stay the same. Certain time expressions often change, e.g. *today → that day.*
1 Use **reported statements** to say what somebody said.	*He said (that) he was tired.* *She told me (that) she hadn't finished.*	Introduce a reported statement with *said,* or *told* + person. NOT ~~She said me …~~ *that* is optional after *said/ told me.*
2 Use **reported questions** to say what somebody asked.	*He asked me what my name was.* *She asked me if/whether I liked sport.*	NOT ~~He asked me what was my name.~~ ~~He asked me did I like sport.~~ **!** The word order is subject + verb.

Reported speech: imperatives: *told / asked* + person + *to* + infinitive

Use	Example	Notes/Problems
Use **reported imperatives and requests** to say what somebody told or asked somebody to do.	*He told us to help him.* *She told them not to wait.* *We asked him to tell us the time.*	NOT ~~He told us that we helped him.~~ The (−) infinitive is *not to (be,* etc.). For requests use *asked* not *told.*

Connectors: *although / though, however, on the other hand, as well, also*

Use	Example	Notes/Problems
Use *although/ though, however,* or *on the other hand* to introduce contrasting information.	*We had a good time, although/though it rained a lot.* *She usually listens to pop music.* *On the other hand,/ However, she likes opera too.*	*although/ though* mean the same but *though* isn't normally used at the beginning of a sentence. *on the other hand/ however* usually go at the beginning of a sentence. They can only be used to introduce a contrasting idea.
Use *also* or *as well* to introduce additional similar information.	*He had some chocolate cake, and he also had an ice cream.* *He had some chocolate cake and an ice cream as well.*	*Also* usually goes <u>before</u> the main verb, but <u>after</u> *be.* *As well* (like *too*) always goes at the end of a phrase or sentence.

in case

Use	Example	Notes/Problems
Use *in case* when you talk about doing something because something <u>might</u> happen later.	*Take a map in case you get lost.* *She **took** her passport in case she **needed** it.*	(− because there's a possibility you'll get lost.) Use the present tense after *in case.* NOT ~~in case you will get lost.~~ You can also use the past after *in case* if the main verb is in the past. **!** Remember *in case* doesn't mean *if.*

FILE 8

Third conditional: *if* + past perfect, *would / wouldn't have* + past participle

Use	Example	Notes/Problems
To speculate about something that happened in the past and how it could have been different.	*If I'd worked harder, I would have passed the exam.* *You wouldn't have been late if you'd got up earlier.*	(= but I didn't work hard so I didn't pass it.) You can use *could* or *might* instead of *would.* **!** Don't use *would have* after *if.* NOT ~~if you would have got up earlier.~~

FILE 1

T1.3

I Have you ever had a serious argument with Andy?

C Yes, I have. Only one, but it was a big one, in fact it almost finished our friendship.

I What was the argument about?

C A girl. She was called Tessa and we met her at a friend's birthday party. Andy was talking to her and I came up and introduced myself. We both talked to her a lot during the evening. We both liked her. Then when the party finished, I asked her for her phone number. And Andy asked her too. But we didn't tell each other. In fact, we didn't say anything about Tessa after the party. Anyway, next day I phoned her and I asked her if she wanted to go out that night and she said, 'OK'. Two hours later Andy called her and asked her out too and she said, 'Oh sorry, I can't. I'm already going out with your friend tonight.' When I saw him the next day, Andy was furious. I've never seen him so angry and we had a terrible argument. I said to him, 'Come on. What's the problem? We both did the same thing – it's just that I did it first.' But we didn't speak to each other for about a month. The funny thing was that later Tessa told me that when I phoned her she wasn't sure if it was me or Andy who she was talking to because she couldn't remember our names.

I Are you and Andy still best friends?

C Well, Tessa and I started going out together but we broke up after a few weeks and little by little, Andy and I started talking again. Yes, we're still best friends but it's a subject that we don't talk about.

T1.9

I So, Jessica, could you tell us about other things that affect our personality?

J Yes, well of course your position in the family isn't the only thing that counts. It also depends on your sex and the sex of the other children in the family. For example, if you're a first child and you're a girl you will be more jealous if the second child is a boy, and vice versa. This is partly because mothers tend to show more interest in the second child if they're a different sex from the first.

If you're a girl in the middle of three girls, you will probably rebel against feminine things and want to wear jeans and play football. On the other hand, if you're a girl in the middle of boys you'll probably do exactly the opposite and like dolls and pretty dresses.

The parent you spend most time with or who you have the closest relationship with will also have an influence on your personality. Girls who have a lot of attention from their fathers in the early years are usually more extrovert and confident. A good example of this is the ex-prime minister of Britain, Margaret Thatcher. And boys who spend most of their time with their mothers, maybe because their parents are separated, are often better at communicating and more sociable than boys who spend most of their time with their fathers.

T1.11

Right, can I have your attention please? Good morning to you all. My name is David Hudson, the Director of Studies. I'm going to speak slowly and clearly so that you can all understand me, but if you don't, don't worry, as you can ask any questions when I've finished. First, I'd like to welcome you all to the Cambridge Language school. We are very happy that you have chosen to study here with us, and we will do all we can to help you enjoy your time with us, and of course to help you learn as much English as possible.

Now, all of you have met your host families. If any of you have got a problem with your family, please go and talk to the accommodation officer, Sharon Black, this afternoon. Her office is next to the reception area, on the left, and she will be there all afternoon from one o'clock until five o'clock. Now in a few moments, you're going to do a short written placement test which will start at 9.30 here in the main hall. This test is so that we can find out what your level of English is. Then there'll be a coffee break at half past ten, and after the break we'll tell you which class you're in and the name of your teacher. Your first class will start at eleven o'clock.

Lunch will be at 1.30 in the canteen, which is on the ground floor and then this afternoon, for those of you who want to go, there is an optional tour of Cambridge for all students, and you'll be visiting some of the university colleges. So if you want to go on the tour, please be outside the main gate of the school at 2.45 where your tour guide, Kevin, will be waiting for you. The tour will start at 3.00 on the dot, so don't be late. If anybody has any questions about anything, you can either ask me now or speak to your teacher. And if you have any problems during the course, my office is on the first floor and the door's always open. So, now it's time for your level test …

FILE 2

T2.3

I How often do you have to work nights?

E I'm on night duty for two weeks out of every five. Quite a lot really.

I What time do you start and finish work when you're on nights?

E We start at 10 o'clock at night and finish at 8 o'clock in the morning.

I So what time do you go to bed?

E As soon as I get home. About 8.30 usually.

I Do you find it difficult to sleep?

E No, not at all. I fall asleep immediately, and I sleep really deeply, at least for the first two or three hours.

I How long do you sleep for?

E It depends. Between four or five hours normally. I wake up at about one o'clock. The problem is that somebody or something always wakes me up, like the phone or the doorbell.

I How do you feel when you wake up?

E If I've slept five hours or more, I feel fine, but if I've only slept three or four, not so good.

I What do you eat or drink during the night?

E Between 1 and 2 o'clock in the morning I have lunch. But only something light like a sandwich, because the canteen's closed.

I Do you have a big breakfast when you finish work?

E Oh, no, I never have breakfast. The only thing I think about when I finish work is going to bed.

I What are the main problems of working nights. For example do you find it difficult to stay awake?

E Yes, I think we all find it difficult to stay awake. Especially between 4.30 and 6 o'clock. That's the worst time. You have to make a real effort not to fall asleep.

I Have you ever fallen asleep at work?

E No, never.

I As a nurse, do you think it's bad for your body to work at night?

E Yes, absolutely. In fact there are studies which show that people who work at night get old more quickly than people who work during the day, which is a bit worrying!

I Apart from feeling tired, what other problems are there?

E The worst thing is that when you're on night duty, you still have to do things in the morning because the world isn't made for people who work at night. For example, the banks are only open in the morning, children have to go to school in the morning and so on. The other big problem is your social life. Sometimes when I'm working nights, friends invite me for lunch because they know I can't go to dinner at night. But they forget that if I meet them for lunch at one o'clock, then I can only sleep for three or four hours that morning. That's a problem.

T2.4

I … So, what do people think of these vegetables? And especially what do children think? What do chocolate carrots really taste like? Well, we've got two top chefs with us today, and a child, James, who, as we speak, is actually eating them … but we'll ask James for his opinion in a moment. Before that, I'd like a quick comment from our two chefs. First, Marco Pierre White from the Hyde Park Hotel. What do you think, Marco?

M Well, I have three young children myself who don't like eating vegetables. But I would not give them chocolate-flavoured carrots. Personally, I think it's much better to bribe children, for example, I promise them a trip to the park if they eat their vegetables. Anything is better than these products. They will destroy children's future eating habits.

I Well, next we have Nico Ladenis from the Chez Nico restaurant. Do you agree with Marco?

N Absolutely. I cannot imagine anybody eating these chocolate carrots. Chocolate and carrots just don't go together. It's a crazy mixture. The colour is horrible. People eat with their eyes, it's the first sense. I'm sure children won't be attracted to them.

I Thanks, Nico. Well, we'll be coming back to our chefs in a minute. But before we go any further, the moment of truth. James, who's eight years old has just been tasting some of the new vegetables. What do you think of the carrots, James?

J They're delicious. They taste like hot chocolate. They're not like the carrots my Mum gives me.

I So, you like them?

J Well, I think the carrots are very nice on their own but I don't think they'd be very nice with chicken or hamburgers.

I And what about the chewing-gum flavoured peas?

J Urgh! They're disgusting. I don't like peas and I don't like chewing gum either. I only had one spoonful, and I didn't want any more.

I So, would you like to have the carrots and the peas again?

J No, thank you.

T2.9

P And now we have this week's edition of *Medicine Today*, presented as usual by Keith Davey.

K Good evening. And our first story tonight on *Medicine Today* is the strange story of Mr Gordon Pringle. Mr Pringle is a man who never has any problems waking up in the morning. Why? Because he never sleeps … Difficult to believe? Well, we've got Mr Pringle and his wife Angela here in the studio to tell us all about it. So tell us Gordon, when was the last time you slept?

G I can tell you exactly. It was 13th September 1987.

K You mean you haven't slept since September 1987.

G That's right.

K And why is that? What happened to you?

G Well, on 14th September 1987 I had an accident. I was cycling home from work and I was hit by a car. I fell off my bike and I suffered head injuries and was taken to hospital.

K And what happened to you there?

G Well, I had an operation, and when I woke up after the operation I found I was suffering from complete insomnia. I couldn't sleep. The doctors gave me all kinds of drugs, but I'm afraid none of them worked. And since then I haven't been able to sleep at all. I often feel exhausted, but I just can't sleep.

K Is this true, Angela?

A Yes, I can honestly say I haven't seen my husband asleep since 1987.

K And is this a problem for you, having a husband who is awake twenty-four hours a day?

A Well it's not ideal, as you can imagine.

K And what do you do with all these extra hours, Gordon. Do you do all the housework?

G No, I don't. At night, I go to bed when my wife goes to bed and I just lie on the bed, relax and meditate. I think about nice things – it's not as good as sleeping but it helps me.

K Gordon, the doctors say that you're perfectly fit and healthy and I must say you look very well. But are you happy about being awake all the time?

G No, not at all. Recently, I've been having tests at the Sleep Research Unit of the local university and I'm hoping that one day the scientists will discover why I can't sleep. I'm sure you can believe me when I tell you I'd give anything for just one good night's sleep.

K Thank you very much, Gordon and Angela Pringle.

FILE 3

T3.1

I Where were you when you heard about Princess Diana's death?

N I was in bed. It was Sunday morning about 7.00. I was asleep and a friend phoned me to tell me the news. I just couldn't believe it at first. It was like a nightmare. She was so young, and so beautiful.

I Did you realize then that your life had changed completely?

N No, I didn't, not at first. I just thought about Diana herself and her two boys. My job didn't seem to matter compared with this terrible tragedy. But then after a few days I started thinking, 'What about me? What do I do now? I'm unemployed.'

I Can you tell us about what you used to do?

N I used to impersonate Princess Diana. That was my job. People used to pay me to pretend to be her.

I How did you get the job?

N Well, physically I looked like Diana a lot, and one day a friend suggested I send my photograph to a model agency where they employed lookalikes. A lookalike is somebody who looks like somebody famous. And I soon got a lot of work.

I What did you do when you were working?

N All kinds of things. I used to open new shops, I used to give interviews on TV, on comedy programmes. I used to give the cheques to lottery winners. That kind of thing.

I How exactly did you use to copy her appearance?

N Well I used to dress like her of course, and I used to have short hair, just like hers. In fact, I used to take a copy of *Hello!* magazine into my hairdresser's, show him a photo of Diana, and say 'Copy that!' I even tried to copy her voice.

I So what are you doing now?

N Well, now I've started doing a computer course and I'm sure I'll be able to find another job in the future.

I Have you changed your appearance since Diana died?

N Yes. The day after her death I went straight to the hairdresser and had my hair cut shorter, and changed the colour. I didn't want to look like her any more.

I Has her death changed you in any other way?

N Yes, it has. I didn't use to spend enough time with my children because I was away working so often. Now, I take them to school every day. And then I think I used to worry too much about the future, and not enough about the present. When Diana died, I realized that what happened to her could happen to any of us. You have to live for today, not for tomorrow.

T3.6

I In England today are schools mixed or single sex?

S Well, there are both. Fifty years ago all schools used to be single sex, I mean girls only or boys only. Then in the 1970s, many schools changed and became mixed because people thought then that it was better for boys and girls to be educated together. So today there are a lot of mixed schools, although there are also single-sex schools.

I Do parents still prefer mixed schools?

S No, things have changed. Today many parents, especially parents of girls, think that their children get a better education in single-sex schools. So single-sex schools have started to become more popular again.

I Is it true that girls do better at single-sex schools?

S Well, academically I don't think there is any difference between single-sex and mixed schools. Generally girls do well at both kinds of schools, and they get the same exam results. But psychologically, I think girls do better at single-sex schools.

I Why is that?

S In my opinion, girls do better psychologically because they learn to be more self-confident and they are less worried about their appearance. In mixed schools, girls worry too much about how attractive they are. For example, in some classes like PE, physical education that is, some girls really suffer. In fact, in the last mixed school where I worked the boys and girls had physical education separately for this reason.

I What about boys?

S Well, with boys, it's often the opposite situation. Today, many parents of boys want to send them to mixed schools. They think that they will do better, because the girls will be a positive influence. They think that girls will make the boys more civilized.

I And is this true?

S Well, yes, I think it is. Boys do better in mixed schools because there is a calmer atmosphere and more discipline. It really does seem that boys behave better when there are girls around.

I So, generally speaking, who does better academically at mixed schools?

S Oh, the girls. They get better exam results than boys in both kinds of schools.

FILE 4

T4.1

Job 1

Well, you need to be good with people. I'd say that's the most important thing. And you need to be really patient. You don't need any qualifications except languages, of course. The more languages you speak, the better.
The good side of the job is definitely the travelling. I've been able to get to know places I never dreamed of seeing, like Bali and Honolulu. And you meet a lot of nice people too.
The bad side is that it's not very well paid. The salary's quite low compared to other jobs. And the job itself *can* sometimes be very stressful. There are nearly always problems – overbooking in hotels, flight delays, luggage that doesn't arrive, people wanting to change their rooms and things like that.
The worst experience I've had was this awful customer who spent at least two hours a day complaining to me, and always about the same things. He complained about the size of the swimming pool, then about the music in the restaurant, then about the food. Finally he even locked me in his room one day to make me listen to his complaints. After that we paid for a plane ticket for him to go home a week early. He was the worst customer I've had.

Job 2

I think the most important thing is that you have to love children, and be good at getting on with them. You don't need any qualifications, you just have to be able to speak a bit of English.
The good side of the job is definitely the children. Although sometimes they're naughty or difficult, most of the time I really enjoy looking after them. And I've learned a lot of English talking to them and playing with them. I also have a lot of free time, so I can go to classes, or go out with my friends at night.
The bad side is the parents of the children. They're not friendly to me and they don't get on with each other. They're always arguing. I don't like them. And I have to do a lot of housework. Too much.
My worst experience was one night when the phone rang, and I picked it up and said 'Hello?' It was a woman and she thought I was the children's mother. She said, 'I'm going to tell you everything. I'm in love with your husband!' Then when I explained that I was only the au pair, she became completely hysterical! That evening, when the wife wasn't there, I told her husband about the phone call. First he laughed and said it was a joke, but then he offered me more money. I didn't accept it.

T4.6

E Good morning, Mr Keeler.

K Good morning, Eve.

E Oh, Mr Keeler, Mr Walford called at nine and asked you to go and see him as soon as you got in.

K Which Mr Walford?

E Senior. The big boss.

K Oh right. I'll go there straight away.

W Come in.

K You called for me, Mr Walford.

W Sit down, Keeler. This man of yours, Stanford …

K Yes, I'm very sorry about him Mr Walford. I tried to stop him coming to see you.

W Yes, but he came. A very emotional young man. A good man too. I asked Mr Bowles in the Personnel Department about him. He said he was the best young man in your department. What a pity. I didn't want to lose him. But after the things he said to me, I couldn't let him stay. He even called me an old …

K I'm terribly sorry, Mr Walford. I didn't want to sack him either. But the Personnel Department knows best …

W Did you get the order from Mr Bowles?

K Yes, sir.

W When?

K On Wednesday. It was in the lift, actually. He told me that Stamford wasn't the right man for the job — "StaMford" — Oh my God.

W Yes, Keeler. Stamford. With an 'm'. You sacked the wrong man. Tell me something, Keeler. How long have you been working here?

T4.11

I was born in 1940, so in 1968, the time of the photo, I was 28. My grandfather was called Count Maurice de Bendern. He was extremely rich – mostly because of all the property and land that he owned in Paris and in Monaco. Well, for some reason – I don't really know why – perhaps because I was pretty – he chose me to be his heir, so when he died I would inherit everything. He paid for me to be educated at all the best boarding schools in England, and his dream was for me to marry someone from a European Royal family, an aristocrat, like him.

But I was a rebel. I went to New York and worked for a short time as a model. After that I went to Paris. It was 1968, and it was a wonderful time. So many things were in the air – freedom, revolution. There was a lot of street fighting, a lot of demonstrations, and the French police were everywhere. I wasn't really interested in politics – I wasn't a communist or an anarchist. But I just became intoxicated with the atmosphere and I took part in all the marches. On May 15th I was with thousands of other young people, walking towards the Place de la Bastille. I was tired, so a friend picked me up and carried me on his shoulders, and someone walking next to us said 'Hey, could you hold the flag?' There was so much happening that I didn't realize there were photographers everywhere and that one of them had taken my photo.

The next day the photo was everywhere. It was on the cover of magazines all over the world.

When my grandfather saw the photo, he immediately ordered me to come to see him. He was furious – really angry – and he said that he had decided now **not** to leave me **any** of his money. I walked out of the room and I never saw him again, because he died six months later. So that was it. I didn't inherit anything!

FILE 5

T5.1

If you're looking for a really relaxing weekend, why don't you go to Lisbon? It's one of the most beautiful and romantic cities in Europe, and the good news is you don't have to spend a fortune. Lisbon is still cheap compared to many other European cities.

So, where should you stay? It's easy to find accommodation in Lisbon, except in August when it's normally very crowded. If you don't want to spend too much, there are small hostels which are cheap and clean but quite basic. If you're looking for something more comfortable then you should try one of the bigger hotels, although these can be expensive.

And what about getting around in the city? Well, despite the hills, Lisbon is a good city for walking, but you **must** take a pair of comfortable shoes and make sure you've got a good map of the city. Public transport is good and cheap – even the taxis aren't expensive but they are not recommended for the nervous! Portuguese taxi drivers drive – well, let's say – very quickly. But really the best way to see Lisbon is to do what the Portuguese do and take a tram and the best tram ride of all is the number 28. I strongly recommend it.

There are lots of interesting places to visit in Lisbon, but if you're only going for a weekend, there are two things which you really **must** see. The first is the castle. It's a long walk to get there but when you arrive, you get the most incredible view over the whole city and the river Tajo. The other place you mustn't miss is the Expo site, which is now a cultural centre with a fine collection of museums.

If you like shopping, you **must** go to the Baixa area. That's B-A-I-X-A, where you'll find not only beautiful old traditional shops but also fashionable new clothes shops, and if you want a typical souvenir, don't forget to buy a bottle of port.

What about nightlife in Lisbon? Well, at night I recommend you get a tram up to the *barrio alto* – the high area – which is where all the best restaurants, bars and clubs are. And if you like dancing, why not go to a Brazilian bar? You can hear great music, and see some fantastic dancers.

Well, that's all the time we've got to tell you about the enchanting city of Lisbon. Next week, we'll be telling you all you need to know about Amsterdam …

T5.5

1 *When did you first learn to drive?*
I didn't start learning to drive until I was 25. That was in 1981. In fact, when I got my driving licence, I had already won an Olympic medal.
2 *Do you like driving?*
No, I don't, not very much. I must admit I prefer running.

3 *What car have you got now?*
I've got an old Opel, but I'm going to get a new car in the next few weeks. I don't know what model, but it has to be big enough for me, my wife, three children and three dogs.
4 *What's your dream car?*
I haven't got one. I never dream about cars. I dream about lots of other things, but not about cars.
5 *What do you hate most about other drivers?*
When they drive right behind me on the motorway. That really annoys me.
6 *Do you ever go over the speed limit?*
Well, yes I do, I'm sorry to say. I've always liked going fast. I used to go very fast when I was a runner and now I do the same when I'm driving.
7 *What's your favourite car advertisement?*
I like the one with the girl who drops the keys to her Volkswagen car in the street. But it was the girl that I remember, of course, not the car.

T5.8

1 What I really hate are drivers who drive slowly in the middle lane on the motorway. They really drive me mad … I don't want to be sexist but they're usually women drivers …

2 What really annoys me is people on trains who talk on mobile phones. I get the train to work every day, from London to Oxford, and nowadays it's impossible to sleep or read a paper because all around me there are people with their mobiles – and they don't just talk, they shout.

3 What I really hate is computer or video manuals which you can't understand. I've just bought a new PC and I can't understand the manual at all. Why can't they write them in normal English for normal people?

4 What really irritates me is shops where the shop assistants are always standing behind you. Especially in clothes shops, when all you want to do is look at the clothes and see how much they cost. There's always a shop assistant saying, 'Can I help you? Would you like to try it on?' I hate it.

5 What drives me mad is advertising leaflets which come inside magazines or newspapers. Nowadays every time you buy a magazine or a Sunday paper as soon as you pick it up something falls out of it. I just throw it away.

6 What I really hate are plastic shopping bags which break. It's usually the ones they give you at the supermarket. The other day I put my shopping in one, and the bag broke when I was walking home. I had some eggs in there and they broke all over the pavement. It was awful.

FILE 6

T6.1

M Did you do anything at the weekend?
W Yeah, I went to the cinema on Saturday night. I saw the new Woody Allen film.
M What's it like?
W Well, I thought it was brilliant. You must see it. You'd love it.
M Oh yeah? I doubt it. What kind of film is it?
W A comedy.
M Yeah, all his films are comedies. The trouble is I don't find them all that funny. Where's it on?
W At the ABC.
M Who's in it?
W Well, Woody Allen of course. Oh, and that guy who was in *When Harry met Sally*.
M Billy Crystal?
W Yeah, that's right. And Demi Moore. And lots of other people.
M Mia Farrow?
W You must be joking. I don't think they talk to each other any more!
M Anyway, what's it about?
W Well, it's about this man and his psychoanalyst …
M Oh no, not again! That's what **all** his films are about.
W Yes, but this one really **is** good. I think it's one of his best. You must see it.

T6.4

… and to finish tonight on *World Sport* we have some more of those incredible statistics for you. Starting with athletics … Did you know that the oldest marathon runner in the world was Dimitrion Yordanidis from Greece? He completed the Athens marathon in 1976 in 7 hours 33 minutes at the incredible age of 98! And if you think that jogging round the park is hard work, why don't you try the triathlon? The triathlon is probably the world's hardest sport because competitors have to – listen to this – swim 3.8 km, then cycle 180 km, and finally run a marathon, which is 42.195km. Now onto basketball. Well, we all know that basketball players are tall, but the tallest basketball player known is Suleiman Ali Nashnush who played for the Libyan national team in 1962. He was – and I promise this is true – 2.45m tall. I bet he has problems finding clothes to fit him.
And the highest number of points scored by one player in a basketball match? Well that record's held by a Swedish player called Mats Wermelin who scored **all** the points in his team's victory in a tournament in Stockholm in 1974. The final score … 272–nil!
And finally, football. Brazilians love football, but did you know that the largest crowd ever at a football match was in the Maracanã municipal stadium in Rio de Janeiro, Brazil on 16th July 1950 for a match between Brazil and Uruguay? There were almost 200,000 spectators there. Imagine that!
And to finish, here's a really unusual statistic for you. Did you know that the heaviest international goalkeeper on record was Willie (Fatty) Foulke who played for England? He was 1.90m tall and weighed 165 kg. They say they once had to stop the game because he broke the bar of the goal! Perhaps he sat on it! That's all we've got time for tonight on *World Sport* …

T6.9

You're not going to believe this story but it really is true! It happened to me when I was on holiday in Singapore. I'd been working in Hong Kong for three years but I hadn't had the chance to travel and see other places in that part of the world. So, when my contract finished, I decided to have a really good holiday before returning to Britain. A couple of friends and I booked five days at one of the most expensive hotels in Singapore.

One morning, my two friends were swimming and I was sunbathing on the beach and listening to a Phil Collins tape on my Walkman. I had my eyes closed as I was half asleep, when suddenly I heard voices and some people sat down on the beach next to me. I opened my eyes to see who it was and I couldn't believe it. It was Phil Collins! He was with a friend and he was sitting right next to me. The first thing I could think of to do was to give him my Walkman. I said, 'Hi. Have a listen to this.' He took the headphones and put them on. When he heard himself singing, he smiled and said, 'Great song – but I don't like the singer much.'

T6.13

B Can I help you?
P Yes, I'd like two tickets for *Miss Saigon* for Saturday night.
B For this Saturday? The 14th?
P That's right.
B Where do you want them? We've got stalls and circle.
P What's the difference?
B The stalls are here. They're downstairs, so they're nearer the stage. But they're more expensive. The circle is here. It's upstairs, and it's a bit cheaper.
P How much are the seats in the stalls?
B They're 80 each.
P And the circle?
B 65.
P OK, I'll have two circle seats then. As near to the front as possible.
B Seats B16 and 17. They're in the second row, and they're quite central. That'll be 130. How would you like to pay?
P By credit card. Visa.
B Can you sign here, please? Thanks. Here you are then. Two tickets for Saturday night.
P Thanks very much.

FILE 7

T7.1

M Oh, look at that man. The one who's talking on the mobile phone. Do you think he's English?
W No, listen. He's speaking in Spanish. He doesn't look Spanish, though.
M He could be South American, I suppose. I hate mobile phones, don't you?
W Yeah, I do. Look at that woman.
M Which one?
W That one over there. I like her dress. She looks very elegant. Where do you think she's from?
M Well, she can't be English. She's probably French or Italian. Look at those two girls over there. They look exhausted.
W Yes, they must be travelling round Europe. They've got enormous backpacks. Ooh, look at that man over there.
M Which one? Oh yes, the one wearing a cowboy hat.
W He **must** be American. They're the only ones who wear hats like that. Look at that couple over there. They don't look very happy.
M No, they don't. I think they might be having an argument. Look at those other two over there. Do you think she's his wife?
W No way. She's much too young for him. She can't be his wife. She must be his daughter.
M Come on. She's not his daughter. Perhaps they're …

T7.2

W Would you like anything else, sir?
J Some more coffee, please.
W Of course… Here you are, sir. Is this your first time here in Athens?
J No, no, I've been many times but not at this time of year, because my wife doesn't really like the heat, and there are so many tourists. This is the first time I've been here in August, though.
W Are you enjoying your holiday?
J Well, actually I'm not on holiday.
W Ah, you're on business then.
J I'm here to write a travel article.
W So, you are a writer then?
J Well, a journalist. I work for *The Times*.
W You are American then?
J No, not the *New York Times*, the *Sunday Times*. I'm British.
W So, you're here on your own this time?
J Yes, well, as I said before, I'm here for work… Just a couple of days.
W Can I get you anything else?
J No, just the bill, please.
W Right away. Well, I hope you enjoy your stay here in Greece.
J Thank you very much. I'll see you again.

T7.5

T Oh, hello. How did you enjoy New York?
J Oh, it was very nice, very nice.
S Well, New York was great. But I'm afraid the hotel was a disaster.

T Oh, I'm sorry to hear that. What exactly was the problem?

S Well, to start with, you told us that we would have a wonderful view of Central Park. The only thing we could see from our room was the back of another hotel.

T Well, I'm very sorry Mrs Williams, but I think you'll find if you read the brochure carefully that it says *most* rooms have a view of the park, so I'm afraid it was just bad luck.

J I told you that, Stella.

S You also said that the hotel was near Broadway and Fifth Avenue. It wasn't. It was …

T No, we never said that it was *very near* Broadway, we said it was *ideally* located. The hotel is in fact, as I'm sure you found out, very near the subway station that takes you to Broadway.

S Well, I think it's disgraceful. Ideally located should mean *near*. And then the rooms. You said that they had been completely redecorated. Well, they hadn't. They were dirty, and the air-conditioning kept going wrong. Even the TV didn't work.

J Well, it worked, but not very well.

S Oh, shut up, Jack.

T Well, but apart from that everything was OK?

S No, it *wasn't* OK. The brochure said that it had one of New York's finest restaurants. Well we thought the food was *awful*.

J It wasn't awful. It wasn't great.

S It *was* awful. I didn't like it at all.

T Well, I'm very sorry you were disappointed madam.

S It's just not good enough. We paid for a first-class hotel and we didn't get one. We want a complete refund.

T Well, I'm afraid we can't possibly do that. We could perhaps offer you …

S We want either a complete refund or a free holiday. And we're not leaving till we get it. Are we Jack?

J Er, no, no we're not.

T I'm sorry you feel like that. Perhaps you should come and talk to the manager. She's in her office …

T7.7

A Excuse me, but can I ask you, are you British?

J Yes, we are.

A I thought so. I love those British accents. Where are you from?

J We're from Sidcup.

A Sidcup? Now, is that where Shakespeare was born?

J Er no, actually. That's Stratford-upon-Avon.

A Oh, yes of course, Stratford. Tell me, have you been to New York before?

J No, this is our first time.

A Your first time! Wow, that's great! And what do you think of the 'Big Apple'?

S Oh, it's very nice. We like it. It's very interesting.

A And do you like our wonderful food?

S Well, it's … different.

A And how long are you staying?

J Only another day, I'm afraid.

A Oh, that's a pity. You'll have to come back and see New York in the fall. New York's really beautiful in the fall.

J Yes, that would be great …

T7.10

Story 1

I was on holiday in Florida a couple of years ago. I was staying in a really nice four-star hotel. Anyway, on the first morning I got up early because the weather was fantastic and I wanted to go sightseeing and take some photos. I was walking down this narrow street – the street was completely empty and suddenly a man's voice behind me said quietly, 'Don't turn round! You've got a gun in your back.' I could feel something very hard pressing into my back. Then he said, 'Don't say a word or you're a dead man. Give me your camera and your money.'
I was absolutely terrified. I didn't turn round of course. I gave him my camera, all my money and all my credit cards. Then he said, 'Don't move and count to twenty.'
Well, I counted to about fifty and when I looked round, I was alone in the street.
I couldn't believe it. I'd only been in Florida for a few hours and I'd been robbed! But the worst thing is that perhaps he didn't really have a gun in my back. Perhaps it was just his hand. I'll never know now.

Story 2

This happened to me a few years ago when I was a student. I was travelling in India, and I didn't have much money so I always stayed in these really cheap hotels. Well, I arrived in Calcutta one evening, and found a small hotel near the station. I'd been travelling all day and I was absolutely exhausted so I went straight to bed. In the middle of the night, I suddenly woke up because I could feel something on my pillow. I switched on the light and I saw that it was an enormous cockroach. It was about 5 or 6 cm long and I promise I'm not exaggerating. I jumped out of bed and then I saw that the whole room was *full* of giant cockroaches, on the walls, on the ceiling, everywhere. So I ran out to reception in my pyjamas and I shouted at the receptionist, 'Come quickly. My room is full of cockroaches.' The receptionist didn't seem at all surprised. He just gave me a can of insect spray and said, 'Here you are. Spray your room with this.' But I couldn't go back in there, so I said, 'No, *you* do it.' In the end he sprayed it, but I was so terrified I spent the night on a chair in reception. Next morning when I went back to my room to get my clothes, the room was just full of dead cockroaches. It was the most disgusting thing I've ever seen.

FILE 8

T8.1

The sinking of the *Titanic*
Sunday, 14th April 1912. 11.30 p.m.
It was a freezing cold night with a sky full of stars. The *Titanic* was travelling across the Atlantic to New York on its first voyage. It was travelling at full speed. The *Titanic* was the biggest, fastest, and most luxurious ship in the world. There were 2,207 people on board. Among them were some of the richest and most famous people in the world, including ten millionaires.

11.40 p.m. Most of the passengers were sleeping or getting ready for bed. Suddenly in the darkness one of the sailors saw an enormous dark object. 'Iceberg ahead!' he shouted. The huge ship turned slowly to avoid it, but it was too late. The *Titanic* hit the side of the iceberg, which made a hole in the side of the ship more than 100 metres long. Water began to rush in … When the engines stopped, the captain went down to see exactly what had happened. With him was the ship's designer, Thomas Andrews.
'What do you think, Thomas? Is it serious?'
'I'm afraid it is, Captain. The ship's going to sink in less than two hours.'
'Sink? Are you sure?'
'I'm certain. You'll have to abandon ship.'
But Captain Smith and Thomas Andrews knew something that none of the passengers knew. The Titanic had only 20 lifeboats, enough for about half the people on board.

12.10 a.m. The two radio officers on the *Titanic* began sending the desperate SOS message, 'We have hit an iceberg. We are sinking fast. Come immediately.' The nearest ship, the *Carpathia*, was four hours away. As soon as it heard the message, it started coming at full speed to help.

12.25 a.m. Captain Smith gave the order to abandon ship – 'Women and children first'. The *Titanic*'s orchestra of eight musicians began playing cheerful dance music on deck to keep the passengers calm. The first lifeboat was lowered into the water.

2.00 a.m. The last lifeboat left the *Titanic*. At the final moment, Bruce Ismay, the director of the company which owned the ship, got into the lifeboat. The men, women and children who were still on the ship now had no hope of rescue. The orchestra continued playing.

2.20 a.m. With an awful noise, the *Titanic* disappeared completely into the sea. Immediately afterwards the people in the lifeboats heard the terrible shouts and screams of the passengers in the freezing water. After half an hour, the noise finally stopped.

3.30 a.m. The *Carpathia* finally arrived an hour and ten minutes after the *Titanic* had sunk, and the 705 passengers in the lifeboats were rescued. The *Carpathia* searched the area where the *Titanic* had sunk, but they found no more survivors. 1,502 people had drowned.

Oxford University Press, Great Clarendon Street,
Oxford OX2 6DP

Oxford New York
Auckland Bangkok Buenos Aires Cape Town
Chennai Dar es Salaam Delhi Hong Kong Istanbul
Karachi Kolkata Kuala Lumpur Madrid Melbourne
Mexico City Mumbai Nairobi São Paulo Shanghai
Taipei Tokyo Toronto

OXFORD and OXFORD ENGLISH
are trade marks of Oxford University Press

ISBN 0 19 436678 2

© Oxford University Press 1999

First published 1999
Fourteenth impression 2003

No unauthorized photocopying

Design and composition by Newton Harris

Printed in China

The Authors would like to thank all those at Oxford
University Press (both in Oxford and around the
world), and the design team who have contributed their
skills and ideas to producing this course.

The Publisher and Authors would like to thank the staff
at the British Institute Valencia for their help and
encouragement, especially Beatriz Martin, Gill
Hamilton, Michael O'Brien, and Ros Rice; special
thanks to Lester Vaughan for many invaluable
comments on the material; special thanks to Christina
and Clive's intermediate students (1997–9) for their
help in trialling all the lessons; the following readers for
their comments on the materials: Stuart Gale (Spain),
Fiona Campbell (Italy), Sandra Possas (Brazil), Marek
Doskocz (Poland), Ann Lee, Kevin Laing (UK); Susan
Powell, Esther Alonso, Dominic Latham-Koenig, and
Kate Chomacki for agreeing to be interviewed.

Finally, very special thanks from Clive to Ma Angeles
and from Christina to Cristina for all their help and
encouragement. Christina would also like to thank her
children Joaquin, Marco, and Krysia for their constant
inspiration.

The Publisher and Authors are grateful to those who
have given permission to reproduce the following
articles, extracts, and adaptations of copyright material:

p.7 from PAIRWORK: Activities for Effective
Communication by Peter Watcyn-Jones (Penguin
Books, 1981) copyright © Peter Watcyn-Jones, 1981.
Reproduced by permission of Penguin Books Ltd; p.18
'Family fortunes' by Andrea Jones appeared in *Options*
May 1992. Reproduced by permission of *Options*; p.19
'The making of you' by Angela Phillips and Jayne
Dowle. Appeared in *Options* August 1994 and
reproduced by permission of Robert Harding
Syndication; p.20 Extracts from the Cambridge
Academy of English brochure with their permission;
p.23 'The time of your life' by Patsy Westcott.
Appeared in *The Sunday Times STYLE London*

24 November 1996 © Patsy Westcott/*The Sunday
Times*, 1996; p.26 'Chocolate carrot could help
tomorrow's adults beat cancer' by Ian Murray.
Appeared in *The Times* 22 April 1997 © Times
Newspapers Limited, 1997; p.28 Ideas taken from *Eat
Yourself Slim* by Michel Montignac, by permission of
Montignac Publishing (UK) Limited; p.36
'Remembrance of things past: Nicky Lilley' by Joanna
Moorhead, 30 December 1997 © *The Guardian*; p.38 ©
Bill Bryson 1989. Extract from *The Lost Continent*
published by Black Swan, a division of Transworld
Publishers Ltd. All rights reserved; p.40 'Classroom
slaves' by Stella Kim appeared in *Marie Claire* 30
December 1997, reproduced with permission; p.44
'Book of the month: *Still me* by Christopher Reeve' by
Margarette Driscoll. Appeared in *The Sunday Times*
3 May 1998 © Times Newspapers Limited, 1998; p.48
AA Hotel Guide 1999 by permission of AA Publishing;
p.53 'You'll have six children, four husbands, and
make a long journey…' by Vicki Snow, reproduced
with her permission. Appeared in *Good Housekeeping*,
January 1998; p.54 'The Firing Line' by Henry Slesar,
reprinted with his permission; p.60 'Money does buy
happiness' by Nick Gardner. Appeared in *The Sunday
Times* 11 January 1998 © Times Newspapers Limited,
1998; p.61 'The image that cost a fortune' by Ben
Macintyre. Appeared in *The Times* 5 February 1998 ©
Times Newspapers Limited, 1998; p.63 Blue Guide
London by permission of A & C Black; p.64 'All set for
the rush-hour Grand Prix' by Alan Copps. Appeared in
The Times 8 June 1996 © Times Newspapers Limited,
1996; p.68 'Good runner with own seat' by Andrew
Pierce. Appeared in *The Times* 27 July 1996 © Times
Newspapers Limited, 1996; p.72 'Is noise driving you
mad?' by Caroline Bloor © *Good Housekeeping
Magazine*/Caroline Bloor. Reproduced by permission
of the National Magazine Company; p.80 Adapted
extract from the article 'Primal screen' by Lesley White.
Appeared in *The Sunday Times Magazine* May 1994 ©
Times Newspapers Limited, 1994; p.82 Records from
The Guinness Book of Records 1997 edition © 1996
Guinness Publishing Ltd. The Guinness Book of
Records is a Trade Mark of Guinness Publishing Ltd;
p.84 'Survival of the fittest' by John Brewer. Appeared
in *The Sunday Times STYLE London* 20 July 1997 ©
John Brewer/*The Sunday Times*, 1997; p.87 *Many Years
From Now*: Paul McCartney Biography by Barry Miles,
published by Martin Secker & Warburg. Extracts
reprinted by permission of Random House UK
Limited; p.90 Classic Musicals leaflet designed and
printed by Dewynters plc London; p.106 *Titanic: An
Illustrated History* by Don Lynch. Copyright © 1992
Don Lynch and Ken Marschall. Reproduced by
permission of Hodder and Stoughton Limited.

p.33 *Moon Over Bourbon Street* Words and Music by
Sting © 1985. Reproduced by permission of EMI Music
Publishing Ltd/Magnetic Music Publishing Ltd,
London WC2H 0EA; p.43 *Another Brick In The Wall
Pt II* by Roger Waters © 1979 Pink Floyd Music
Publishers Limited; p.89 *Let it be* by Lennon &
McCartney published by Sony ATV Music Publishing
Ltd.

Although every effort has been made to trace and
contact copyright holders before publication, this has
not always been possible. We apologize for any
apparent infringement of copyright and if notified, the
publisher will be pleased to rectify any errors or
omissions at the earliest opportunity.

The Publishers would like to thank the following for
their kind permission to reproduce photographs and
other copyright material:

Allsport UK Ltd pp.69 (T Duffy), 82 (IOC/Jesse
Owens); Apex p. 68; Mauricio J. Barriobero Pérez de
Soto p.108 (Víctor Peñasco and Josefa Pérez de
Soto);Bruce Coleman Ltd p.74 (H Reinhard);
Comstock Picture Library pp.16, 18; Corbis pp.45
(Everett/Superman II), 52–3 (zodiac), 57, 107
(newsboy), 112 (McDonalds); Dewynters p.90
(*Phantom of the Opera*); Greg Evans International
pp.72 (alarm), 93 (G B Evans), 98; Mary Evans Picture

Library pp.46 (J L Charmet), 106 (Bruce Ismay,
Captain Smith); First Choice Holidays p.50 (tour rep);
The Ronald Grant Archive pp.78 (*The Full Monty,
Nightmare on Elm Street, The Prince of Egypt, Saving
Private Ryan, The Sound of Music*), 79, 80 (*Manhattan
Murder Mystery*), 81 (*Annie Hall*), 137 (*Psycho*); Robert
Harding Picture Library pp.96 (skating), 112 (M
Chillmaid/schoolchildren); Nigel Hillier p.84 (sit-ups);
The Image Bank pp.43 (P Eden), 50 (A Chambon/air
traffic controller), 96 (Buillaty/Lorneo/Central Park,
Guido A/Fifth Avenue), 113 (L Gatz/cruise); INS
Reading pp.60–61 (John Madejski); Katz Pictures p.86
(D Borris/McCartney, M Wong/Outline/Gallaghers),
87 (B Bernstein/Outline/Wings); The Kobal Collection
pp.80–81 (1997 Fine Line Features/*Deconstructing
Harry*, 1989, Orion/*Crimes and Misdemeanours*), 137
(*Chariots of Fire, Star Wars*, C Coote/*101 Dalmatians*);
London Features International pp.86 (J
Furmonowsky/Bob Marley), 91 (*Cats, Les Misérables*),
96 (D Van Tine/Jekyll & Hyde club); Madison Press
p.106 (K Marschall/Titanic painting); Mirror
Syndication p.87 (Chloë fashion show); Montignac
Publishing p.28 (Michel Montignac); Moviestore
Collection p.23; Network Photographers p.61 (Rapho/J
P Rey/Caroline de Bendern); News Team International
p.26; PA News pp.60–61 (B Batchelor/Marquis of
Bath); Pictor International Ltd pp 67 (Lisbon, statue),
89; Pictorial Press Ltd pp.78 (*The Fifth Element*), 81
(Woody Allen in uniform), 90 (*Miss Saigon*), 137 (*Ben
Hur, Titanic*); Retna Pictures p.14; Rex Features Ltd
pp.10 (M Beddall/Three Tenors), 36 (B Beirne, N
Jorgensen, The Sun), 44 (A Di Crollalanza/Christopher
Reeve , B Strong/Christopher Reeve), 87 (McCartney
and Lennon, R/Young/McCartney); The Stock Market
pp.28 (cheeseburger), 44 (P Barton/man in café), 84
(M Daley/runner), 112 (J Zaruba/kitchen); Tony Stone
Images pp.10 (P Dokus/men dancing), 28
(C Everard/salad), 30 (J Darrell), 33 (T Shonnard), 44
(J Riley/man at home), 50 (V Oliver/father), 52–53
(L Wies/crystal ball), 63 (A Errington), 72
(D E Myers/aeroplane, S Rands/road worker), 84
(L Adamski Peek/tennis, J McBride/canoeist,
D Madison/football), 94 (D E Boyer/Hawaii)96 (J
Lamb/Limo), 112 (L Adamski Peek/father and son),
113 (couch potato, D Joel/swimmers, Z
Kaluzny/tourists); Sygma pp.10
(G Schachmes/Pavarotti), 45 (J Ohlinger/Superman),
82 (D Hudson/swimmers), 87 (The Beatles), 107
(M Polak/Titanic underwater); Telegraph Colour
Library pp.7 (Masterfile), 17 (FPG), 44 (A
Tilley/woman, N White/teenagers), 48, 67 (W
Otto/tram), 72 (M Wilson-Smith/traffic), 84 (FPG
J T Turner/shot putter); Times Newspapers Ltd
pp.60–61 (F Guidicini/Elaine Thompson), 64 (T
White).

We are unable to trace the copyright holders of the
photographs on pp.40, 108 (children) and would be
grateful for any information which would enable us to
do so.

Picture research by Diane Jones

Cover illustration by: Sarah Jones/Debut Art

Illustrations by:

Rowan Barnes-Murphy pp.11, 29, 30, 31, 38, 39, 52, 53,
71, 79, 95, 101, 109, 135; Philip Bishop/Illustration
pp.54, 55, 56, 132; Michelle Blackmore pp.26, 27;
Stefan Chabluk pp.25, 139; Rowie Christopher pp.15,
47, 51, 59, 111; Jonty Clark pp.17, 100, 122, 126; Paul
Dickinson pp.33, 109; Mark Draisey p.92; Martin Fish
pp.12, 75; David Gifford p.131; Neil Gower pp.77, 92,
136, 138, 139; Sarah Jones/Debut Art p6; David
Shephard/Illustration pp.54, 97, 99; Simon Spilsbury
pp.19, 21, 37, 68, 69, 76, 88, 110; Katherine Walker
pp.13, 34, 35, 42, 43, 62, 73, 102, 130, 133; Bob Wilson
pp.49, 59, 66, 70, 82, 131, 134; Annabel Wright p.32.

Commissioned photography by:

Gareth Boden pp.9, 20, 24, 90, 93
Mark Mason pp.52, 58, 69, 103, 104, 123, 127, 135
Rob Judges p.34